# SILVER POETS OF THE SIXTEENTH CENTURY

Edited by Lisa Roy

# SILVER POETS OF THE SIXTEENTH CENTURY

**Edited by Lisa Roy**

/ith Complete Introduction, Biography, Author's Background, Complete Text, Select Criticism and Bibliography]

**Lisa Roy**
M.A. English, B.Ed.
Calcutta University

**ANMOL PUBLICATIONS PVT. LTD.**
**NEW DELHI - 110 002 (INDIA)**

**ANMOL PUBLICATIONS PVT. LTD.**

*H.O.:* 4374/4B, Ansari Road, Darya Ganj,
New Delhi-110 002 (India)
Ph.: 23278000, 23261597

*B.O.:* No. 1015, Ist Main Road, BSK IIIrd Stage
IIIrd Phase, IIIrd Block
Bangalore - 560 085 (India)
*Visit us at:* www.anmolpublications.com

*Silver Poets of the Sixteenth Century*

First Published, 2009



PRINTED IN INDIA

Printed at Mehra Offset Press, Delhi.

# Contents

# Preface

This edition of Silver Poets of 16th century is widely acknowledged and is the best available. It features biographies, works and critical essays on the popular silver poets of 16th century. To make things more comprehensive and informative, you will also be provided timelines and selected works of the poets.

Sir Thomas Wyatt, Henry Howard Earl of Surrey, Sir Walter Raleigh and Sir John Davies are popularly known as the 16th century Silver Poets. It will include devotional poetry, musings on the cult of Elizabeth, love lyrics and apocalyptic prophecies.

Author

# Chapter 1

# Introduction: Edmund Spenser

Born in or near 1552 to a family of modest means, Edmund Spenser was possibly the son of John Spenser, a free journeyman cloth maker resident in East Smithfield in London, though this relationship is far from certain. Whatever his parentage, it is likely that the Spenser's (or Spencer's) originated in Lancashire, where they would have been connected with prominent local families such as the Nowells and Towneleys. Spenser seems to have had at least one sister, Sarah, and a number of brothers. As a boy, the future poet entered the Merchant Taylors' school, probably at its opening in 1561 under the celebrated humanist and pedagogical writer Richard Mulcaster; his place there may have been secured by the patronage of one Nicholas Spenser, the warden of the Taylors' Company at the time and possibly a relation. While at the school, Spenser was supported at least in part by the generous bequest of Robert Nowell, brother of Alexander Nowell, dean at St. Paul's.

The curriculum of the school, entirely at the discretion of its headmaster, seems to have pursued the standard humanist course of the day: boys were taught and examined on the works of Cato, Caesar, Horace, Lucan, and Homer; nursed on the rhetorical models of Cicero, Erasmus, and Vives; and trained assiduously in Latin language and composition. The boys of the school may also have received a few years of training in Greek and Hebrew, slightly unusual for the time. Spenser later wrote in The Shepheardes Calender (December, 37-42) that it was his 'shepherd peres' at the Merchant Taylors' school and Mulcaster (probably the 'good olde shephearde,

Wrenock') who first encouraged him to write verse. In May 1569, Spenser left school and matriculated as a sizar at Pembroke Hall (now Pembroke College), Cambridge, receiving a further ten shillings from the Nowell bequest to support him. Although he had to work for his meals and accommodation, and may often have been ill during his studies, this appears to have been an important and productive time for the young poet. At Pembroke, Spenser came to know the master John Young, later Bishop of Rochester, and probably met Lancelot Andrewes, the future Bishop of London and privy councilor, who had also been at the Merchant Taylors' school.

The most important influence on Spenser during this period, though, was undoubtedly his intimate friendship with Gabriel Harvey, himself admitted as a Fellow of Pembroke Hall in 1570. While Spenser's relationship with Harvey was later satirized by fellow students in a play titled Pedantius, Harvey appears to have introduced Spenser to a number of important connections and potential patrons, including Robert Dudley, Earl of Leicester.

After taking his B.A. (1573) and M.A. (1576), Spenser left Cambridge for Kent, where he acted as secretary for John Young, recently created Bishop of Rochester. It was there that the poet probably composed The Shepheardes Calender, which seems to represent the Kentish landscape and certainly refers to Harvey (as Hobbinol), Young (as Roffy), Archbishop of Canterbury Grindal (as Algrind), and Spenser himself (as Colin Clout); The Shepheardes Calender was printed in 1579.

Spenser may have been employed by the Earl of Leicester as early as 1577, perhaps carrying messages to Leicester's brother-in-law Sir Henry Sidney, then Lord Deputy in Ireland; this speculation is very uncertain, though Spenser claims to have witnessed the execution of Murrogh O'Brien in July of that year. By spring 1579, at any rate, Spenser had been accepted into the employment of the Earl of Leicester, and was living in Leicester House on the Strand. While in Leicester's home and service, Spenser came into contact with Sir Philip Sidney and Sir Edward Dyer, then young men at the centre of an artistic culture in Elizabeth's court. With several others, including Harvey, Daniel Rogers, and Thomas Drant, these men seem to have constituted an informal intellectual society called the 'Areopagus', discussing matters of law, philosophy, and poetry.

It was at this time that the well-known printer Henry Bynneman put out two short volumes containing letters exchanged between Spenser and Harvey, letters that discuss trendy intellectual topics of the day and give a good deal of biographical information about Spenser's new contacts in London.

Probably through Leicester's influence, Spenser was in July 1580 appointed secretary to Arthur, fourteenth Lord Grey de Wilton, then leaving England to take up office as Lord Deputy of Ireland. Arriving shortly thereafter in Dublin, Spenser accompanied Grey on his famous and tortuous overland march to Munster, where the Lord Deputy's forces besieged, captured, and executed a much larger and better provisioned Papal and Spanish force in the Fort d'Oro at Smerwick. In March 1581, Spenser was appointed clerk of the Chancery for Faculties in Dublin, probably a sinecure post inherited from Lodowick Bryskett, a former travelling companion of Sidney's.

He obtained a lease of Lord Baltinglas's Dublin home in 1582, and in August 1582 leased New Abbey, County Kildare, serving as Commissioner of Musters for Kildare in May 1583 and July 1584. When the lands of the attainted Earl of Desmond were set out in plantation in 1586, Spenser was allotted 3,028 acres near Doneraile, including the old castle at Kilcolman. He seems to have moved to Munster sometime within the following two years, perhaps in the company of his sister Sarah, although the royal grant of his estate was not confirmed by fiant until 1591. In June 1588 he inherited, again from Lodowick Bryskett, the post of Clerk of the Council of Munster, by which time he certainly appears to have been resident near Cork, where the Council met.

Spenser was at this time, and for many years following, involved in protracted legal wrangles with Maurice Viscount

Roche of Fermoy, an Old English neighbour financially and socially threatened by the incursions of the New English undertakers in the area. By 1589 at the latest, Spenser appears to have made the acquaintance of Sir Walter Ralegh, at that time living on his Munster estate and serving as mayor of the city Yougal. It was Ralegh who, reading through Spenser's draft of The Faerie Queene, encouraged him to join him on a trip to London in 1590, where he presented the celebrated poet to the Queen.

Spenser used his time in London to publish the first three books of The Faerie Queene, and seems to have attempted to secure enough court patronage to make it possible for him to remain in England. Although the Queen promised him a handsome pension for his labours, her generosity was questioned and moderated by the intercession of Lord Burghley, whom Spenser went on to lampoon in Complaints, printed and almost immediately suppressed (or 'called in') in 1591. Judging from a commentary on the scandal recently discovered in a contemporary letter, Spenser seems to have returned to Ireland in the early months of 1591 as a direct result of the offense he had caused to Burghley. Resuming his residence at Kilcolman, the poet shortly thereafter fell in love with and courted Elizabeth Boyle, daughter of James Boyle, himself a kinsman of Richard Boyle, later first earl of Cork. On 11th June 1594, the couple were married, an event celebrated in Spenser's Amoretti and Epithalamion, published in London in the following year.

According to Amoretti 80, the poet had completed the second instalment (Books IV-VI) of The Faerie Queene shortly before the marriage, although it was not to be printed until 1596. Spenser returned to London for the publication of the second half of The Faerie Queene, and probably remained there for almost a year, living in Essex House (formerly Leicester House) in the Strand as a guest of the Earl of Essex.

It was probably during this stay that he began work on a view of the present state of Irelands, a treatise on the social and political reformation of Ireland. Shorter works published during this period include Fowre Hymnes and Prothalamion.

By the time that A view appeared on the Stationers' Register in April 1598, Spenser was probably back in Munster, disappointed with his failure, once again, to secure court favors. By order of the Privy Council, he was in September 1598 appointed Sheriff for County Cork; the letter of appointment described him as 'a gentleman dwelling in the county of Cork who is well known unto you all for his good and commendable parts, being a man endowed with good knowledge and learning, and not unskilful or without experience in the wars'. His tenure of this post, which itself might well have led to further elevation, was destined to be short.

The 'upstart' Earl of Tyrone, Hugh O'Neill, had defeated the Queen's army at the Yellow Ford of the Blackwater in August of 1598; by the following month, all of Munster was in rebellion, and Spenser and his family fled to the city of Cork for safety. He was shortly thereafter dispatched by the President of Munster, Sir Thomas Norris, to London with messages for the Privy Council. Arriving late in 1598, he took up residence in King's Street, and died there, according to Ben Jonson 'for lake of bread', on a Saturday in January 1599. It is not clear how a poet so well loved by so many, an official so highly-regarded by so many, and a man so politically well-connected to so many, could have died in the fabled penury to which Jonson later testified. Camden recorded that the Earl of Essex paid for his funeral, and that poets carried his coffin, throwing their verses and pens, along with many tears, into his grave. His tomb is situated, appropriately enough, adjacent to that of Geoffrey Chaucer in Westminster Abbey.

Spenser was known to his contemporaries as 'the prince of poets', as great in English as Virgil in Latin. He left behind him masterful essays in every genre of poetry, from pastoral and elegy to epithalamion and epic. Although his prose treatise on the reformation of Ireland was not published until 1633, it showed even then a shrewd comprehension of the problems facing English government in Ireland, and a capacity for political office as thorough as his literary ability. Milton was later to claim Spenser as 'a better teacher than Aquinas', and generations of readers, students, and scholars have admired him for his subtle use of language, his unbounded imagination, his immense classical and religious learning, his keen understanding of moral and political philosophy, and his unerring ability to synthesize and, ultimately, to delight.

### A Chronology

1552 Spenser born, probably to a London family of modest means.

1561 Merchant Taylors' School founded, September. Spenser was probably among the first pupils, along with Thomas Kyd, Lancelot Andrewes, and Thomas Lodge.

1569 Spenser matriculates as a sizar at Pembroke Hall, May Jan van der Noot's A theatre for Worldlings, including poems translated from Spenser from French sources, published in London by Henry Bynneman.

1573 Spenser graduates B.A. from Pembroke, eleventh in a list of one hundred and twenty students.

1576 Spenser receives M.A., sixty-sixth in a list of seventy

1578 Spenser serving as secretary to John Young, Bishop of Rochester, in Kent.

1579 Spenser back in London, in the employment of the Earl of Leicester.

The Shepheardes Calender entered into the Stationers' Register, December.

1580 Spenser-Harvey correspondence entered into the Stationers' Register, June Spenser appointed secretary to Arthur, fourteenth Lord Grey de Wilton, upon his departure from England to become Lord Deputy of Ireland.

Grey defeated by O'Byrne at Glenmalure, August

Spenser accompanies Grey on a military expedition to encounter Papal forces at Smerwick

Fort surrenders and 600 captives executed, 9 November.

Spenser returns thereafter with Grey to Dublin, arriving by the end of the year.

1581 Spenser appointed clerk of the Faculties in the Court of Chancery,
March Spenser and Lodowick Bryskett with Grey during negotiations with Turlogh Lynagh O'Neill at the Blackwater. Spenser subsequently accompanies Grey on an expedition against Baltinglas and Feagh McHugh

1582 Lodowick Bryskett later records, in A Discourse of Ciuill Life, that Spenser was present at a gathering of friends at Bryskett's cottage outside Dublin. Spenser allegedly asked those present-including Sir Robert Dillon, Warham St. Leger, Thomas Norris, and Christopher Carleill-to excuse him from Bryskett's request that he treat them to a discourse on moral philosophy Sir John Desmond killed and his head sent to Dublin for display, January
Spenser leases New Abbey, County Kildare, August
Grey recalled, Spenser discharged from secretaryship, end of August.

1583 Bryskett receives patent for the Clerkship of Munster. Spenser serves as his deputy
Earl of Desmond killed near Tralee, November.

1586 Articles for the Munser Undertakers drawn up and confirmed by the Queen, June. Most of the land initially put under the disposition of Sir Walter Ralegh

1587 Spenser in attendance, as Bryskett's deputy, at meetings of the Munster Council.

1588 Spanish Armada wrecked in a storm off the Irish coast, February Spenser occupies Kilcolman, perhaps as early as September.

1589 Official confirmation of Spenser's right to Kilcolman and its 3,028 acres, May The Faerie Queene entered into the Stationers' Register, December.

1590 Spenser writes his 'Letter of the Authors, to Sir Walter Ralegh', January Spenser obtains royal grant of Kilcolman in fee farm, OctoberThe Faerie Queene, Books I-III, published in LondonComplaints entered into Stationers' Register.

1591 Spenser granted a life pension of £50 per annnum by Elizabeth, February Spenser completes Colin clouts come home againe while at Kilcolman, December

1592 Publication of Daphnaïda in London, January
Cuthbert Burbie publishes the pseudo-Platonic dialogue Axiochus, the translation of which is attributed to 'Edw: Spenser'

1593 Death of Arthur, Lord Grey de Wilton

1594 Spenser serving as Queen's Justice for County Cork
Spenser marries Elizabeth Boyle, June 11th
Amoretti and Epithalamion entered in Stationers' Register, November

1595 Hugh O'Neill, Earl of Tyrone, proclaimed a traitor
Publication of Amoretti and Epithalamion, Colin clouts come home againe, and Astrophel

1596 Books IV-VI of The Faerie Queene entered in the Stationers' Register, January
Earl of Essex raids Spanish fleet at Cadiz and sacks the city, June
Fowre Hymnes dedicated from the court at Greenwich
Publication of the first six books of The Faerie Queene, Fowre Hymnes, Prothalamion

1597 Spenser acquires Renny in south Cork, on behalf of his son Peregrine
Spenser probably completes A vewe of the present state of Irelande sometime this year

1598 A vewe of the present state of Irelande entered in Stationers' Register, April, 'to be prynted when he do bringe other authoritie'. The authority is presumably not brought, as the treatise is not published until 1633, in Dublin
Royal forces routed by the Earl of Tyrone at the Yellow Ford, August
Spenser designated Sheriff of Cork, September
Kilcolman sacked, October. Spenser and his family flee to the city of Cork
Spenser leaves Cork for London, carrying messages from Sir THomas Norris to the Privy Council

1599 Spenser dies at Westminster, 13th January
Spenser buried in Westminster Abbey, 16th January. Funeral expenses are paid by the Earl of Essex

## Chapter 2

# Shakespeare: Introduction

Information about the life of William Shakespeare is often open to doubt. Some even doubt whether he wrote all plays ascribed to him. From the best available sources it seems William Shakespeare was born in Stratford on about April 23rd 1564. His father William was a successful local businessman and his mother Mary was the daughter of a landowner. Relatively prosperous it is likely the family paid for Williams education, although there is no evidence he attended university. In 1582 William, aged only 18, married an older woman named Anne Hathaway. Soon after they had there first daughter, Susanna. They had another two children but William's only son Hamnet died aged only 11. After his marriage information about the life of Shakespeare is sketchy but it seems he spent most of his time in London writing and performing in his plays. It seemed he didn't mind being absent from his family. Only returning home during Lent when all theatres were closed. It is generally thought that during the 1590s he wrote the majority of his sonnets. This was a time of prolific writing and his plays developed a good deal of interest and controversy. Due to some well timed investments he was able to secure a firm financial background leaving time for writing and acting. The best of these investments was buying some real estate near Stratford in 1605, this soon doubled in value. Some academics known as the "oxfords" claim that Shakespeare never actually wrote any plays they suggest names such as Edward de Vere. They contend Shakespeare was actually just a successful businessman. Nevertheless there is some evidence of Shakespeare in theatres as he received a variety of criticism from people such as Ben Johnson and Robert Greene.

*Shakespeare the Poet*

William Shakespeare wrote 154 Sonnets mostly in the 1590s. Fairly short poems they deal with issues such as lost love. His sonnets have an enduring appeal with his characteristic skill with language and words.

*"Let me not to the marriage of true minds*
*Admit impediments. Love is not love*
*Which alters when it alteration finds,*
*Or bends with the remover to remove:"*
*- Sonnet C15I*

*The Plays of Shakespeare*

The plays of Shakespeare have been studied more than any other writing in the English language and have been translated into numerous languages. He was rare as a playwright for excelling in tragedies, comedies and histories. He deftly combined popular entertainment with a rare poetic capacity for expression, which is almost mantic in quality.

*"This above all: to thine ownself be true,*
*And it must follow, as the night the day,*
*Thou canst not then be false to any man.*
*Farewell: my blessing season this in thee!"*
*—Lord Polonius, Hamlet Act I, Scene 3*

During his lifetime Shakespeare was not without controversy, but he also received lavish praise for his plays which were very popular and commercially successful.

Shakespear3 died in 1664 it is not clear how he died although his vicar suggested it was from heavy drinking. His tombstone is marked with the following epitaph;

*Good friend for Jesus sake forbeare*
*To digg the dust encloased heare*
*Blessed by y man y spares hes stones*
*And curst be he y moves my bones*

It is true to say that each line of Shakespeare has been poured over by scholars and students no idea or concept has been left unturned. Shakespeare has left a profound and lasting impact on literature, cinema and theatre.

## Chapter 3

# William Shakespeare–Biography

### Shakespeare's Ancestry

As a brief introductory detail, it should be mentioned that, during the sixteenth century, there were many families with the name Shakespeare in and around Stratford. "Shakespeare" appears countless times in town minutes and court records, spelled in a variety of ways, from Shags ere to Casper. Unfortunately, very few records reveal William Shakespeare's relationship to or with the many other Stratford Shakespeare's. Genealogists claim to have discovered one man related to Shakespeare who was hanged in Gloucestershire for theft in 1248, and Shakespeare's father, in an application for a coat of arms, claimed that his grandfather was a hero in the War of the Roses and was granted land in Warwickshire in 1485 by Henry VII.

No historical evidence has been discovered to corroborate this story of the man who would be William Shakespeare's great-grandfather, but, luckily, we do have information regarding his paternal and maternal grandfathers. The Bard's paternal grandfather was Richard Shakespeare (d. 1561), a farmer in Snitterfield, a village four miles northeast of Stratford. There is no record of Richard Shakespeare before 1529, but details about his life after this reveal that he was a tenant farmer, who, on occasion, would be fined for grazing too many cattle on the common grounds and for not attending manor court.

There is no record of Richard Shakespeare's wife, but together they had two sons (possibly more), John and Henry.

Richard Shakespeare worked on several different sections of land during his lifetime, including the land owned by the wealthy Robert Arden of Wilmecote, Shakespeare's maternal grandfather. Robert Arden (d. 1556) was the son of Thomas Arden of Wilmecote, Shakespeare's maternal great-grandfather, who probably belonged to the aristocratic family of the Arden's of Park Hall.

He was catholic and married more than once (we know the name of his second wife — Agnes Hill) and he fathered no fewer than eight daughters. He became the stepfather of Agnes' four children. Robert Arden had accumulated much property, and when he died, he named his daughter (Shakespeare's mother) Mary, only sixteen at the time, one of his executors. He left Mary some money and, in his own words, "all my land in Willmecote cawlide As byes and the crop apone the grounde, sowne and tyllide as hitt is".

**Shakespeare's Parents**

Shakespeare's father, John, came to Stratford from Snitterfield before 1532 as an apprentice glover and tanner of leathers. John Shakespeare prospered and began to deal in farm products and wool.

It is recorded that he bought a house in 1552 (the date that he first appears in the town records), and bought more property in 1556. Because John Shakespeare owned one house on Greenhill Street and two houses on Henley Street, the exact location of William's birth cannot be known. Sometime between 1556 and 1558, John Shakespeare married Mary Arden, the daughter of the wealthy Robert Arden of Wilmecote and owner of the sixty-acre farm called Asbies.

The wedding would have most likely taken place in Mary Arden's parish church at Aston Cantlow, the burial place of Robert Arden, and, although there is no evidence of strong piety on either side of the family, it would have been a Catholic service, since Queen Mary I was the reigning monarch. We assume neither John nor Mary could write — John used a pair of glovers' compasses as his signature while Mary used a running horse — but it did not prevent them from becoming important members of the community. John Shakespeare was elected to a multitude of civic positions, including ale-taster of the borough (Stratford had a long-reaching reputation for its brewing) in 1557, chamberlain of the borough in 1561, alderman in 1565, (a position which came with free education for his children at the Stratford Grammar School), high bailiff, or mayor, in 1568, and chief alderman in 1571.

Due to his important civic duties, he rightfully sought the title of gentleman and applied for his coat-of-arms in 1570. However, for unspecific reasons the application was abruptly withdrawn, and within the next few years, for reasons just as mystifying, John Shakespeare would go from wealthy business owner and dedicated civil servant to debtor and absentee council member. By 1578, he was behind in his taxes and stopped paying the statutory aldermanic subscription for poor relief. In 1579, he had to mortgage Mary Shakespeare's estate, Asbies, to pay his creditors. In 1580, he was fined 40 pounds for missing a court date and in 1586, the town removed him from the board of aldermen due to lack of attendance. By 1590, John Shakespeare owned only his house on Henley Street and, in 1592, he was fined for not attending church.

However, near the very end of John Shakespeare's life, it seems that his social and economic standing was again beginning to flourish. He once again applied to the College of Heralds for a coat-of-arms in 1596, and, due likely to the success of William in London, this time his wish was granted. On October 20 of that year, by permission of the Garter King of Arms (the Queen's aid in such matters) "the said John Shakespeare, Gentlemen, and...His children, issue and posterity" were lawfully entitled to display the gold coat-of-arms, with a black banner bearing a silver spear (a visual representation of the family name "Shakespeare"). The coat-of-arms could then be displayed on their door and all their personal items.

The motto was "Non sans droict" or "not without right. The reason cited for granting the coat-of-arms was John Shakespeare's grandfather's faithful service to Henry VII, but no specifics were given as to what service he actually performed. The coat-of-arms appears on Shakespeare's tomb in Stratford. In 1599, John Shakespeare was reinstated on the town council, but died a short time later, in 1601. He was probably near seventy years old and he had been married for forty-four years. Mary Shakespeare died in 1608 and was buried on September 9.

## Shakespeare's Birth

The baptismal register of the Holy Trinity parish church, in Stratford, shows the following entry for April 26, 1564: Gulielmus filius Johannes Shakespeare. The actual date of Shakespeare's birth is not known, but, traditionally, April 23, St George's Day has been Shakespeare's accepted birthday, and a house on Henley Street in Stratford, owned by William's father, John, is accepted as Shakespeare's birthplace. However, the reality is that no one really knows when the great dramatist was born.

According to the Book of Common Prayer, it was required that a child be baptized on the nearest Sunday or holy day following the birth, unless the parents had a legitimate excuse. As Dennis Kay proposes in his book Shakespeare

If Shakespeare were indeed born on Sunday, April 23, the next feast day would have been St. Mark's Day on Tuesday the 25. There might well have been some cause, both reasonable and great — or perhaps, as has been suggested, St. Mark's Day was still held to be unlucky, as it had been before the Reformation, when altars and crucifixes used to be draped in black cloth, and when some claimed to see in the churchyard the spirits of those doomed to die in that year....but that does not help to explain the christening on the twenty-sixth. No doubt, Shakespeare's true birthday will remain a mystery forever. However, the assumption that the Bard was born on the same day of the month that he died lends an exciting esoteric highlight to the otherwise mundane details of Shakespeare's life.

## Shakespeare's Siblings

William Shakespeare was indeed lucky to survive to

adulthood in sixteenth-century England. Waves of the plague swept across the countryside, and pestilence ravaged Stratford during the hot summer months.

Mary and John Shakespeare became parents for the first time in September of 1558, when their daughter Joan was born. Nothing is known of Joan Shakespeare except for the fact that she was baptized in Stratford on September 15, and succumbed to the plague shortly after. Their second child, Margaret, was born in 1562 and was baptized on December 2. She died one year later.

The Shakespeare's' fourth child, Gilbert, was baptized on October 13, 1566, at Holy Trinity. It is likely that John Shakespeare named his second son after his friend and neighbour on Henley Street, Gilbert Bradley, a glover and the burgess of Stratford for a time.

Records show that Gilbert Shakespeare survived the plague and reached adulthood, becoming a haberdasher, working in London as of 1597, and spending much of his time back in Stratford. In 1609, he appeared in Stratford court in connection with a lawsuit, but we know no details regarding the matter. Gilbert Shakespeare seems to have had a long and successful career as a tradesman, and he died a bachelor in Stratford on February 3, 1612. In 1569, John and Mary Shakespeare gave birth to another girl, and named her after her first-born sister, Joan. Joan Shakespeare accomplished the wondrous feat of living to be seventy-seven years old — outliving William and all her other siblings by decades. Joan married William Hart the hatter and had four children but two of them died in childhood.

Her son William Hart (1600-1639) followed in his famous uncle's footsteps and became an actor, performing with the King's Men in the mid-1630s. His most noted role was that of Falstaff. William Hart never married, but the leading actor of the restoration period, Charles Hart, is believed to have been William Hart's illegitimate son and grandnephew to Shakespeare.

Due to the fact that Shakespeare's children and his other siblings did not carry on the line past the seventeenth century, the descendants of Joan Shakespeare Hart possess the only genetic link to the great playwright. Joan Shakespeare lost her husband William a week before she lost her brother William in 1616, and she lived the rest of her life in Shakespeare's birthplace. Joan died in 1646, but her descendants stayed in Stratford until 1806. Undoubtedly already euphoric that Joan had survived the precarious first few years of childhood, the Shakespeare's' joy was heightened with the birth of their fourth daughter, Anne, in 1571, when William was seven years old.

Unfortunately, tragedy befell the family yet again when Anne died at the age of eight. The sorrow felt by the Shakespeare's' over the loss of Anne was profound, and even though they were burdened by numerous debts at the time of her death, they arranged an unusually elabourate funeral for their cherished daughter.

Anne Shakespeare was buried on April 4, 1579. In 1574, Mary and John Shakespeare had another boy and they named him Richard, probably after his paternal grandfather. Richard was baptized on March 11 of that year, and nothing else is known about him, except for the fact that he died, unmarried, and was buried on February 4, 1613 — a year and a day after the death of Gilbert Shakespeare. Mary gave birth to one more child in 1580. They christened him on May 3 and named him Edmund, probably in honour of his uncle Edmund Lambert. Edmund was eager to follow William into the acting profession, and when he was old, enough he joined William in London to embark on a career as a "player".

Edmund did not make a great reputation for himself as an actor, but, in all fairness, cruel fate, and not his poor acting abilities, was likely the reason. Edmund died in 1607 — not yet thirty years old. He was buried in St. Savior's Church, in Southwark, on December 31 of that year. His funeral was costly and magnificent, with tolling bells heard across the Thames.

It is most likely that William planned the funeral for his younger brother because William would have been the only Shakespeare wealthy enough to afford such an expensive tribute to Edmund. In addition, records show that the funeral was held in the morning, and as Dennis Kay points out, funerals were usually held in the afternoon. It is probable that the morning funeral was arranged so that Shakespeare's fellow actors could attend the burial of Edmund.

## Shakespeare's Education and Childhood

Shakespeare probably began his education at the age of six or seven at the Stratford grammar school, which is still standing only a short distance from his house on Henley Street and is in the care of the Shakespeare Birthplace Trust. Although we have no record of Shakespeare attending the school, due to the official position held by John Shakespeare it seems likely that he would have decided to educate young William at the school, which was under the care of Stratford's governing body. The Stratford grammar school had been built some two hundred years before Shakespeare was born and in that time the lessons taught there were, of course dictated primarily by the beliefs of the reigning monarch. In 1553, due to a charter by King Edward VI, the school became known as the King's New School of Stratford-upon-Avon.

During the years that Shakespeare attended the school, at least one and possibly three headmasters stepped down because of their devotion to the Catholic religion proscribed by Queen Elizabeth. One of these masters was Simon Hunt, who, in 1578, according to tradition, left Stratford to pursue his more spiritual goal of becoming a Jesuit, and relocated to the seminary at Rheims. Hunt had found his true vocation: when he died in Rome seven years later he had raised to the position of Grand Penitentiary.

Like all of the great poets and dramatists of the time, Shakespeare learned his basic reading and writing skills from an ABC, or hornbook. Robert Speight in his book, Shakespeare: The Man and His Achievement, describes this book as a primer framed in wood and covered with a thin plate of transparent horn. It included the alphabet in small letters and in capitals, with combinations of the five vowels with b, c, and d, and the Lord's Prayer in English. The first of these alphabets, which ended with the abbreviation for 'and' began with the mark of the cross. Hence the alphabet was known as 'Christ cross row'

— the cross-row of Richard III, I, i, 55. A short catechism was often included in the ABC book (the 'absey book' of King John, I, i, 196). In 'The Merry Wives of Windsor', there is a comical scene in which the Welsh headmaster tests his pupil's knowledge, who is appropriately named William. There is little doubt that Shakespeare was recalling his own experiences during his early school years. As was the case in all Elizabethan grammar schools, Latin was the primary language of learning. Although Shakespeare likely had some lessons in English, Latin composition and the study of Latin authors like Seneca, Cicero, Ovid, Virgil, and Horace would have been the focus of his literary training.

One can see that Shakespeare absorbed much that was taught in his grammar school, for he had an impressive familiarity with the stories by Latin authors, as is evident when examining his plays and their sources. Even though scholars, basing their argument on a story told more than a century after the fact, accept that Shakespeare was removed from school around age thirteen because of his father's financial and social difficulties. There is no reason whatsoever to believe that he had not acquired a firm grasp of both English and Latin and that he had continued his studies elsewhere. The famous quotation from Nicholas Rowe's notoriously inaccurate biography of Shakespeare (written in 1709), where he claims that Shakespeare "acquired that little Latin he was Master of" and that Shakespeare was prevented by his father's poor fortune from "further Proficiency in that Language", should be read with an extremely critical eye.

There are other fragmented and dubious details about Shakespeare's life growing up in Stratford. He is supposed to have worked for a butcher, in addition to helping run his father's business. There is a fable that Shakespeare stole a deer from Sir Thomas Lucy at Charlecote, and instead of serving a prison sentence, fled from Stratford. Although this surely is a fictitious incident, a few verses of a humourous ballad mocking Lucy have been connected to Shakespeare. "Edmond Malone records a version of two verses of the Lucy Ballad collected by one of the few great English classical scholars, Joshua

Barnes, at Stratford between 1687 and 1690. Barnes stopped overnight at an inn and heard an old woman singing it. He gave her a new gown for the two stanzas which were all she remembered":

*Sir Thomas was so covetous*
*To covet so much deer*
*When horns enough upon his head*
*Most plainly did appear*
*Had not his worship one deer left?*
*What then? He had a wife*
*Took pains enough to find him horns*
*Should last him during life.*

Shakespeare's daily activities after he left school and before he re-emerged as a professional actor in the late 1580s are impossible to trace. Suggestions that he might have worked as a schoolmaster, lawyer, or glover with his father and brother, Gilbert, are all plausible. So too is the argument that Shakespeare studied intensely to become a master at his literary craft, and honed his acting skills while traveling and visiting playhouses outside of Stratford. However, it is from this period known as the "lost years" that we obtain one vital piece of information about Shakespeare: he married a pregnant orphan named Anne Hathaway.

## Shakespeare's Marriage and Children

Recordings in the Episcopal register at Worcester on the dates of November 27 and 28, 1582, reveal that Shakespeare desired to marry a young girl named Anne. There are two different documents regarding this matter, and their contents have raised a debate over just whom Shakespeare first intended to wed. Were there two Anne's? Was Shakespeare in love with one but in lust with the other? Was Shakespeare ready to join in matrimony with the Anne of his dreams only to have an attack of conscience and marry the Anne with whom he had carnal relations? To discuss the controversy properly we should look at the documents in question. The first entry in the register is the following record of the issue of a marriage license to one Wm Shakespeare:

Anno Domini 1582...Novembers...27 die eiusdem mensis. Item eodem die supradicto emanavit Licentia inter Wm Shaxpere et Annam Whateley de Temple Grafton.

The next entry in the episcopal register records the marriage bond granted to one Wm Shakespeare:

Noverint universi per praesentes nos Fulconem Sandells de Stratford in comitatu Warwici agricolam et Johannem Rychardson ibidem agricolam, teneri et firmiter obligari Ricardo Cosin generoso et Roberto Warmstry notario publico in quadraginta libris bonae et legalis monetae Angliae solvend. eisdem Ricardoet Roberto haered. execute. et assign at. suis ad quam quidem solucionem bene et fideliter faciend. obligamus nos et utrumque nostrum per se pro toto et in solid. haired. executor. et administrator. nostros firmiter per praesentes sigillis nostris sigillat. Dat. 28 die Novem. Anno regni dominae nostrae Eliz. Dei gratia Angliae Franc. et Hiberniae Reginae fidei defensor &c.25.2 The condition of this obligation is such that if hereafter there shall not appear any lawful let or impediment by reason of any precontract, consanguinity, affinity or by any other lawful means whatsoever, but that William Shagspere on the one party and Anne Hathwey of Stratford in the diocese of Worcester, maiden, may lawfully solemnize matrimony together, and in the same afterwards remain and continue like man and wife according unto the laws in that behalf provided...

Three possible conclusions can be reached from the above records: 1) The Anne Whateley in the first record and the Anne Hathaway in the second record are the same woman. Some scholars believe that the name Whateley was substituted accidentally for Hathwey into the register by the careless clerk. "The clerk was a nincompoop: he wrote Baker for Barber in his register and Darby for Bradley, and Dock for Lock and Anne Whitely for Anne Hathaway. A lot of ingenious ink has been spilt over this error, but it is surely a simple one. The name whitely occurs in a tithe appeal by a vicar on the same page of the register; the clerk could not follow his own notes, or he was distracted". Moreover, some believe that the couple selected Temple Grafton as the place for the wedding for reasons of privacy and that is why it is recorded in the register instead of Stratford. 2) The Wm Shaper and the Anna Whateley who wished to marry in Temple Grafton were two different people entirely from the Wm Shagspere and Anne Hathwey who were married in Stratford. This argument relies on the assumption that there was a relative of Shakespeare's living in Temple Grafton, or a man unrelated but sharing Shakespeare's name (which would be extremely unlikely), and that there is no trace of this relative after the issue of his marriage license. 3) The woman Shakespeare loved and the woman Shakespeare finally married were two different Anne's. Not many critics support this hypothesis, but those that do use it to portray Shakespeare as a young man torn between the love he felt for Anne Whateley and the obligation he felt toward Anne Hathwey and the child she was carrying, which was surely his. In Shakespeare, Anthony Burgess constructs a vivid scenario to this effect:

It is reasonable to believe that Will wished to marry a girl named Anne Whateley. The name is common enough in the Midlands and is even attached to a four-star hotel in Horse Fair, Banbury. Her father may have been a friend of John Shakespeare's, he may have sold kidskin cheap, there are various reasons why the Shakespeare's and the Whateleys, or their nubile children, might become friendly. Sent on skin-buying errands to Temple Grafton, Will could have fallen for a comely daughter, sweet as May and shy as a fawn. He was eighteen and highly susceptible. Knowing something about girls, he would know that this was the real thing. Something, perhaps, quite different from what he felt about Mistress Hathaway of Shottery.

But why, attempting to marry Anne Whateley, had he put himself in the position of having to marry the other Anne? I suggest that, to use the crude but convenient properties of the old women's-magazine morality-stories, he was exercised by love for the one and lust for the other. I find it convenient to imagine that he knew Anne Hathaway carnally, for the first time, in the spring of 1582...

Whichever argument one chooses to accept, it is fact that

Shakespeare, a minor at the time, married Anne Hathaway, who was twenty-six and already several months pregnant. Anne was the eldest daughter, and one of the seven children of Richard Hathaway, a twice-married farmer in Shottery. When Richard died in 1581, he requested his son, Bartholomew, move into the house we now know as Anne Hathaway's Cottage, and maintain the property for his mother, Richard's second wife and Anne's stepmother. Anne lived in the cottage with Bartholomew, her stepmother, and her other siblings.

No doubt, she was bombarded with a barrage of household tasks to fill her days at Hew land Farm, as it was then called. After her marriage to Shakespeare, Anne left Hew land Farm to live in John Shakespeare's house on Henley Street, as was the custom of the day. Preparations for the new bride were made, and for reasons unknown, her arrival greatly bothered John Shakespeare's current tenant in the house, William Burbage. A heated fight ensued, and John refused to release Burbage from his lease, so Burbage decided to take the matter to a London court. On July 24, 1582, lawyers representing both sides met and resolved the matter — John would release William Burbage from his lease.

The Shakespeare's' first child was Susanna, christened on May 26, 1583, and twins arrived in January 1585. They were baptized on February 2 of that year and named after two very close friends of William—the baker Hamnet Sadler and his wife, Judith. The Sadlers became the godparents of the twins and, in 1598, they, in turn, named their own son William. Not much information is known about the life of Anne and her children after this date, except for the tragic fact that Hamnet Shakespeare died of an unknown cause on August 11, 1596, at the age of eleven. By this time, Shakespeare had long since moved to London to realize his dreams on the English stage (a time in the Bard's life that will be covered in depth later on) and we do not know if he was present at Hamnet's funeral in Stratford. We can only imagine how deeply the loss of his only son touched the sensitive poet, but his sorrow is undeniably reflected in his later work, and, particularly, in a passage from King John, written between 1595 and 1597:

*Young Arthur is my son, and he is lost:*
*I am not mad: I would to heaven I were!*
*For then, 'tis like I should forget myself:*
*O, if I could, what grief should I forget!*
*Preach some philosophy to make me mad,*
*And thou shalt be canonized, cardinal,*
*For being not mad but sensible of grief,*
*My reasonable part produces reason*
*How I may be deliver'd of these woes,*
*And teaches me to kill or hang myself:*
*If I were mad, I should forget my son,*
*Or madly think a babe of clouts were he:*
*I am not mad; too well, too well I feel*
*The different plague of each calamity....*
*I tore them from their bonds and cried aloud*
*'O that these hands could so redeem my son,*
*As they have given these hairs their liberty!'*
*But now I envy at their liberty,*
*And will again commit them to their bonds,*
*Because my poor child is a prisoner.*
*And, father cardinal, I have heard you say*
*That we shall see and know our friends in heaven:*
*If that be true, I shall see my boy again;*
*For since the birth of Cain, the first male child,*
*To him that did but yesterday suspire,*
*There was not such a gracious creature born.*
*But now will canker-sorrow eat my bud*
*And chase the native beauty from his cheek*
*And he will look as hollow as a ghost,*
*As dim and meagre as an ague's fit,*
*And so he'll die; and, rising so again,*
*When I shall meet him in the court of heaven*
*I shall not know him: therefore never, never*
*Must I behold my pretty Arthur more. (III.iv.45-91)*

## Chapter 4

# Shakespeare as Actor and Playwright

We know very little about Shakespeare's life during two major spans of time, commonly referred to as the "lost years." The lost years fall into two periods: 1578-82 and 1585-92. The first period covers the time after Shakespeare left grammar school until his marriage to Anne Hathaway in November of 1582. The second period covers the seven years of Shakespeare's life in which he must have been perfecting his dramatic skills and collecting sources for the plots of his plays. "What could such a genius accomplish in this direction during six or eight years? The histories alone must have required unending hours of labour to gather facts for the plots and counter-plots of these stories.

When we think of the time he must have spent in reading about the pre-Tudor dynasties, we are at a loss to estimate what a day's work meant to him. Perhaps he was one of those singular geniuses who absorb books. George Douglas Brown, when discussing Shakespeare, often used to say he knew how to 'pluck the guts' out of a tome".

No one knows for certain how Shakespeare first started his career in the theatre, although several London players would visit Stratford regularly, and so, sometime between 1585 and 1592, it is probable that young Shakespeare could have been recruited by the Leicester's or Queen's men. Whether an acting troupe recruited Shakespeare in his hometown or he was forced on his own to travel to London to begin his career, he was nevertheless an established actor in the great city by the end of 1592. In this year came the first reference to Shakespeare in the world of the theatre.

The dramatist Robert Greene declared in his death-bed autobiography that, "There is an upstart crow, beautified with our feathers, that with his Tigers heart wrap in a Players hide supposes he is as well able to bombast out a blank verse as the best of you; and, being an absolute Johannes Factotum, is in his own conceit the only Shake-scene in a country." After Green's death, his editor, Henry Chettle, publicly apologized to Shakespeare in the Preface to his Kind-Heart's Dream:

About three months since M. Robert Greene died, leaving many papers in sundry booksellers' hands, among other his Groatsworth of Wit, in which a letter written to divers playmakers is offensively by one or two of them taken, and because on the dead they cannot be avenged, they willfully forge in their conceits a living author. With neither of them, that take offence was I acquainted, and with one of them, I care not if I never be.

The other, whom at that time I did not so much spare as since I wish I had, for that, as I have moderated the heat of living writers and might have used my own discretion (especially in such a case, the author being dead), that I did not I am as sorry as if the original fault had been my fault, because myself have seen his demeanor no less civil than he excellent in the quality he professes. Besides, the divers of worship have reported his uprightness of dealing, which argues his honesty and his facetious grace in writing that approves his art.

Such an apology indicates that Shakespeare was already a respected player in London with influential friends and connections. Records also tell us that several of Shakespeare's plays were popular by this time, including Henry VI, The Comedy of Errors, and Titus Andronicus. The company that staged most of the early productions of these plays was Pembroke's Men, sponsored by the Earl of Pembroke, Henry Herbert. The troupe was very popular and performed regularly at the court of Queen Elizabeth. Most critics conclude that Shakespeare spent time as both a writer and an actor for

Pembroke's Men before 1592. The turning point in Shakespeare's career came in 1593. The theatres had been closed since 1592 due to an outbreak of the plague and, although it is possible that Shakespeare toured the outlying areas of London with acting companies like Pembroke's Men or Lord Strange's Men, it seems more likely that he left the theatre entirely during this time to work on his non-dramatic poetry. The hard work paid off, for by the end of 1593, Shakespeare had caught the attention of the Earl of Southampton.

Southampton became Shakespeare's patron, and on April 18, 1593, Venus and Adonis were entered for publication. Shakespeare had made his formal debut as a poet. The dedication Shakespeare wrote to Southampton at the beginning of the poem is impassioned and telling, "phrased with courtly deference"

TO THE RIGHT HONOURABLE HENRY WRIOTHESLEY, EARL OF SOUTHAMPTON, AND BARON OF TICHFIELD.

RIGHT HONOURABLE,

I KNOW not how I shall offend in dedicating my unpolished lines to your lordship, nor how the world will censure me for choosing so strong a prop to support so weak a burden only, if your honour seem but pleased, I account myself highly praised, and vow to take advantage of all idle hours, till I have honoured you with some graver labour. But if the first heir of my invention prove deformed, I shall be sorry it had so noble a god-father, and never after ear so barren a land, for fear it yield me still so bad a harvest. I leave it to your honourable survey, and your honour to your heart's content; which I wish may always answer your own wish and the world's hopeful expectation.

*Your honour's in all duty,*

Although there is no concrete proof that Shakespeare had a long and close friendship with Southampton, most scholars agree that this was the case, based on Shakespeare's writings, particularly the early sonnets.

Shakespeare returned to the theatre in 1594, and became

a leading member of the Lord Chamberlain's Men, formally known as Lord Strange's Men. The manuscript account of the treasurer of the royal chamber in the public records office tells us the following:

To William Kempe, William Shakespeare, and Richard Burbage, servants to the Lord Chamberlain, upon the council's warrant dated at Whitehall 15 die March 1594 for two several comedies or interludes showed by them before her Majesty in Christmas time last past, viz; upon St. Stephan's day and Innocent's day, xiiij li. vj s. viij d. and by way of her Majesty's reward...

This is proof that Shakespeare had performed with the Chamberlain's Men before Elizabeth I on several occasions. As payment for their performance, the actors each received 10 pounds. During his time with the Chamberlain's Men Shakespeare wrote many plays, including Romeo and Juliet, Richard II, King John, and Love's Labour's Lost. As G.E. Bentley points out in Shakespeare and the Theatre, Shakespeare had by this time become immersed in his roles as actor and writer. He was "more completely and more continuously involved in theatres and acting companies than any other Elizabethan dramatist. [Shakespeare is] "the only one known who not only wrote plays for his company, acted in the plays, and shared the profits, but who was also one of the housekeepers who owned the building. For seventeen years he was one of the owners of the Globe theatre and for eight years he was one of the housekeepers of the company's second theatre, the Black friars, as well".

During the years Shakespeare performed with the Chamberlain's Men, before their purchase of the Globe in 1599, they played primarily at the well-established theatres like the Swan, the Curtain, and the Theatre. The troupe would also give regular performances before Elizabeth I and her court, and tour the surrounding areas of London. Some important events in Shakespeare's personal life also take place during this period. The Shakespeare has finally received a coat of arms 1596 (see "Shakespeare's Parents" for more information on the coat-of-arms), and on August 11 of the same year,

Shakespeare's son, Hamnet, died at the age of eleven. Shakespeare no doubt returned to Stratford for the burial, although we have no documented proof. In 1597, Shakespeare purchased the second largest house in Stratford: New Place. The house stood at the corner of Chapel Lane and Chapel Street, north of the Guild Chapel and right across from the very school he attended in his youth. He bought it from William Underhill for the low price of 60 pounds. And below is the actual deed (translated from the original Latin) transferring New Place from Underhill to Shakespeare on May 4, 1597.

Between William Shakespeare, complainant, and William Underhill, deforciant [wrongful occupier, supposed by the legal fiction on which the fine method of transfer was based to be keeping the complainant out of his rightful property], concerning one dwelling house, two barns, and two gardens with their appurtenances in Stratford-on-Avon, in regard to which a plea of agreement was broached in the same court. Namely, that the said William Underhill acknowledged the said tenements with their appurtenances to be the right of W. Shakespeare as being those which the same William Shakespeare has by gift of the said W. U., and remitted and waived claim to them from himself and his heirs to the said W.S. and his heirs forever....and agreement the same W.S. has given the foresaid W./U. sixty pounds sterling.

Many theorize that Shakespeare renewed his interest in Stratford only after the death of Hamnet and that, for the many years he was away in London, he neglected his family back home. However, it is just as likely that he made frequent yet unrecorded trips to Stratford while he was trying to find success in London.

## Chapter 5

# William Shakespeare–Timeline

1564 Born in Stratford-upon-Avon. to tanner and glove maker, John Shakespeare and his wife, Mary (Arden). His actual birthday is unknown but assumed to be April the 23 rd. His baptism was recorded in the Parish register of Holy Trinity Church on April the 26th.

1571 If Shakespeare went to school this is when he would have started because children in Stratford began their schooling at the age of seven. He would have gone to the local grammar school.

1582 Shakespeare marries Anne Hathaway November the 27th at Temple Grafton, a village near Stratford.

1583 Susanna, his first child is born

1585 Judith and Hamnet, twins, are born, February 2 nd. Shakespeare goes to London and starts his theatrical career.

1589 -92 Shakespeare establishes his career and begins to make a name for himself. Henry VI, 1,2,3 The Comedy of Errors Titus Andronicus The Taming of the Shrew Richard III

1593 Dedicates *Venus and Adonis* and *The Rape of Lucrece* to Henry Wriothsley, Earl of Southampton - thought to be the beautiful youth of the Sonnets 1593 Venus and Adonis Begins writing the Sonnets, Two Gentlemen of Verona Love's Labour's Lost

1594 Founding member of the Lord Chamberlain's

| | |
|---|---|
| | Men, an acting company. The Rape of Lucrece (published) |
| 1596-97 | Hamnet dies 1597Shakespeare purchases New Place, a large house in Stratford, 1597. A Midsummer Night's Dream Romeo and Juliet Richard II Merchant of Venice |
| 1597-99 | The Globe Theater built on Bankside 1599. Shakespeare is a shareholder. Henry IV,1,2 The Merry Wives of Windsor As You Like It Much Ado About Nothing Henry V Julius Caesar |
| 1600-08 | The Great Tragedies 1601 Shakespeare's father dies 1603 The Lord Chamberlain's Men become The King's Men and perform regularly at court. 1607 Susanna Shakespeare marries Dr. John Hall 1608 The King's Men begin playing at the Blackfriars 1608 Shakespeare's mother dies. Twelfth Night Hamlet Troilus & Cressida Alls Well That Ends Well Measure for Measure Othello King Lear Macbeth Antony and Clepatra Coriolanus Timon of Athens |
| 1609-11 | 1609 the Sonnets published. The Romances Pericles Prince of Tyre Cymbeline The Winter's Tale The Tempest |
| 1612-16 | Shakespeare retires from the theatre and returns to live in Stratford. Works on new plays with his friend, John Fletcher 1616 Judith Shakespeare married Thomas Quiney. Henry VIII The Two Noble Kinsmen Cardenio |
| 1616 | Shakespeare dies 23 rd April (on his birthday) and is buried in Holy Trinity Church. |

Chapter 6

# William Shakespeare–List of Works

### *Comedy*

- All's Well That Ends Well
- As You Like It
- The Comedy of Errors
- Cymbeline
- Love's Labours Lost
- Measure for Measure
- The Merry Wives of Windsor
- The Merchant of Venice
- A Midsummer Night's Dream
- Much Ado About Nothing
- Pericles, Prince of Tyre
- Taming of the Shrew
- The Tempest
- Troilus and Cressida
- Twelfth Night
- Two Gentlemen of Verona
- Winter's Tale

### *History*

- Henry IV, part 1
- Henry IV, part 2
- Henry V
- Henry VI, part 1
- Henry VI, part 2
- Henry VI, part 3
- Henry VIII
- King John
- Richard II
- Richard III

### *Tragedy*

- Antony and
- Coriolanus
- Julius Caesar
- Macbeth
- Romeo and Juliet
- Titus Andronicus
- Cleopatra
- Hamlet
- King Lear
- Othello
- Timon of Athens

### *Poetry*

- The Sonnets
- Complaint
- Lucrece
- Funeral Elegy by W.S.
- A Lover's
- The Rape of
- Venus and Adonis

# Chapter 7

# George Herbert: Introduction

George attended Trinity College, Cambridge, and became the Public Orator of the University, responsible for giving speeches of welcome in Latin to famous visitors, and writing letters of thanks in Latin, to acknowledge gifts of books for the University Library. This brought him to the attention of King James I, who granted him an annual allowance, and seemed likely to make him an ambassador. However, in 1625 the king died, and George Hebert, who had originally gone to college with the intention of becoming a priest, but had head turned by the prospect of a career at Court, determined anew to seek ordination. In 1626, he was ordained, and became vicar and then rector of the parish of Bemerton and neighbouring Fugglestone, not far from Salisbury.

He served faithfully as a parish priest, diligently visiting his parishioners and bringing them the sacraments when they were ill, and food and clothing when they were in want. He read Morning and Evening Prayer daily in the church, encouraging the congregation to join him when possible, and ringing the church bell before each service so that those who could not come might hear it and pause in their work to join their prayers with his. He used to go once a week to Salisbury to hear Evening Prayer sung there in the cathedral. On one occasion, he was late because he had met a man whose horse had fallen with a heavy load, and he stopped, took off his coat, and helped the man to unload the cart, get the horse back on its feet, and then reload the cart. His spontaneous generosity and good will won him the affection of his parishioners.

Today, however, he is remembered chiefly for his book

of poems, *The Temple,* which he sent shortly before his death to his friend Nicholas Ferrar, to publish if he thought them suitable. They were published after Herbert's death, and have influenced the style of other poets, including Samuel Taylor Coleridge. Several of them have been used as hymns, in particular "Teach me, my God and King," and "Let all the world in every corner sing." Another of his poems contains the lines:

*Prayer, the Church's banquet, Angel's age,*
*God's breath in man returning to his birth,*
*The soul in paraphrase, the heart in pilgrimage,*
*The Christian plummet sounding heav'n and earth.*

*He died on 1 March 1633, but is commemorated two days earlier, to avoid conflict with other commemorations.*

## Chapter 8

# Edmund Spenser

EDMUND SPENSER, English poet, author of *The Faery Queen*, was born in London about the year 1552. The received date of his birth rests on a passage in sonnet lx. of the *Amoretti*. He speaks there of having lived forty-one years; the *Amoretti* was published in 1595, and described on the titlepage as "written not long since"; this would make the year of his birth 1552 or 1553. We know from the *Prothalamion* that London was his birthplace. This at least seems the most natural interpretation of the words "Merry London, my most kindly nurse, That to me gave this life's first native source." In the same poem he speaks of himself as taking his name from "an house of ancient fame." Several of his pieces are addressed to the daughters of Sir John Spencer, head of the Althorp family; and in *Colin Clout's Come Home Again* he describes three of the ladies as "The honour of the noble family Of which I meanest boast myself to be." Mr R. B. Knowles, however, is of the opinion (see the Spending of the Money of Robert Nowell, privately printed, 1877) that the poet's kinsmen must be sought among the humbler Spencers of north-east Lancashire.

Robert Nowell, a London citizen, left a sum of money to be distributed in various charities, and in the account-books of his executors among the names of other beneficiaries has been discovered that of "Edmund Spensore, scholar of the Merchant Taylor School, at his going to Pembroke Hall in Cambridge." The date of this benefaction is the 28th of April 1569. As the poet is known to have been a sizar of Pembroke, the identification is beyond dispute. Till this discovery it was not known where Spenser received his school education.

The speculations as to the poet's parentage, started by the Nowell MS., are naturally more uncertain.

Mr Knowles found three Spensers in the books of the Merchant Taylors, and concluded that the poorest of them, John Spenser, a "free journeyman" in the "art or mystery of clothmaking," might have been the poet's father, but he afterwards abandoned this theory. Dr Grosart, however, adhered to it, and it is now pretty generally accepted. The connexion of Spenser with Lancashire is also supported by the Nowell MS. - several Spensers of that county appear among the "poor kinsfolk" who profited by Nowell's bounty. The name of the poet's mother was Elisabeth, and he notes as a happy coincidence that it was borne by the three women of most consequence to him - wife, queen and mother.

It is natural that a poet so steeped in poetry as Spenser should show his faculty at a very early age; and there is strong reason to believe that verses from his pen were published just as he left school at the age of sixteen or seventeen.

Certain pieces, translations from Du Bellay and Petrarch, afterwards included in a volume of poems by Spenser published in 1591, are found in a miscellany, *Theatre for Worldings,* issued by a Flemish Protestant refugee, John van der Noodt, on the 25th of May 1569. The translations from Du Bellay appear in blank verse in the miscellany, and are rhymed in sonnet form in the later publication, but the diction is substantially the same; the translations from Petrarch are republished with slight variations.

Poets were so careless of their rights in those days and publishers took such liberties that we cannot draw the conclusion that would be inevitable if the facts were of more modern date.

But the probabilities are that these passages in Van der Noodt's *Theatre,* although the editor makes no acknowledgment, were contributed by the schoolboy Spenser. As the exercises of a schoolboy writing before our poetic diction was enriched by the great Elizabethans, they are remarkable for a sustained command of expression which many schoolboys might exhibit in translation now, but which was a rarer and more significant accomplishment when Surrey and Sackville were the highest models in post-Chaucerian English.

Little is known of Spenser's Cambridge career, except that he was a sizar of Pembroke Hall, took his bachelor's degree in 1572, his master's in 1576, and left Cambridge without having obtained a fellowship. Dr Grosart's inquiries have elicited the fact that his health was not good - college allowances while he was in residence being often paid "Spenser legrotanti." One of the fellows of Pembroke strongly influenced his destiny. This was Gabriel Harvey, a prominent figure in the university life of the time, an enthusiastic educationist, vigorous, versatile, not a little vain of his own culture and literary powers, which had gained him a certain standing in London society.

The revival and advancement of English literature was a passion of the time, and Harvey was fully possessed by it. His fancy for reforming English verse by discarding rhyme and substituting unrhymed classical meters, and the tone of his controversy with Thomas Nash, have caused him to be regarded as merely an obstreperous and pragmatic pedant; but it is clear that Spenser, who had sense enough not to be led astray by his eccentricities, received active and generous help from him and probably not a little literary stimulus. Harvey's letters to Spenser[2] throw a very kindly light on his character. During his residence at the university the poet acquired a knowledge of Greek, and at a later period offered to impart that language to a friend in Ireland (see Ludowick Bryskett, *Discourse of Civil Life*, London, 1606, written twenty years previously). Spenser's affinity with Plato is most marked, and he probably read him in the original.

Three years after leaving Cambridge, in 1579, Spenser issued his first volume of poetry, the *Shepherd's Calendar*. Where and how he spent the interval has formed subjects for elabourate speculation. That most of it was spent in the study of his art we may take for granted. That he lived for a time in the "north parts" of England; that there or elsewhere he fell in love with a lady whom he celebrates under the anagram of "Rosalind". Who was most likely Rose, a daughter of a yeoman named Dyneley, near Clitheroe; that his friend Harvey urged him to return south, and introduced him to Sir Philip Sidney; that Sidney took to him, discussed poetry with him, introduced him at court, put him in the way of preferment - are ascertained facts in his personal history. Dr Grosart conjectures with considerable plausibility that he was in Ireland in 1577. The words "for long time far estranged" in E.K.'s preface to the *Shepherd's Calendar* point that way. Spenser undoubtedly entered the service of the Earl of Leicester either in 1578 or a year earlier (Carew Papers).

The interest of the *Shepherd's Calendar* is mainly personal to Spenser. Its twelve poems continue to be read chiefly because they were the first published essays of the author of the *Faery Queen*, the poems in which he tried and disciplined his powers. They mark no stage in the history of pastoral poetry. The title, borrowed from a French almanack of the year 1496, which was translated into English in 1503 and frequently reprinted, is attractive but hardly tallies with the subject. It may have been an afterthought. Spenser had too strong a genius not to make his own individuality felt in any form that he attempted, and his buoyant dexterity in handling various schemes of verse must always afford delight to the connoisseur in such things. But a reader not already interested in Spenser, or not already familiar with the artificial eclogue, would find little to attract him in the *Shepherd's Calendar*.

The poems need a special education; given this, they are felt to be full of charm and power, a fresh and vivid spring to the splendid summer of the Faery Queen. The diction is a studiously archaic artificial compound, partly Chaucerian, partly North Anglian, partly factitious; and the pastoral scenery is such as may be found in any country where there are sheep, hills, trees, shrubs, toadstools and running streams. That Spenser, having been in the north of England, should have introduced here and there a touch of north country colour is natural enough, but it is not sufficient to give a character to the poems as pastoral poems. As such they follow continuously and do not violently break away from Latin, Italian and French predecessors, and Professor George Saintsbury is undoubtedly right in indicating Marot as the most immediate model.

At the same time one can quite understand on historical grounds why the *Shepherd's Calendar* was hailed with enthusiasm as the advent of a "new poet." Not only was it a complete work in a form then new to English literature, but the execution showed the hand of a master. There had been nothing so finished, so sustained, so masterful in grasp, so brilliant in meter and phrase, since Chaucer. It was felt at once that the poet for whom the age had been waiting had come. The little coterie of friends whose admiration the young poet had won in private were evidently concerned lest the wider public should be bewildered and repelled by the unfamiliar pastoral form and rustic diction.

To put the public at the right point of view the poems were published with a commentary by "E.K." - supposed to be one Edward Kirke, who was an undergraduate with Spenser at Pembroke. This so-called "glosse" explained the archaic words, revealed the poet's intentions, and boasted that, as in the case of Virgil, the pastoral poetry of the "new poet" was but "a proving of the wings for higher and wider flights." The "new poet's" name was withheld; and the identification of the various "shepherds" - of Cuddie and Roffy and Diggon Davie, and the beauteous golden-haired "widow's daughter of the glen" - was fortunately reserved to yield delight to the ingenious curiosity of a later age.

On the subject of Spenser's obligations the "glosse" is very misleading. An eclogue drawn almost entirely from Virgil is represented as jointly inspired by Virgil and Theocritus and chiefly by the latter. Marot is belittled and his claim to be a poet called in question. As regards the twelfth eclogue suggested by and in part translated from his poetry, his influence is ignored. The stanzas Professor Hales cites as autobiographical are actually taken from Marot's eclogue, *Au Roi sous les noms de Pan et Robin*. Dr Grosart falls into the same error.

*The Shepherd's Calendar* was published at Gabriel Harvey's instance, and was dedicated to Sir Philip Sidney. It was one out of many poetical schemes on which the young poet was busy in the flush of conscious power and high hopes excited by the admiration of the literary authorities whose approval was then most to be coveted. His letters to Harvey and Harvey's letters to him furnish hints for a very engaging fancy picture of Spenser at this stage of his life - looking at the world through rose-coloured spectacles, high in favour with Sidney and Leicester, dating his letters from Leicester House, gaily and energetically discussing the technicalities of his art, with some provision from his powerful friends - certain, but the form of it delightfully uncertain - going to court in the train of Leicester, growing pointed beard and mustachios of fashionable shape, and frightening his ever-vigilant friend and mentor Harvey by the light courtier-like tone of his references to women.

The studious pastoral poet from "north parts" had blossomed with surprising rapidity in the image of the gay fortune-seeking adventurers who crowded the court of the virgin queen in those stirring times. Some of the poems which he mentions to Harvey as then completed or on the anvil - his *Dreams*, his *Nine Comedies*, his *Dying Pelican* and his *Stemmata dudleiana* (singing the praises of the noble family which was befriending him) - have not been preserved, at least in any form that can be certainly identified. Among the lost works was his *English Poet* - a contribution to literary criticism. He had sent Harvey a portion of the *Faery Queen*, which he was eager to continue; but Harvey did not think much of it - a judgment for which Harvey is often ridiculed as a dull pedant, as if we knew for certain that what was submitted to him was identical with what was published ten years later.

Spenser was appointed secretary to the lord-deputy of Ireland in 1580, and was one of the band of adventurers who, with mixed motives of love of excitement, patriotism, piety and hopes of forfeited estates, accompanied Lord Arthur Grey of Wilton to Ireland to aid in the suppression of Desmond's rebellion. Regret is sometimes expressed that the author of the *Faery Queen*, who ought to have been dreamy, meditative, gentle and refined, should have been found in such company, and should have taken part in the violent and bloody scenes of Lord Grey's two years' attempt at "pacification." But such things must be judged with reference to the circumstances and the spirit of the time, and it must be remembered that England was then engaged in a fierce struggle for existence against the Catholic powers of the Continent.

Of Lord Grey's character his secretary was an enthusiastic admirer, exhibiting him in the *Faery Queen* as Arthegal, the personification of justice; and we know exactly what were his own views of Irish policy, and how strongly he deplored that Lord Grey was not permitted to carry them out. Spenser's *View of the State of Ireland* drawn up after fourteen years' experience, but first printed in 1633 by Sir James Ware, who complains of Spenser's harshness and inadequate knowledge (*History of Ireland*, appendix), is not the work of a gentle dreamer, but of an energetic and shrewd public official.

*The View* is not a descriptive work; there is nothing in the style to indicate that it was written by a poet; it is an elabourate state paper, the exposition in the form of a dialogue of a minutely considered plan for the pacification of Ireland, written out of zeal for the public service for the eyes of the government of the day. A very thoroughgoing plan it is. After passing in review the history and character of the Irish, their laws, customs, religion, habits of life, armour, dress, social institutions and finding "evil usages" in every department, he propounds his plan of "reformation." Reformation can be effected only by the sword, by the strong hand. The interlocutor in the dialogue holds up his hands in horror. Does he propose extermination? By no means; but he would give the Irish a choice between submission and extermination.

The government had vacillated too long, and, fearing the cost of a thorough operation, had spent twice as much without in any way mending matters. Let them send into Ireland 10,000 foot and 1000 horse, disperse them in garrisons - a complete scheme of localities is submitted - give the Irish twenty days to come in; if they did not come in then, give no quarter afterwards, but hunt them down like wild beasts in the winter time when the covert is thin; "if they be well followed one winter, ye shall have little work to do with them the next summer"; famine would complete the work of the sword; and in eighteen months' time peace would be restored and the ground cleared for plantation by English colonists. There must be no flinching in the execution of this plan - "no remorse or drawing back for the sight of any such rueful object as must thereupon follow, nor for compassion of their calamities, seeing that by no other means it is possible to recover them, and that these are not of will but of very urgent necessity." The government had out of foolish compassion drawn back before when Lord Grey had brought the recalcitrant Irish to the necessary extremity of famine; the gentle poet warns them earnestly against a repetition of the blunder.

Such was Spenser's plan for the pacification of Ireland, propounded not on his own authority, but as having support in "the consultations and actions of very wise governors and counselors whom he had sometimes heard treat thereof." He knew that it was "bloody and cruel"; but he contended passionately that it was necessary for the maintenance of English power and the Protestant religion. The method was repugnant to the kindly nature of average Englishmen; from the time of Lord Grey no English authority had the heart to go through with it till another remorseless zealot appeared in the person of Cromwell.

That Cromwell knew the treatise of "the sage and serious Spenser," perhaps through Milton, is probable from the fact that the poet's Irish estates were secured to his grandson by the Protector's intervention in 1657. These estates had been granted to Spenser as his share in the redistribution of Munster - 3000 acres of land and Kilcolman Castle, an ancient seat of the Desmonds, in the north of the county of Cork. The elabourate and business-like character of the *View* shows that the poet was no sinecurist, but received his reward for substantial political services. He ceased to be secretary to the lord-deputy when Lord Grey was recalled in 1582; but he continued in the public service, and in 1586 was promoted to the onerous position of clerk to the council of Munster.

Amidst all the distractions of his public life in Ireland Spenser kept up his interest in literature, and among proper subjects for reform included Irish poetry, of which he could judge only through the medium of translations. He allows it some merit - "sweet wit," "good invention," "some pretty flowers" - but laments that it is "abused to the gracing of wickedness and vice." Meanwhile he seems to have proceeded steadily with the composition of the *Faery Queen*, translating his varied experience of men and affairs into the picturesque forms of his allegory, and expressing through them his conception of the immutable principles that ought to regulate human conduct.

He had, as we have seen, conceived a work of the kind and made a beginning before he left England. The conception must have been very much deepened and widened and in every way enriched by his intimate daily contact with the actual struggle of conflicting individuals and interests and policies in a great crisis. Some four or five years later, being asked in a mixed company of English officials in Ireland (as recorded in Lodowick Bryskett's *Discourse of Civil Life*) to give off-hand a short sketch of "the ethical part of moral philosophy" and the practical uses of the study, Spenser explained to these simpleminded men that the subject was too intricate for an impromptu exposition, but that he had in hand a work called the *Faery Queen* in which an ethical system would be exhibited in action.

The respect paid by his official brethren to Spenser as a man, "not only perfect in the Greek tongue, but also very well read in philosophy, both moral and natural," is an interesting item in his biography. Some years later still, when Spenser was settled at Kilcolman Castle, Sir Walter Raleigh found him with three books of the *Faery Queen* completed, and urged him to come with them to London. London accordingly he revisited in 1589, after nine years' absence. There is a very pretty record of this visit in *Colin Clout's Come Home Again*, published in 1595, but written in 1591, immediately after his return to Kilcolman. The incidents of the visit, by that time matters of wistful memory, are imaged as a shepherd's excursion from his quiet pastoral life into the great world. Colin Clout calls round him once again the masked figures of the *Shepherd's Calendar*, and describes to them what he saw, how he fared, and whom he met at the court of Cynthia, and how, through the influence of "the Shepherd of the Ocean," he was admitted at timely hours to play on his oaten pipe in the great queen's presence.

How much is pure fiction and how much veiled fact in this picture cannot now be distinguished, but it is undoubted that Spenser, though his chief patrons Leicester and Sidney were now dead, was very graciously received by the great world on his return to London. Not only did the queen grant him an audience, but many ladies of the court, several of whom he afterwards honoured with dedications, honoured him with their patronage. The first three books of the *Faery Queen,* which were entered at Stationers' Hall on the 1st of December 1589, were published in 1590, and he was proclaimed at once with remarkable unanimity by all the writers of the time as the first of living poets.

From the first week of its publication the literary world has continued unanimous about the *Faery Queen,* except on minor points. When romanticism was at its lowest ebb Pope read Spenser in his old age with as much delight as in his boyhood. Spenser speaks himself of having had his detractors, of having suffered from the venomous tooth of the Blatant Beast, and he seems to have had in more than ordinary share the poet's sensitiveness to criticism; but the detraction or indifference have generally been found among men who, like the lord high treasurer Burghley, have no liking for poetry of any kind.

The secret of Spenser's enduring popularity with poets and lovers of poetry lies specially in this, that he excels in the poet's peculiar gift, the instinct for verbal music. Shakespeare, or the author of the sonnet usually assigned to him, felt and expressed this when he drew the parallel between "music and sweet poetry": "Thou lovest to hear the sweet melodious sound That Phoebus' lute, the queen of music, makes; And I in deep delight am chiefly drowned Whenas himself to singing he betakes." This is an early word in criticism of Spenser, and it is the last word about his prime and unquestionable excellence - a word in which all critics must agree. Whether he had imagination in the highest degree or only luxuriant fancy, and whether he could tell a story in the highest epic manner or only put together a richly varied series of picturesque incidents, are disputable points; but about the enchantment of his verse there can be no difference of opinion. It matters not in the least that he gains his melody often by archaic affectations and licences of diction; there, however purchased, the marvelously rich music is.

In judging of the structure of the *Faery Queen* we must always remember that, long and diffuse as it is, what we have is but a fragment of the poet's design, and that the narrative is regulated by an allegorical purpose. But, however intricate, however confused, the reader may feel the succession of incidents to be, when he studies the succession of incidents, it is only at the call of duty that he is likely to occupy himself with such a study in reading Spenser.

The ethical value of the allegory has been very variously estimated. The world would probably never have divined that there was any allegory if he had not himself drawn attention to it in a prose dedication and in doggerel headings to the cantos. It was apparently at his friend Raleigh's suggestion that the poet condescended to explain his ethical purpose in *A Letter of the Author's* addressed to Sir Walter and dated the 23rd of January 1589-1590; otherwise it would have been as problematical as the similar intention in the case of the *Idylls of the King* before that intention was expressly declared.

It is almost to be regretted, as far as the allegory is concerned, that the friendly "E. K." was not employed to furnish a "glosse" to the *Faery Queen* as he had done to the *Shepherd's Calendar*. Undoubtedly the peculiar "poetic luxury" of the *Faery Queen* can be enjoyed without any reference to the allegory; even Professor Dowden, the most eloquent champion of Spenser's claims as a "teacher," admits that it is a mistake to look for minute correspondence between outward symbol and underlying sense, and that the poet is least enjoyable where he is most ingenious. Still the allegory governs the structure of the poem, and Spenser himself attached great importance to it as determining his position among poets.

The ethical purpose is distinctive of the poem as a whole; it was foremost in Spenser's mind when he conceived the scheme of the poem, and present with him as he built up and articulated the skeleton; it was in this respect that he claimed to have "overpassed" his avowed models Ariosto and Tasso. If we wish to get an idea of Spenser's imaginative force and abundance, or to see his creations as he saw them, we must not neglect the allegory.

It is obvious from all that he says of his own work that in his eyes the ethical meaning not only heightened the interest of the marvellously rich pageant of heroes and heroines, enchanters and monsters, but was the one thing that redeemed it from romantic commonplace. For the right appreciation of many of the characters and incidents a knowledge of the allegory is indispensable. For example, the slaughter of Error by the Red Cross knight would be merely disgusting but for its symbolic character. The iron Talus and his iron flail is a revolting and brutally cruel monster if he is not regarded as an image of the executioner of righteous law; the Blatant Beast, a purely grotesque and ridiculous monster to outward view, acquires a serious interest when he is known to be an impersonation of malignant detraction.

Notwithstanding its immense range, the *Faery Queen* is profoundly national and Elizabethan, containing many more or less cryptic allusions to contemporary persons and interests. It has never been popular abroad, as is proved by the fact that there is no complete translation of it in any of the Continental languages. This is doubtless on account of a certain monotony in the subject-matter, which is only partially relieved by subtle variations.

The same objection applies to the famous "Spenserian stanza" with its concluding Alexandrine. It was by no means a happy invention, but its infelicity is disguised by its author's marvellous skill in rhythm, and thus recommended it was adopted by Byron and Keats. In his own day Spenser was criticized by Sidney, Ben Jonson, Daniel and others for the artificiality of his language, his "aged accents and untimely words," but Ben Jonson went further - "Spenser's stanza pleased him not, nor his matter." Milton, on the other hand, duly appreciated "our sage and serious poet," and he has been followed by a long line of distinguished judges. It was Charles Lamb who named Spenser "the poet's poet."

After the publication of the *Faery Queen* Spenser seems to have remained in London for more than a year, to enjoy his triumph. It might be supposed, from what he makes the Shepherd of the Ocean say in urging Colin Clout to quit his banishment in Ireland, that Raleigh had encouraged him to expect some permanent provision in London. If he had any such hopes, they were disappointed.

The thrifty queen granted him a pension of £50, which was paid in February 1591, but nothing further was done for him. Colin Clout's explanation that the selfish scrambling and intriguing of court life were not suited to a lowly shepherd swain, and that he returned to country life with relief, may be pastoral convention, or it may have been an expression of the poet's real feelings on his return to Kilcolman, although as a matter of fact there seems to have been as much scrambling for good things in Munster as in London. Certain it is that he did return to Kilcolman in the course of the year 1591, having probably first arranged for the publication of *Daphnaida* and *Complaints*.

*Daphnaida* is a pastoral elegy on the death of the niece of the mistress of the robes. The fact implied in the dedication that he was not, personally, known to the lady has more than once provoked the solemn remark that the poet's grief was assumed. Of course it was assumed; and it is hardly less obvious that sincerity of personal emotion, so far from being a merit in the artificial forms of pastoral poetry, the essence of which lies in its dreamy remoteness from real life, would be a blemish and a discord. Any suggestion of the poet's real personality breaks the charm; once raise the question of the poet's personal sincerity, and the pastoral poem may at once be thrown aside. The remark applies to all Spenser's minor poetry, including his love sonnets; the reader who raises the question whether Spenser really loved his mistress may have a talent for disputation, but none for the full enjoyment of hyperbolical poetry. *Complaints*, also published in 1591, is a miscellaneous collection of poems written at different periods.

The volume contained *The Ruins of Time; The Tears of the Muses; Virgil's Gnat; Mother Hubbard's Tale; The Ruins of Rome; Muiopotmos; Visions of the World's Vanity; Bellay's Visions; Petrarch's Visions.* Some of these pieces are translations already alluded to and interesting only as the exercises of one of our greatest masters of melodious verse; but two of them, *The Tears of the Muses* and *Mother Hubbard's Tales,* have greater intrinsic interest. The first is the complaint of the decay of learning alluded to in *Midsummer Night's Dream,* v. i. 52 "The thrice three Muses mourning for the death Of Learning late deceased in beggary."

The lament, at a time when the Elizabethan drama was "mewing its mighty youth," was not so happy as some of Sperser's political prophecies in his *View of Ireland;* but it is idle work to try to trace the undercurrents and personal allusions in such an occasional pamphlet. *Mother Hubbard's Tale,* a fable in Chaucerian couplets, shows a keenness of satiric force not to be paralleled in any other of Spenser's writings, and suggests that he left the court in a mood very different from Colin Clout's.

Spenser returned to London probably in 1595. He had married in the interval a lady whose Christian name was Elizabeth - Dr Grosart says Elizabeth Boyle. The marriage, celebrated on the 11th of June 1594, was followed by a rapid succession of publications. The first was a volume (entered at Stationers' Hall, on the 19th of November 1594; published 1595) containing the *Amoretti,* a series of exquisite sonnets commemorative of the moods and incidents of his courtship, and the magnificent *Epithalamion,* incomparably the finest of his minor poems. As in the case of the *Complaints,* the publisher for obvious reasons issued this volume nominally without his authority. *Colin Clout's Come Home Again* was published in the same year, with a dedication to Sir Walter Raleigh, dated 1591. Early in 1596 the second three books of the *Faery Queen* were entered in the register of Stationers' Hall, and in the course of the same year were published his *Four Hymns,* his *Prothalamion,* and his *Astrophel,* a pastoral lament for Sir Philip Sidney, which he dedicated to the countess of Essex.

That Spenser wrote more of the *Faery Queen* during the last two years of his life, and that the MS. perished in the sack of Kilcolman Castle by the rebels, may plausibly be conjectured, but cannot be ascertained. During those years he would seem to have been largely occupied with political and personal cares. He describes himself in the *Prothalamion* as a disappointed suitor at court. He drew up his *View of Ireland* in 1596 when he was in London, and from various circumstances it is evident that he had hopes of some kind from the favour of Essex.

The *View*, with its urgent entreaty that Essex should be sent to Ireland, was entered at Stationers' Hall in April 1598, but he did not obtain leave to publish it. Burghley, who had long stood in his way, died in August of that year, and next month Spenser, who seems to have returned to Ireland in 1597, was appointed sheriff of Cork. In October, Tyrone's rebellion broke out, and Spenser's house was sacked and burned. The poet himself escaped, and in December was sent to London with dispatches. Again, he ventured to urge upon the queen his plan for the thorough "reformation" of Ireland. But his own end was near. On 16 January 1599, he died at Westminster, ruined in fortune, if not heart-broken, and was buried in Westminster Abbey, near his master Chaucer. Ben Jonson asserted that he perished for lack of bread, and that when the earl of Essex, hearing of his distress, sent him "20 pieces," the poet declined, saying that he had no time to spend them.

The author of The Return from Parnassus mentions this report of his end also, but, having regard to Spenser's position in the world, it is inherently improbable. Still there is an ugly possibility of its truth. The poet left three sons and a daughter. A pedigree of the family appeared in the *Gentleman's Magazine* for August 1842.

## Chapter 9

# Johnson, Spenser and Literary Progress

Neat "meta-narratives" of literary history are a favorite target of recent critics, justly suspicious of teleological accounts of literary development. One of the most significant of these meta-narratives is the Renaissance, the progression from medieval barbarism toward modern enlightenment, but this notion of an emergence from rudeness to refinement has come under fire from recent critics. The nineteenth century has so far provided much of the ammunition for this reversionary assault, and it is only natural that Schiller, Burckhardt, Pater, Hegel, and Marx should be central in the project. But Augustan critics were formulating their own ideas about the Renaissance, and we can gain a great deal of insight by looking at their approach to, say, Shakespeare or Milton. We can perhaps gain even more by looking at the problem cases. The third member of the English Renaissance poetic triumvirate, Edmund Spenser, was manifestly one of these problems, and he fit uneasily in the eighteenth century's progressive version of the Renaissance.

Spenser was much on the mind of Samuel Johnson, one of the most active and important of those developing our notion of the Renaissance — not in any extended treatment, but in scattered comments from the 1730s through the '80s. Spenser's position in Johnson's thought has received little attention, but tugging on these Spenserian loose ends reveals a thread woven across the entire fabric of Johnson's criticism. Focusing on Johnson and his age may help us better understand the meta-narrative called the Renaissance, and focusing on the rise of the Renaissance may in turn help us better understand Johnson and his age.

The word "Renaissance" was not englished until around 1840, but the lack of the term did not prevent Johnson's contemporaries from recognizing the phenomenon. Johnson himself refers, for instance, to "the Revival of Learning in Europe," and dates "the golden age of our language" from "the accession of Elizabeth."

The metaphors used for this period show the importance of progression: "refinement," for instance, a metaphor from metallurgy, suggests that modern purity came from burning away the imperfections of the past; "cultivation" suggests our arable land once lay fallow. Impressing readers with the darkness of the Dark Ages was *de rigueur* for early eighteenth-century writers such as Addison, for whom the Middle Ages were a time of "Darkness and Superstition." Critics whose interest in medieval authors extended beyond mere antiquarianism valued only their anticipation of what was to come. Winstanley, for instance, finds Gower "the first refiner of our *English* Tongue," and praises Chaucer's "earnest desire to enrich and beautifie our *English* Tongue, which in those days was very rude and barren." Writers who were not part of this march from rudeness to refinement were ill regarded. Skelton, for example, is "now accounted only a Rhymer," and "Whoso reads him, will find he hath a miserable, loose, rambling Style;... yet were good Poets so scarce in his Age, that he had the good fortune to be chosen Poet Laureat."

Like Skelton, Spenser sat uncomfortably in a tradition that valued forward-looking authors, and he was therefore a problem for the eighteenth century. Spenser, somewhere between medieval rudeness and modern civilization, perversely refused to let go of what appeared to be vulgar errors, and could not be reconciled with progressive Augustan critical bromides. This peculiar failure of Spenser's judgment led to scathing attacks, of which Addison's dismissal is typical: "But now the mystic tale, that pleas'd of yore,/ Can charm an understanding age no more."

The lapses in Spenser's taste can be arranged under three heads: design, allegory, and language. Most upsetting is his disregard for the Aristotelian unity of action. The romance design, with its Ariostan *entrelacement* and multiple heroes, was no more appreciated by early eighteenth-century critics than by those of the Renaissance. Allegory, another holdover from the Dark Ages, was also scorned: as Addison complains, "The long-spun allegories fulsome grow,/ While the dull moral lies too plain below." And Spenser's metrical "imperfections" and his archaic diction were considered more perverse than charming before mid-century.

This paradox frustrated eighteenth-century critics, who found that his poetical power, for all its faults, could be neither denied nor resisted. Spenser, educated in the classics in an enlightened age, rejected many aesthetic principles the eighteenth century held not only dear but self-evident. Johnson's censure of Spenser's "studied barbarity" is one expression of this frustration; Hughes's account is another: "It may seem strange indeed, since *Spenser* appears to have been well acquainted with the best Writers of Antiquity, that he has not imitated them."

Even Spenser's defenders had to admit he was incompatible with the Renaissance-as-progression paradigm, and this contributed to the changes in critical sensibility over the course of the century. Hughes was among the first to formulate an aesthetics different from the classical inheritance, an early stage in the development of a new Romantic sensibility. He begins with an architectural metaphor picked up from Rymer, who confesses "I have thought our Poetry of the last Age was as rude as our Architecture." What was censure in Rymer is praise in Hughes:

Indeed the whole Frame of it wou'd appear monstrous, if it were to be examin'd by the Rules of Epick Poetry.... But... the Author never design'd it by these Rules.... To compare it therefore with the Models of Antiquity, wou'd be like drawing a Parallel between the *Roman* and the *Gothick* Architecture.... Tho the former is more majestick in the whole, the latter may be very surprizing and agreeable in its Parts.

This Gothic aesthetic grew, with the help of others like Warton and Hurd, over the course of the century. Spenser provided, along with Percy's ballads, a rallying-cry for a generation of Romantic critics engaged in rewriting the eighteenth century's version of literary history.

Samuel Johnson not only witnessed this change; he was a major participant in it. But he was also an important representative of the earlier sensibility, who in many ways agrees with the progressive paradigm for the Renaissance. He contrasts the na‹vet, of earlier ages with Elizabethan enlightenment: in the Preface to the *Dictionary*, for instance, he writes, "Every language has a time of rudeness antecedent to perfection." Likewise the Preface to Shakespeare: "Nations, like individuals, have their infancy.... The study of those who then aspired to plebeian learning was laid out upon adventures, giants, dragons, and enchantments." The best Renaissance writers slew these dragons, and "*Sidney*'s work" is therefore "the boundary, beyond which I make few excursions. From the authors, which rose in the time of *Elizabeth*, a speech might be formed adequate to all the purposes of use and elegance."

Spenser is a major figure in this age of awakening, and Johnson's interest—even fascination—with Spenser was eternal. In *Idler* 91, for instance, Johnson "considers the whole succession [of poets] from Spenser to Pope, as superior to any names which the continent can boast." Spenser appears nearly three thousand times in the *Dictionary*, and gives Johnson his designation for "the writers before the restoration, whose works I regard as *the wells of English undefiled*."

But for all his fondness of Spenser, Johnson saw the same problems as his contemporaries, and they produced in him the same tensions. He refused, however, to let *a priori* notions of periodization direct his reading. His comment on the object of critical inquiry is well known: "It is... the task of criticism to establish principles; to improve opinion into knowledge." This task includes rendering the past intelligible by building historical narratives. But though the rules and schemata have their place, the empiricist critic must also distinguish those means of pleasing which depend upon known causes and rational deduction, from the nameless and inexplicable elegancies... which may well be termed the enchantresses of the soul. Criticism reduces those regions of literature under the dominion of science, which have hitherto known only the anarchy of ignorance, the caprices of fancy, and the tyranny of prescription.

Johnson wants, where possible, to explain away the "enchantresses of the soul" by annexing their territory into the realm of literary history, but he recognizes—perhaps uncomfortably — that some authors cannot, and should not, be subdued. Guarding against "the tyranny of prescription," therefore, is as important as reducing literature to rules.

Of the three categories considered above—design, allegory, and language—Johnson says nothing about Spenser's design, but we can speculate on his opinion. Though he was instrumental in removing the unities of time and place from English criticism, he preserved one Neoclassical unity—"nothing is essential to the fable, but unity of action" and here Spenser is manifestly deficient. But up rises Johnson's empiricism: "Since the end of poetry is pleasure, that cannot be unpoetical with which all are pleased," and this critical honesty accounts for his fondness for Medieval romances.

This honesty accounts for many of his departures from the taste of his age. Though allegory was widely condemned, Spenser the allegorist was dear to Johnson. Boswell notes that he "praised John Bunyan highly," and that Johnson said "There is reason to think that he had read Spenser." His own allegorical writings owe much to Spenser; the personified Truth and Falsehood of *Rambler* 96, for instance, and "the 'Gulph of Intemperance,' a dreadful whirlpool, interspersed with rocks"31 in *Rambler* 102 echo specific passages in *The Faerie Queene*. His *Vision of Theodore* is especially reminiscent of Spenser's allegory, while the title of his never-completed *"Palace of Sloth, — a vision"* has an unmistakable Spenserian ring. Language is a more considerable problem than design or allegory. No party-line ancient or modern, Johnson considers language neither degenerative nor progressive, but he does see in it a kind of development or trajectory: "Every language has a time of rudeness antecedent to perfection, as well as of false refinement and declension." This is not historical relativism but its opposite; it suggests a trans-historical linguistic ideal, an ideal to which ages succeed or fail in attaining. The Renaissance marks the beginning of this linguistic perfection.

Johnson's concern for this ideal made him uneasy at seeing "the imitation of Spenser... likely to gain upon the age," and Spenser's unmusical stanza and versification were especially loathsome: the imitators seem to conclude, that when they have disfigured their lines with a few obsolete syllables, they have accomplished their design.... Perhaps... the stile of Spenser might by long labour be justly copied; but life is surely given us for higher purposes than to gather what our ancestors have wisely thrown away.

Johnson here is able to "consider the metrical art simply as a science," a positivist science in which the clear failures of the past should be abandoned, and in which modern poets can advance by degrees beyond their precursors.

Johnson also faults Spenser's diction, which he, like Ben Jonson, found to be "no language." *The Shepheardes Calender* draws Johnson's scorn for its "obsolete terms and rustick words, which they very learnedly call Dorick"; this "studied barbarity" calls forth Johnson's most devastating sarcasm: "Surely at the same time that a shepherd learns theology," he writes acidly, "he may gain some acquaintance with his native language." Johnson's dismissal of Spenser's archaism shows the critical tension Johnson felt at discovering major failings in a major poet, a poet who could not be rescued from "the nameless and inexplicable elegancies which appeal wholly to the fancy." It shows, in short, the limits of systematic criticism.

That Spenser could draw both the highest approbation and the most stinging sarcasm leads us to seek Johnson's particular notion of the Renaissance, one that admits Spenserian allegory but not Spenser's language. A candidate for the kind of progress he saw in the Renaissance appears throughout his works; one especially clear statement comes in his praise of Homer: His positions are general, and his representations natural, with very little dependence on local or temporary customs, on those changeable scenes of artificial life, which, by mingling original with accidental notions, and crowding the mind with images which time effaces, produce ambiguity in diction, and obscurity in books. To this open display of unadulterated nature it must be ascribed, that Homer has fewer passages of doubtful meaning than any other poet either in the learned or in modern languages.

Here is one of Johnson's favorite pairs of polar opposites, generality *versus* "accident," and I suggest Johnson saw the Renaissance as Europe's passage from one pole to the other. Faux Medieval diction is a recollection of the "remote allusions and obscure opinions" of a justly forgotten age. These are Johnson's targets in his attacks on Spenser's obfuscator archaism, which leads only to "obscurity in books," and which time justly "effaces."

Generality and "unadulterated nature," on the other hand, are dissociated from "changeable scenes of artificial life" with their "accidental notions" — the very business of allegory, which works by moving from the specific to the general. Allegory educates us in generality, teaching us not to depend on the "local and temporary customs" of the Middle Ages. The "revival of learning" amounts to the revival of general nature, the nature that appears in Shakespeare at his most "universal."

The Renaissance is therefore Europe's maturity, its accession to general nature, its abandonment of the peculiarities of archaism. But even the most mature literature has room for the generality of allegory, the bridge between the details consigned to antiquarians and the universal nature valuable to every reader, just as the Renaissance is the bridge between darkness and light. Spenser more than any other poet is the wedge that splits allegory from archaism, and forces Johnson's empirical criticism to come to terms with Renaissance poetic progress.

## Chapter 10

# Christopher Marlowe

English dramatist, the father of English tragedy, and instaurator of dramatic blank verse, the eldest son of a shoemaker at Canterbury, was born in that city on the 6th of February 1564. He was christened at St George's Church, Canterbury, on the 26th of February, 1563/4, some two months before Shakespeare's baptism at Stratford-on-Avon. His father, John Marlowe, is said to have been the grandson of John Morley or Marlowe, a substantial tanner of Canterbury. The father, who survived by a dozen years or so his illustrious son, married on the 22nd of May 1561 Catherine, daughter of Christopher Arthur, at one time rector of St Peter's, Canterbury, who had been ejected by Queen Mary as a married minister. The dramatist received the rudiments of his education at the King's School, Canterbury, which he entered at Michaelmas 1578, and where he had as his fellow-pupils Richard Boyle, afterwards known as the great earl of Cork, and Will Lyly, the brother of the dramatist. Stephen Gosson entered the same school a little before, and William Harvey, the famous physician, a little after Marlowe. He went to Cambridge as one of Archbishop Parker's scholars from the King's School, and matriculated at Benet (Corpus Christi) College, on the 17th of March 1571, taking his B.A. degree in 1584, and that of M.A. three or four years later.

Francis Kett, the mystic, burnt in 1589 for heresy, was a fellow and tutor of his college, and may have had some share in developing Marlowe's opinions in religious matters. Marlowe's classical acquirements were of a kind, which was then extremely common, being based for the most part upon a minute acquaintance with Roman mythology, as revealed in Ovid's *Metamorphoses*. His spirited translation of Ovid's *Amores* (printed 1596), which was at any rate commenced at Cambridge, does not seem to point to any very intimate acquaintance with the grammar and syntax of the Latin tongue. Before 1587 he seems to have quitted Cambridge for London, where he attached himself to the Lord Admiral's Company of Players, under the leadership of the famed actor Edward Alleyn, and almost at once began writing for the stage.

Of Marlowe's career in London, apart from his four great theatrical successes, we know hardly anything; but he evidently knew Thomas Kyd, who shared his unorthodox opinions. Nash criticized his verse, Greene affected to shudder at his atheism; Gabriel Harvey maligned his memory. On the other hand Marlowe was intimate with the Walsinghams of Scadbury, Chiselhurst, kinsmen of Sir Francis Walsingham. He was also the personal friend of Sir Walter Raleigh, and perhaps of the poetical earl of Oxford, with both of whom, and with such men as Walter Warner and Robert Hughes the mathematicians, Thomas Harriott the notable astronomer, and Matthew Royden, the dramatist is said to have met in free converse. Either this free converse or the licentious character of some of the young dramatist's tirades seems to have sown a suspicion among the strait-laced that his morals left everything to be desired. It is probable enough that this attitude of reprobation drove a man of so exalted a disposition as Marlowe into a more insurgent attitude than he would have otherwise adopted. He seems at any rate to have been associated with what was denounced as Sir Walter Raleigh's school of atheism, and to have dallied with opinions, which were then regarded as putting a man outside the pale of civilized humanity.

As the result of some depositions made by Thomas Kyd under the influence of torture, the Privy Council were upon the eve of investigating some serious charges against Marlowe when his career was abruptly and somewhat scandalously terminated. The order had already been issued for his arrest, when a man variously named (Archer and Ingram) at

Deptford, at the end of May 1593, slew him in a quarrel and he was buried on the 1st of June in the churchyard of St Nicholas at Deptford. The following September Gabriel Harvey referred to him as "dead of the plague." The disgraceful particulars attached to the tragedy of Marlowe in the popular mind would not seem to have appeared until four years later (1597) when Thomas Beard, the Puritan author of *The Theatre of God's Judgements*, used the death of this playmaker and atheist as one of his warning examples of the vengeance of God. Upon the embellishments of this story, such as that of Francis Meres the critic, in 1598, that Marlowe came to be "stabbed to death by a bawdy servingman, a rival of his in his lewde love". That of William Vaughan in the *Golden Grove* of 1600, in which the unfortunate poet's dagger is thrust into his own eye in prevention of his felonious assault upon an innocent man, his guest, it is impossible now to pronounce.

We really do not know the circumstances of Marlowe's death. The probability is he was killed in a brawl, and his atheism must be interpreted not according to the ex parte accusation of one Richard Baines, a professional informer (among the Privy Council records), but as a species of rationalistic antinomianism, dialectic in character, and closely related to the deflection from conventional orthodoxy for which Kett was burnt at Norwich in 1589. A few months before the end of his life there is reason to believe that he transferred his services from the Lord Admiral's to Lord Strange's Company, and may have thus been brought into communication with Shakespeare, who in such plays as Richard II and Richard III owed not a little to the influence of his romantic predecessor.

Marlowe's career as a dramatist lies between the years 1587 and 1593, and the four great plays to which reference has been made were *Tamburlaine the Great*, an heroic epic in dramatic form divided into two parts of five acts each (1587, printed in 1590); *Dr Faustus* (1588, entered at Stationers' Hall 1601); *The Famous Tragedy of the Rich Jew of Malta* (dating perhaps from 1589, acted in 1592, printed in 1633); and *Edward the Second* (printed 1594). The very first words of *Tamburlaine* sound the trumpet note of attack in the older order of things dramatic: "From jigging veins of riming mother wits And such conceits as clownage keeps in pay We'll lead you to the stately tent of war, Where you shall hear the Scythian Tamburlaine Threatening the world with high astounding terms And scourging kingdoms with his conquering sword."

It leapt with a bound to a place beside Kyd's *Spanish Tragedy*, and few plays have been more imitated by rivals (Greene's *Alphonsus of Aragon*, Peele's *Battle of Alcazar*) or more keenly satirized by the jealousy and prejudice of out-distanced competitors. With many and heavy faults, there is something of genuine greatness in Tamburlaine the Great; and for two grave reasons it must always be remembered with distinction and mentioned with honour. It is the first play ever written in English blank verse, as distinguished from mere rhymeless decasyllabics.

It contains one of the noblest passages, perhaps indeed the noblest, in the literature of the world, ever written by one of the greatest masters of poetry in loving praise of the glorious delights and sublime submission to the everlasting limits of his art. In its highest and most distinctive qualities, in unfaltering and infallible command of the right note of music and the proper tone of colour for the finest touches of poetic execution, no poet of the most elabourate modern school, working at ease upon every consummate resource of luxurious learning and leisurely refinement, has ever excelled the best and most representative work of a man who had literally no models before him and probably or evidently was often if not always compelled to write against time for his living.

The just and generous judgment passed by Goethe on the *Faustus* of his English predecessor in tragic treatment of the same subject is somewhat more than sufficient to counterbalance the slighting or the sneering references to that magnificent poem which might have been expected from the ignorance of Byron or the incompetence of Hallam. Of all great poems in dramatic form it is perhaps the most remarkable for absolute singleness of aim and simplicity of construction; yet is it wholly free from all possible imputation of monotony or aridity. *Tamburlaine* is monotonous in the general roll and flow of its stately and sonorous verse through a noisy wilderness of perpetual bluster and slaughter; but the unity of tone and purpose in *Doctor Faustus* is not unrelieved by change of manner and variety of incident.

The comic scenes, written evidently with as little of labour as of relish, are for the most part scarcely more than transcripts, thrown into the form of dialogue, from a popular prose *History of Dr Faustus,* and therefore should be set down as little to the discredit as to the credit of the poet. Few masterpieces of any age in any language can stand beside this tragic poem—it has hardly the structure of a play—for the qualities of terror and splendour, for intensity of purpose and sublimity of note. In the vision of Helen, for example, the intense perception of loveliness gives actual sublimity to the sweetness and radiance of mere beauty in the passionate and spontaneous selection of words the most choice and perfect.

Likewise, the sublimity of simplicity in Marlowe's conception and expression of the agonies endured by Faustus under the immediate imminence of his doom gives the highest note of beauty. The quality of absolute fitness and propriety, to the sheer straightforwardness of speech in which his agonizing horror finds vent ever more and more terrible from the first to the last equally beautiful and fearful verse of that tremendous monologue which has no parallel in all the range of tragedy. It is now a commonplace of criticism to observe and regret the decline of power and interest after the opening acts of *The Jew of Malta.* This decline is undeniable, though even the latter part of the play (the text of which is very corrupt) is not wanting in rough energy; but the first two acts would be sufficient foundation for the durable fame of a dramatic poet. In the blank verse of Milton alone — who perhaps was hardly less indebted than Shakespeare was before him to Marlowe as the first English master of word-music in its grander forms — has the glory or the melody of passages in the opening soliloquy of Barabbas been possibly surpassed. The figure of the hero before it degenerates into caricature is as finely touched as the poetic execution is excellent; and the rude and rapid sketches of the minor characters show at least some vigour and vivacity of touch.

In *Edward the Second* the interest rises and the execution improves as visibly and as greatly with the course of the advancing story as they decline in *The Jew of Malta*. The scene of the king's deposition at Kenilworth is almost as much finer in tragic effect and poetic quality as it is shorter and less elabourate than the corresponding scene in Shakespeare's *King Richard II*. The terror of the death-scene undoubtedly rises into horror; but this horror is with skilful simplicity of treatment preserved from passing into disgust. In pure poetry, in sublime and splendid imagination, this tragedy is excelled by *Doctor Faustus*; in dramatic power and positive impression of natural effect it is certainly the masterpiece of Marlowe. It was almost inevitable, in the hands of any poet but Shakespeare, that none of the characters represented should be capable of securing or even exciting any finer sympathy or more serious interest than attends on the mere evolution of successive events or the mere display of emotions (except always in the great scene of the deposition) rather animal than spiritual in their expression of rage or tenderness or suffering. The exact balance of mutual effect, the final note of scenic harmony, between ideal conception and realistic execution is not yet struck with perfect accuracy of touch and security of hand; but on this point also Marlowe has here come nearer by many degrees to Shakespeare than any of his other predecessors have ever come near to Marlowe.

Of *The Massacre at Paris* (acted in 1593, printed 1600?) it is impossible to judge fairly from the garbled fragment of its genuine text which is all that has come down to us. To Mr. Collier, among numberless other obligations, we owe the discovery of a noble passage excised in the piratical edition which gives us the only version extant of this unlucky play, and which, it must be allowed, contains nothing of quite equal value. This is obviously an occasional and polemical work, and being as it is overcharged with the anti-Catholic passion of the time has a typical quality, which gives it some empirical significance and interest. That antipapal ardour is indeed the only note of unity in a rough and ragged chronicle, which shambles and stumbles onward from the death of Queen Jeanne of Navarre to the murder of the last Valois. It is possible to conjecture, what it would be fruitless to affirm, that it gave a hint in the next century to Nathaniel Lee for his far superior and really admirable tragedy on the same subject, issued ninety-seven years after the death of Marlowe.

In the tragedy of *Dido Queen of Carthage* (completed by Thomas Nash, produced and printed 1594), a servile fidelity to the text of Virgil's narrative has naturally resulted in the failure which might have been expected from an attempt at once to transcribe what is essentially inimitable and to reproduce it under the hopelessly alien conditions of dramatic adaptation. The one noble passage in a generally feeble and incomposite piece of work is, however, uninspired by the unattainable model to which the dramatists have been only too obsequious in their subservience. It is as nearly certain as anything can be which depends chiefly upon cumulative and collateral evidence that the better part of what is best in the serious scenes of *King Henry VI* is mainly the work of Marlowe. That he is at any rate the principal author of the second and third plays passing under that name among the works of Shakespeare, but first and imperfectly printed as *The Contention between the two Famous Houses of York and Lancaster*, can hardly be now a matter of debate among competent judges.

The crucial difficulty of criticism in this matter is to determine, if indeed we should not rather say to conjecture, the authorship of the humourous scenes in prose, showing as they generally do a power of comparatively high and pure comic realism to which nothing in the acknowledged works of any pre-Shakespearian dramatist is even remotely comparable. Yet, especially in the original text of these scenes as they stand unpurified by the ultimate revision of Shakespeare or his editors, there are tones and touches, which recall rather the clownish horseplay and homely ribaldry of his predecessors than anything in the lighter interludes of his very earliest plays. We find the same sort of thing, which we find in their writings, only better done than they usually do it, rather than such work as Shakespeare's a little worse done than usual. And even in the final text of the tragic or metrical scenes, the highest note struck is always, with one magnificent and unquestionable exception, rather in the key of Marlowe at his best than of Shakespeare while yet in great measure his disciple. *A Taming of a Shrew*, the play on which Shakespeare's comedy was founded, has been attributed, without good reason, to Marlowe.

The passages in the play borrowed from Marlowe's works provide an argument against, rather than for his authorship; while the humourous character of the play is not in keeping with his other work. He may have had a share in *The Troublesome Raigne of King John* (1591), and Fleay conjectured that the plays *Edward III* and *Richard III* usually included in editions of Shakespeare are at least based on plays by Marlowe. *Lust's Dominion*, printed in 1657, was incorrectly ascribed to him, and a play no longer extant, *The True History of George Scanderbage*, was assumed by Fleay on the authority of an obscure passage of Gabriel Harvey to be his work. *The Maiden's Holiday*, assigned to Day and Marlowe, was destroyed by Warburton's cook. Day was considerably Marlowe's junior, and collabouration between the two is not probable.

Had every copy of Marlowe's boyish version or perversion of Ovid's *Elegies* (*P. Ovidii Nasonis Amorum compressed into three books*) deservedly perished in the flames to which it was judicially condemned by the sentence of a brace of prelates. It is possible that an occasional bookworm, it is certain that no poetical student would have deplored its destruction, if its demerits could in that case have been imagined. His translation of the first book of Lucan alternately rises above the original and falls short of it,— often inferior to the Latin in point and weight of expressive rhetoric, now and then brightened by a clearer note of poetry and lifted into a higher mood of verse.

Its terseness, vigour and purity of style would in any case have been praiseworthy, but are nothing less than admirable, if not wonderful, when we consider how close the translator has on the whole (in spite of occasional slips into inaccuracy) kept himself to the most rigid limit of literal representation, phrase by phrase and often line by line. The startling force and felicity of occasional verses are worthier of remark than the inevitable stiffness and heaviness of others, when the technical difficulty of such a task is duly taken into account.

One of the most faultless lyrics and one of the loveliest fragments in the whole range of descriptive and fanciful poetry would have secured a place for Marlowe among the memorable men of his epoch, even if his plays had perished with himself. His *Passionate Shepherd* remains ever since unrivalled in its way—a way of pure fancy and radiant melody without break or lapse. Marlowe's poem of *Hero and Leander* (entered at Stationers' Hall in September 1593; completed and brought out by George Chapman, who divided Marlowe's work into two sestiads and added four of his own, 1598), closing with the sunrise which closes the night of the lovers' union, stands alone in its age, and far ahead of the work of any possible competitor between the death of Spenser and the dawn of Milton. In clear mastery of narrative and presentation, in melodious ease and simplicity of strength, it is not less pre-eminent than in the adorable beauty and impeccable perfection of separate lines or passages. It is doubtful whether the heroic couplet has ever been more finely handled.

The place and the value of Christopher Marlowe as a leader among English poets it would be almost impossible for historical criticism to over-estimate. To none of them all, perhaps, have so many of the greatest among them been so deeply and so directly indebted. Nor was ever any great writer's influence upon his fellows more utterly and unmixed an influence for good. He first, and he alone, guided Shakespeare into the right way of work; his music, in which there is no echo of any man's before him, found its own echo in the more prolonged but hardly more exalted harmony of Milton's. He is the greatest discoverer, the most daring and inspired pioneer, in all our poetic literature. Before him, there was neither genuine blank verse nor a genuine tragedy in our language. After his arrival the way was prepared, the paths were made straight, for Shakespeare.

Chapter 11

# George Herbert's Approach to God: The Faith and Spirituality of a Country Priest

The spirituality of George Herbert, the seventeenth-century poet and priest, has been associated with classical Anglicanism. It pursues the via media (which is supposed to be both catholic and evangelical). It celebrates creation viewed in continuity with redemption. It focuses on the incarnation as the prime example of the positive value of creation. Its theology is experienced in word and sacrament (in the public worship of the daily office and liturgy of the Book of Common Prayer). Such a summary of Herbert's spirituality is not mistaken, but it encourages us too easily to imagine him as a happy anticipation of the current sacramental and liturgical "experientialism" that passes for spirituality in much contemporary Anglicanism.

This sanctions Herbert's poetry as a forerunner of the primacy of religious."experience" only to the extent that it ignores the actual content of Herbert's writings. At the same time, there is nothing particularly Anglican about the appeal to the primacy of "experience." Designated "experiential-expressivism" by George Lindbeck, variations pervade contemporary spirituality.1 The primary characteristic of experiential-expressivism is the separation and priority of "religious experience" over linguistic interpretation. "Religious experience" is viewed as prethematic, prelinguistic, and (generally speaking) culturally universal. Religious symbols, practices, narratives, and doctrines are viewed as consequent attempts to articulate this prior experience linguistically. Hermeneutically, the contemporary goal is to peel away layers of interpretive enculturation to retrieve and reappropriate the original experience.

Despite its pervasive influence, I find the experientialist model unhelpful, because it offers a misleading and inaccurate account of the relationship between theology and spirituality. It is inconsistent with the self-understanding and actual practices of most Christians in history who have prayed and worshiped. It imposes a paradigm on Christian spirituality that does not fit well with the actual historical texts and studies of Christian spiritual writers.

In place of the "experientialist" paradigm, I find a "cultural-linguistic" (Lindbeck) or "religious contextual" (McGinn) sup approach to spirituality to be more faithful to the actual relationship among theology, religious beliefs and practices, and "spirituality" (which term I prefer to the expression "religious experience"). Rather than religious practices and beliefs expressing prior unthematic religious experiences, the opposite is the case. There simply are no experiences that are not made possible by languages, narratives, and traditions. All experiences (not just religious experiences) are epistemologically mediated in complex ways. Particular religious traditions, with their accompanying narratives, rituals, and practices, form religious experience and make it possible; religious experiences are, accordingly, specific to particular cultural contexts. Buddhists have Buddhist religious experiences; Jews have Jewish religious experiences; Christians have Christian religious experiences.

I think George Herbert's spirituality is better understood in such a contextualist paradigm. He does indeed have much to teach us about a thoughtful, self-critical spirituality that does, after all, value creation, incarnation, sacraments, liturgy, and the catholic and evangelical traditions of the church; but, at the same time, Herbert's spirituality provides a corrective to the dominant paradigm of contemporary spirituality. In this discussion, I examine George Herbert's approach to God as expressed in his short work, The Country Parson, and his collection of religious poetry, The Temple, tracing the relationships among Herbert's religious practices, his theology, and his spirituality.

**Practices**

*The Virtues:* George Herbert's life as a "country parson" for the less than three years that he lived at Bemerton, a village near Salisbury (26 April 1630-1 March 1633), has caused him to be considered an "exemplar" of the Anglican pastor. As a priest, Herbert seems to have transferred his disillusioned idealistic hopes of reforming England through political service to reform-ing it through the Body of Christ, the church. (Herbert spent a period serving in Parliament and for several years sought unsuccessfully to serve with the crown. His brief service as a parish priest was cut short by his death from tuberculosis.)

The themes of Herbert's small treatise, The Country Parson, and his collection of poems, The Temple, seem to reflect the experiences of a rural priest in the Church of England; nonetheless, it has been speculated that he wrote most of these works before his ordination and only edited them and added some poems afterwards. Herbert's method in both works is catechetical and didactic.

**Cross Currents of the Renaissance**

IF Chaucer's Poor Parson could have compared his religious and philosophical beliefs with those of a typical Renaissance figure such as Castiglione's Courtier of a century later, he would have found under their different terminologies a considerable measure of agreement. Both would have agreed, in the first place, that God created the universe to show forth his own goodness, and that without his perpetual support it would dissolve once more into the formless chaos from whence it came. They would have agreed, moreover, that the Universe was a great hierarchy, ranging from the most perfect celestial spirits at the top to the most corruptible matter at the bottom, and that every rank had its precise position and function in the total scheme. In this great system of Nature, man's position was at the junction of the spiritual and the material, a little lower than the angels and a little higher than the beasts; and, as the link between the two, his function was to follow the angelic pattern as far as his material nature would permit. They would have agreed, too, that before the Fall, the system was complete from highest to lowest, with each rank embodying the divine image at its own level and the whole hierarchy reflecting in its diversity what God himself possessed in his unity. After the Fall, however, it seemed that man had a permanent tendency to follow his animal instead of his spiritual leanings, thus causing a gap in nature and endangering the completeness of the whole system. For this reason, human sin was something of more than merely local importance, and threatened the whole order of Nature just as a single broken link will endanger the whole chain.

At this point, the Poor Parson and the Courtier would begin to differ over questions of interpretation and emphasis, though their basic beliefs would be substantially the same. The Fall meant a great deal more to the Middle Ages than it did to the Renaissance.

The mediaeval Church had had a long fight to lift mankind out of the ruins of the pagan world, and sin naturally formed a major part of this experience. Its basic assumption, therefore, was that Adam fell, and that Christ's incarnation, though absolving man from the penalties of the original lapse from Grace, yet left him with the free will to sin again. So prone was man to sin that his best safety lay in flight, and, for this reason, asceticism was rated more highly than worldly success, and the monastic life of celibacy, self-denial and prayer remained the theoretic ideal of the Middle Ages long after its practice had become an impossibility.

Towards the ordinary man who had to live in the world and carry it on, the mediaeval Church acted with humane realism, accepting the inevitability of his sinfulness and offering him the seven sacraments to rescue him from the worst consequences of his nature, as well as the conception of Purgatory to soften the terrors of a final and irrevocable Hell.

The Church was a kind parent, taking sin for granted, and striving to save the sinner in his fall, even between the horse and the ground. It did not expect too much and accepted with amused tolerance the grosser animal propensities of the human body which the Renaissance tended to ignore or to idealize. The Wife of Bath has no place in the *Faerie Queene*.

The tolerance of the Church is nowhere better shown than in its treatment of love which, as it is the most ubiquitous of passions, is a challenge to morality which religion cannot ignore. The Church's attitude towards sexual love contained a certain ambiguity. While, on the one hand, marriage was a sacrament, yet virginity was held to be the nobler state, and the clergy, who were the guides and judges in moral matters, were condemned to celibacy. Sexual love was at once a necessary thing which the Church had to accept and sanctify, and at the same time something so fraught with temptation that even marriage could lapse into sin if its object became pleasure rather than the extension of God's kingdom.

The sinful aspect of love was embodied most explicitly in the tradition of Courtly Love which first arose among the Provençal Troubadours of the XIIth century and found its archetypal expression in the *Romance of the Rose*. It was still a living thing in the XVIth century, and a word about its nature will not be out of place. Courtly Love represents the survival of a fundamental paganism which the Church domesticated but could never totally subdue, and which was only biding its time to burst out in the Renaissance with renewed vitality. In essence it was a religion of love, what C. S. Lewis in his *Allegory of Love* has called "an extension of religion, a rival religion, an escape from religion".

It derived in part from Ovid *Art of Love*, in part from older, more primitive fertility rites and May-day orgies, and its essential paganism was covered by a veneer of Christian terminology which brought it very near to the cult of the Virgin within the Church itself. The Courtly lover had to adore his profane mistress with all the fervour which the Christian offered to the Virgin Mary and to show in her service the loyalty which the feudal man offered to his overlord. He had to devote the Christian virtues of patience, humility and constancy to the service of a love which was carnal, unprocreative and in most cases adulterous.

The Church was tolerant of Courtly Love, partly because it was a form of sin productive of much incidental heroism, and partly, too, because the lovers themselves admitted it to be sinful. Even Sir Launcelot, "the truest lover of a sinful man that ever loved a woman", failed to see the vision of the Holy Grail which was granted to the virgin Sir Galahad. The orthodox attitude is shown at its finest in Chaucer *Troilus and Criseyde* when, after four books of tremulous wooing and rapturous enjoyment, the love affair comes to its unhappy and inevitable end. The closing verses of this tragedy for which Fortune alone is to blame contain no moral criticism, but only pity for the dilemma of youth, helpless between the irresistible demands of the God of Love and the immovable pressure of mortality:

*O yonge fresshe folkes, he or she,*
*In whiche ay love up-groweth with your age,*
*Repeireth horn fro worldly vanite,*
*And of your herte up-casteth the visage*
*To thilke God that after his image*
*You made; and thinketh al n'is but a faire*
*This world, that passeth sone as floures faire. (V. 1835.)*

The mediaeval Church was all-inclusive; it took for granted all the inescapable qualities of human nature and graded them precisely, in terms of moral value. The term "Renaissance" is difficult to define since it is used to describe developments which are by no means uniform in different countries of Europe and at different periods. If, however, we turn to Italy at the end of the XVth century as the fountainhead of the new ideas which spread through Europe during the next hundred years, we find a very different emphasis from that of the Middle Ages. Italy in 1500 was in the later stages of a renaissance of classical learning which had begun almost two hundred years earlier, and which had culminated in a revival of Neo-Platonism, often frankly pagan and, at best, uneasily grafted on to Christianity. It bore little relationship to the teaching of Plato himself, having absorbed many alien elements on its way down; and it lacked the asceticism which was a feature of genuine Platonism and mediaeval Christianity alike. Man's natural element had become this world instead of the next, and the active life took precedence over the contemplative. This elevation of the active life forms one of the main distinctions between the modern and the mediaeval world. The ideal man of the Renaissance in every country of Europe was no longer the saint but the man of the world, the courtier or the magistrate, Elyot's Governor or Machiavelli's Prince. The models of the new age were men like Sidney—courtier, soldier, statesman, scholar all in one; its apologist might have been Bacon and its symbol the dissolution of the monasteries and the marriage of the clergy. It is symptomatic of the times that one of the most widely read of XVIth-century books should have been Castiglione *Book of the Courtier*, first published in 1528 but translated into almost every European language during the next fifty years.

Basically it is a manual of etiquette and social behaviour, in which the qualities proper to the courtier are discussed. We learn that he must have a "comely shape of person" and a consciousness of his own merits which he must not be ashamed to acknowledge to the world. His main function is to advise his prince on matters of government, but in his spare time he must be orator, poet, painter and musician, though he is advised to avoid those wind instruments which disfigure the features in the playing. He must be able to converse gallantly with ladies, to dance, to make witty conversation and to wear his clothes with an air. It is an ideal of purely secular behaviour such as Chesterfield would have understood, and a far cry from the *Parson's Tale* or the *Divine Comedy*.

There is little sense of original sin or human mortality in the *Courtier*, and the Italian Renaissance was markedly idealistic in its attitude to the world. To Ficino and his Platonic Academy at Florence, from whence most of the Renaissance Platonism flowed, the fall of man counted for little in comparison with the fact that God created man in his own image. The Neo-Platonists were above all conscious of God's immanence in his creation, and their favourite symbol was that of the block of stone in whose heart lies the perfect statue which only the artist can see and release. To use the Neo-Platonic terminology, God imposed his divine "Ideas" upon formless Chaos, and the conjunction of form and first matter produced the universe which, by the very nature of its existence, is "full of the splendour which the spiritual world imparts to the corporeal", as Leone describes it in his manual of Renaissance Platonism, *The Philosophy of Love.*

The Platonists were acutely aware of the love of God in their brave new world of the senses; they saw it as the incarnation of God, sustained by the miracle of his all-embracing love. Atom cohered with atom and the stone fell to the ground for the love they bore each other, and as matter struggled upwards in its desire for ever purer form, so the divine love met it and completed the circle by perpetually seeking fresh incarnation in matter. Love held the world together in a very literal sense for the Renaissance Platonist, and Othello's speech to Desdemona has a terrifying irony for this reason:

*Perdition catch my soul*
*But I do love thee and when I love thee not*
*Chaos is come again.... (III, III. 91.)*

This change of emphasis naturally affected the attitude towards physical love. The Renaissance man was as anxious as his mediaeval counterpart to transcend the limits of the flesh, with this difference, however, that the body seemed a ladder rather than a stumbling block. Beauty was the divine Idea in the material object; love, the perception of that Idea. Where then could a lover find the ideal truth more immanent than in the beauty of his mistress, and by what better means could he ascend to higher things than by his love for her? Bembo, in his great defence of love at the end of the *Courtier*, bids his lover take physical love "for a stayre (as it were) to climbe up to another farre higher than it.... And thus shall he beholde no more the particular beautie of one woman, but an universall, that decketh out all bodies" (pp. 317-318). The lover was amorous with a religious fervour and derived from the worship of his mistress' beauty the sort of strength that Sir

Galahad gained from his asceticism and which Birowne so feelingly described in his fine speech on love in Act IV, Sc. III, of *Love's Labour's Lost*.

The ennobling effects of love had been a commonplace of the Middle Ages, and this aspect of Neo-Platonism was only an idealization of Courtly Love which had been freed from the taint of sinfulness. Love had become orthodoxy, and the Renaissance lover no longer needed to forswear reason as his counterpart in the *Romance of the Rose* had done. Procreation had always had the approval of religion but now the Renaissance gave it fresh philosophic sanction. As God first contemplated his own beauty and after reproduced it in the universe, so the lover might do the same. "Love sometimes would contemplate, sometimes do." There are two Venuses, the heavenly and the earthly, and the latter, "This fruitfull love that loves to get things like itself", is as good as her sister.

These ideas of the Italian Renaissance were slow to penetrate into England, and in the meantime English thought had developed in a different direction. From the first, the English Renaissance had taken a moral and Christian bias, and its first fruits were Colet's sermons or Tyndale's English Bible which are closer to the Reformation than to the Renaissance. Both Reformation and Renaissance accepted the superiority of the active life, and Milton's famous defence of active virtue in the *Areopagitica* speaks for the XVIth century as well as for his own: "I cannot praise a fugitive and cloistered virtue, unexercised and unbreathed, that never sallies out and sees her adversary, but shrinks out of the race where that immortal garland is to be run for not without dust and heat." But the struggle and conflict which Milton's metaphor implies shows neither the tolerance of the Middle Ages nor the optimism of the Renaissance, and the English Protestant had a thornier path to tread than the Italian Platonist.

Calvinism, the most militant of the Protestant creeds, was based on a more austere and uncompromising conception of Original Sin than the mediaeval Church had ever countenanced. At the same time, it followed Luther in banning the external aids to salvation by which the Roman Catholic had been comforted. Admittedly it offered the Bible as a guide, but, in view of the inadequate critical knowledge of the times, this was not always a help, as we can see from Bunyan's struggles to reconcile conflicting texts in his *Grace Abounding*. The very accessibility of the Bible threw a new responsibility onto the individual by forcing him to test his daily actions by the touchstone of the Scriptures with a thoroughness which had not previously been demanded of the layman.

To those who were conscious of being numbered among the Elect, Calvinism offered a fresh and personal assurance of the love of God, but the less confident followers found some cause for uneasiness in a creed which predestined the greater part of mankind to eternal damnation, no matter what their actions. Whereas the mediaeval man who chose the religious calling had available to him a well-trod path with every kind of theological and social support to make his religious idealism practicable, the new Protestant had to thread his uncertain way through the world by the light of his own interpretation of the Bible and the ardour of his own faith, no longer sheltered in the bosom of a ghostly community which safeguarded him from the minute of his birth to the last moment of Extreme Unction, and even beyond.

Calvinism, though not inherently ascetic, was a strenuous religion and a breeder of chronically guilty consciences. It gave rise inevitably to that self-mortification and fear of cakes and ale, which we have come to associate with the term "Puritan"

By 1580, Calvinism was on the increase and, at the same time, the ideas of the Italian Renaissance were making headway in England. Neo-Platonism and its poetical counterpart, Petrarchism, were becoming the most fashionable types of philosophy and verse, manifesting themselves in Sidney *Defence of Poesie* or the poetry of Spenser and the sonneteers. The more sensuous aspect of Italian humanism showed itself increasingly in the imitation by Marlowe and his fellows of the later Greek poetry and Ovid no longer moralized. Religion was faced once more with the old paganism in its new form, and the conflict between Renaissance and Reformation intensified. To the Puritan, the world was becoming more full of pitfalls; to the humanist, religion seemed increasingly intolerant.

The thinking man was driven more and more to choose one and reject the other, to decide between the claims of the love song and the song of good life. The new tension can be felt in Nashe's famous lyric, written in time of plague, and expressing the tug-of-war between human beauty and human mortality with a poignancy rarely found before:

*Brightness falls from the air,*
*Queens have died young and fair,*
*Dust hath closed Helen's eye,*
*I am sick, I must die,*
*Lord, have mercy on us.*
(*Summer's last Will and Testament.*)

All the longing of Courtly Love and the beauty of Renaissance Italy are contained in the symbol of Helen, and Nashe's rejection of the world is sadder than Chaucer's at the end of *Troilus*, because he cares more for it and has, at the same time, a greater fear of "Hell's executioner".

The comprehensiveness of mediaeval religion had been lost and life was becoming more a matter of choice and exclusion. The end of the century saw a greater opulence coupled with a greater sense of the Death's-head, and violent lives concluded by equally violent death-bed repentances, of which Greene in fact and Doctor Faustus in fiction are the classic examples. Though Calvinism was far from universal, its leaven made itself felt in a new urgency, at times amounting to hysteria, which attached itself to morality. Bunyan in the next century was only an extreme case of what many a late Elizabethan was beginning to feel. His *Grace Abounding* is the record of a man faced with vital questions to which he does not know the answers, and rejecting everything rather than risk a mistake. The Mediaeval *Everyman,* in contrast, has the dignity and restraint which comes from being sure of oneself; the sins are clearly known and the recognized remedies brought out at the right time and in the right order.

What the late XVIth century needed, once more, was a philosophy capable of integrating these jarring elements and a code by which the active life could be moral without being inhuman. The enormous increase in gnomic verse and the increasingly uncritical appeal to allegory as a means of justifying what might otherwise have to be rejected as sinful are symptoms of the quest. At no other time, perhaps, has the famous phrase about the bee gathering honey from the flower in which the spider finds only poison been so widely and indiscriminately applied. Gascoigne divided his *Posies* into flowers to comfort, herbs to cure and weeds to avoid: "Beware, therefore, lustie gallants," he writes in the Preface to the *Posies*, "how you smell to these posies." Though there is little obvious difference between the separate sections, and it is not always clear which are the flowers and which are the weeds, yet there is honey in all if one knows how to find it.

The moral interpretations which Sir John Harington appended to his translation of the *Orlando Furioso* must not be dismissed as mere hypocrisy; the Elizabethan age was passionately concerned to find moral justification for the ordinary active life in the world of men. The greatest writers were all striving to reconcile life with religion; Spenser *Faerie Queene* offers a comprehensive and workable religion for most phases of human activity, and Shakespeare embodies in his tragedies a scale of absolute moral values which are yet within the reach of the Lears and Macbeths of every-day life. All are seeking the same thing, a religious ethic which begins with the assumption that the active life is not intrinsically sinful. A precarious balance was, in fact, achieved between the conflicting forces of humanism and religion, until Puritanism, the Counter Reformation and the New Science destroyed it between them. Poetry was inevitably involved in the fray, with results that affected its fundamental status. To the Middle Ages, it had been a form of "honest recreation" and no more; but with the rise of humanism, it was recognized as the finest product of the human mind, the most powerful persuader to action and the sole means of immortality in a mortal world:

*Yet do thy worst, old Time; despite thy wrong,*<br>
*My love shall in my verse ever live young.*<br>
*(Shakespeare, Sonnet XIX.)*

These exalted claims for poetry had to be justified against the attack of traditional and of reformed religion, with the result that the defence of poetry became a recognized genre of Renaissance criticism. Sidney, following in the steps of Aristotle and the Italian humanists, claimed for the poet the status of "maker" and seer. The poet alone sees beyond the material phenomena to the divine Ideas on which they are founded, and, possessing something of the power of all-creating Nature, himself creates a golden world which is nearer to reality than that in which we live. In the same way, Puttenham called the poets the first philosophers, and Spenser compared the Mount of Contemplation from which the Red Cross Knight saw the Heavenly City, to Mount Parnassus:

*On which the thrise three learned Ladies play*
*Their hevenly notes, and make full many a lovely lay.*
*(Faerie Queene, I, x. LIV.)*

For this reason, Renaissance poetry was far more didactic than that of the Middle Ages, and Sidney defended it on the grounds that it showed virtue exalted and vice punished. "Our poet," he says in a justly famous passage of the *Defence*, "doth not only show the way, but giveth so sweete a prospect into the way, as will entice anie man to enter into it... hee cometh to you with words set in delightful proportion... and with a tale forsooth he cometh unto you, with a tale which holdeth children from play, and old men from the Chimney corner; and pretending no more, doth intend the winning of the minde from wickedness to vertue."

Poetry lacking this serious moral purpose was never taken very seriously, however much it was enjoyed and practised, but poetry possessing it aroused an almost Arnoldian reverence as the arbiter and touchstone of values. Daniel great poem, Musophilus, is an argument between a lover of poetry (which Daniel equates with knowledge in its most persuasive form) and a practical man of affairs, an Elizabethan Philistine who prefers action to thought:

*Whilst timorous knowledge stands considering,*
*Audacious ignorance hath done the deed.*

The lover of the Muses replies in terms which are a curious

anticipation of Culture and Anarchy in the middle of the XIXth century. The times, he says, are full of confusion, with everyone busy, but to what end or by what criteria of values nobody knows:

*Gath'ring, incroching, wresting, joining to,*
*Destroying, building, decking, furnishing,*
*Repairing, altring, and so much a do*
*To his soules toile, and bodies travailing:*
*And all this doth he little knowing who*
*Fortune ordaines to have th'inheriting.*

Poetry alone can separate the true from the false and give to human action coherency and moral value, taking the true degree

*Of the just height of swolne mortalitie*
*Right as it is, not as it seemes to be.*
*It is a proud boast, but one of which*
*later Elizabethan poetry showed itself worthy.*

## Society and the Poet

GREAT changes of thought do not occur in a vacuum, and the ideas of the XVIth century which had taken at least two centuries to ripen were accompanied and, in part, caused by a social revolution equally profound and equally gradual. A glance at the bloody catalogue of the Mirror for Magistrates will show how conscious were the Elizabethan historians of the selfdestruction of the old Feudal Nobility in the Wars of the Roses.

In its place, a new power was forming, the Bourgeoisie, consisting of the merchants, the well-to-do guildsmen, the minor scions of noble families, the lawyers and professional classes who had quietly extended their privileges by judicious loans, or struck an opportunist blow on the winning side during the barons' wars and who, at the end, were ready to fill the gap caused by the decay of the old nobility. The Dissolution of the Monasteries hastened their rise to political ascendancy by throwing onto the market large quantities of Church lands in which the middle class quickly invested their money.

Their sons went to the university and Inns of Court in increasing numbers, and marriage into the remnants of the old nobility rapidly produced a new nobility and a new landed gentry. Men of this class, like Thomas Cromwell, were especially useful to the Tudors since they were free from the inherited loyalties of the Wars of the Roses, and under Elizabeth they formed the great new families from which she drew her counsellors. The Sidneys, the Herberts (an illegitimate branch of an old family raised to new nobility under Edward VIth), the Dudleys (descended from Henry VIIIth's notorious tax-collector), the Cavendishes, the Cecils and the Greshams all rose in this way. Few of the great Elizabethan families could trace their titles back further than the reign of Henry VIIth.

The new class inevitably supported the reformed religion, since in many cases the fortunes of its members had been founded on the spoils of the old Church. As the successors of the old nobility, they had little respect for the conception of feudal loyalty, and having risen in the social hierarchy by means of the sober realities of dynastic marriage, they were equally contemptuous of the traditions of Courtly Love and of the extremes of Neo-Platonism.

Like all new classes, they were great supporters of a fixed social hierarchy once they were firmly established in it, and the conception of degree was almost an obsession with the XVIth century because of the need they felt to retain the structure of class at a time when there was so much fluidity in the membership.

Above all, they were the supporters of a strong monarchy and the new Tudor dynasty rested on their shoulders. With the destrution of the old feudal and ecclesiastical hierarchies, the Crown alone stood between them and anarchy; the doctrine of Divine Right, which grew prestige under the Tudors, was a rationalization of the desire for peace and stability which only a strong central authority could give.

The Tudors certainly seized their opportunity, and the Court rose to a new importance in the XVIth century as the seat of government, religion and learning, centring on itself all the functions which had previously been shared between the monarch, the Church and the feudal nobility.

In the same way, the Crown inherited much of the reverence and loyalty which had formerly belonged to the others, and Elizabeth, in particular, succeeded in drawing to herself all the floating emotion which had lost its traditional objects. Possibly her virgin state aided her in this, for she attracted to herself something of the religious adoration which had previously been paid to the Virgin Mary and to the mistresses of Courtly Love, thus harnessing two great forces of emotion to a political end.

The XVIth century, and especially the reign of Elizabeth, was a period of great expansion in which new trading connections were established and new industries set up. In such an environment the philosophy of the active life was naturally accepted, and the Elizabethans were very Victorian in their faith in the value of "making good", with the financial as well as the moral implications of the phrase.

Like the Victorians, too, they attached great importance to education, both as a means of access to the Bible and as a source of the literate apprentices which industry so greatly needed. The second half of the century was a great age for the founding of Grammar schools, and by the end of the reign, the havoc caused by the destruction of the old educational system based on the church had been more than repaired by a host of new and secular foundations, of which Christ's Hospital is one of the more famous.

The school curriculum itself reveals the new emphasis. Rhetoric, for example, had been studied in the Middle Ages as a technique for the handling of Latin. With the Renaissance it still continued to be so, but with this difference, that its object became the training of orators who could apply what they had learned from Cicero in the vernacular. "It is eloquence that prevaileth in an active life," wrote Bacon, and the Governor or the Courtier of the new age needed rhetoric to make a speech in Council or to turn an oration in the presence of the Queen.

The new English Rhetorics, which appeared in such

quantities in the XVIth century, were written with an essentially practical object in view, and the enormous prestige of Cicero reflected a need for oratory as a living, non-academic thing. Coxe dedicated his Art and Craft of Rhetoryke in 1524"to the profyte of yonge students... to make some propre worke of the ryghte pleasaunt and persuadyble art of Rhetoryke which, as it is very necessary to all suche as wyll eyther be advocates and proctours in the lawe, or else apte to be sente in theyr Prynces Ambassades or to be techars of goddes worde in suche maner as may be most sensyble and accepte to theyr audience, and finally to all them that have anything to prepose or to speake afore any company whatsomever they be...." The Tudor world set great store by the art of persuasion, and rhetoric recovered the position as a living thing in government and daily life which it had not held since the great days of the Roman Senate.

The far-reaching effects of this fact on XVIth-century poetry will be discussed in the next chapter. It is enough to notice now that the governing classes, who were the most ardent supporters of the new rhetoric, were also the main patrons and practitioners of poetry. Sidney, who was both the most imitated of poets and the most followed of patrons, was a member of the new nobility, as were his sister, the Countess of Pembroke, and such patrons as Leicester, Cecil and Southampton. It is remarkable, too, how many of the writers sprang from the lower levels of the same class, being the sons of tradesmen who turned to letters after the university. The so-called "University Wits" are a case in point. This important but short-lived group of writers who first broke into print in the '80's had strong middle-class connections; Lodge's father was an eminent member of the grocers' guild and one time Lord Mayor of London; Marlowe's, a well-to-do member of the guild of shoemakers; Greene was, in all probability, the son of a Norwich saddler; Peele, the son of the Clerk of Christ's Hospital. In addition to these, Webster's father was a merchant-tailor; Harvey's, a ropemaker, and Donne's, an ironmonger.

They represent a new social phenomenon, the second

generation of the new bourgeoisie going to the university and abandoning their fathers' professions for a life of letters. Shakespeare, without going to the university, yet followed the pattern, and beginning as the son of an agricultural merchant, rose to a position of solid wealth and a coat of arms. The only serious poet of the century who came from the old aristocracy was Surrey, and he was symbolic of his class in that he was executed while still a young man.

The effect on poetry of this predominance of the middle class was very great and Spenser, the greatest non-dramatic poet of the century, embodied most of its values in the greatest poem of his age. His reasonable Puritanism, his belief in the active life, his insistence on the dignity of marriage, his admiration for gentility and his cult of Gloriana all reflect the aspirations of the new society. The Faerie Queene was doing for its age what Tennyson Idylls of the King attempted in a narrower, less philosophical way for a later recrudescence of the middle class. Admittedly, Spenser could not speak for all; the extreme Puritan minority did not approve of poetry in any form, or only read the versified Psalms which, appearing in such numbers from the time of Wyatt onwards, reflected the zeal for the English Bible.

But the influence of the City was very widespread and appears even in such esoteric forms as the sonnet, where one would least expect to find it. Much sonnet imagery, for example, is drawn from the world of trade and business:

*Oft taking pen in hand, with words to cast my woes,*
*Beginning to account the sum of all my cares,*
*I well perceive my griefe innumerable growes,*
*And styll in reckonings rise more millions of despayres.*
*The payments of my love I read, and reading crosse,*
*And in substracting, set my sweets unto my sowres,*
*Th'arerage of my joyes, directs me to my losse....*
*(Drayton, Ideas Mirrour, Amour 10.)*

This is a sonnet which any shopkeeper could understand as he worked out his balance sheet. The image of conveyancing, too, which was a special favourite with the sonneteers, had its origin in Tudor real estate:

*These eyes (thy Beauty's Tenants) pay due tears*
*For occupation of mine Heart, thy Freehold,*
*In Tenure of Love's services! If thou behold*
*With what exaction, it is held through fears;*
*And yet thy Rents, extorted, daily, bears....*
*(Barnes, Parthenophil., XX.)*

The rapid turnover of land and the increase of rents was a wellknown feature of the post-Reformation society, and the fact that so many of the sonneteers were Inns of Court men with a professional knowledge of such matters was a factor of real importance for poetry.

The sensitivity of XVIth-century poetry to changes in society was also affected by the spread of printing. During the first seventy years of printing, from the time when Caxton set up his press in Westminster until 1557, printing had little direct effect on the writing of verse. It was a business affair, dependent on its profits, and the early publishers were naturally unwilling to risk their money on uncertain sales in a new and untried market when there were certainties to hand. Most of the early books, therefore, were printed either on commission or else were of a kind guaranteed to sell, such as religious works, translations or accepted classics like Chaucer and Lydgate. Some of the livelier poetry, such as Skelton's satires or the polemic verse of the Reformation, was printed, but serious verse, as a whole, remained in manuscript to be circulated amongst friends.

With the more settled days of Elizabeth, the number of presses increased and as the population of London grew from 100,000 to over 200,000 during her reign, so an increasing flood of books poured out to meet the new demands. In general, however, the demand was for books of a practical and educative nature, for the Elizabethan age was a great period for self-help. There were books on religion, law and grammar for the man in the street; manuals of etiquette for those who hoped to rise in the world; text-books of navigation, accountancy and the processes of trade for the apprentice who wished to improve his position. The large number of books on housewifery and purely feminine topics shows that women formed an appreciable part of the reading public, while the increasing spate of romances and popular songs tells us how the average Elizabethan spent his spare time. By the end of the century, the printed book had become familiar enough to enter the field of popular poetic imagery:

*Ay me, what act,*
*That roars so loud, and thunders in the index?*
*(Hamlet, III, iv. 52.)*

Serious poetry had difficulty in competing with this flood of utilitarian or popular print, and for this reason, Tottel's Miscellany—or, to give it its proper title, "Songes and Sonettes written by the ryght honourable Lorde Henry Haward late Earle of Surrey, and other"—is a milestone in the history of poetry and printing. Tottel was a well-known publisher who, realizing the possibilities of the private collections of favourite poems which educated people kept in their scrap-books, conceived the idea in 1557 of publishing such a collection as a popular anthology. His Miscellany is the first attempt to popularize serious verse in print, and his choice of materials is calculated to interest as wide a public as possible.

The Preface points out that the verse is in "small parcelles", so that it is easy to read, memorable and capable of being sung; the forces of patriotism are invoked to promote the sales of a volume published "to the honour of the Englishe tong", and the subjects are all drawn from love and the good life, the two great traditional themes of poetry. Every reader would be at home among poems with titles such as "The lover sheweth his wofull state, and prayeth pitye" on the one hand, or "Of the wretchedness in this world" on the other; such topics were the commonplaces of Chaucer and Lydgate and the XVth-century lyric. Yet these well-worn themes were brought up to date with a veneer of fashionable novelty; the love-lyrics were coloured by the influence of Petrarch, so that the lovers, though assuming the same postures and enduring the same agonies as in the past, yet did so with fresh conviction and in terms of the new poetic conceits; the moral poems, as a result of the Reformation, avoided matters of doctrine and went for wise saws and proverbs such as suited the more secular and practical morality of the new age. Whatever was new and fashionable found a place in the Miscellany, and over all was thrown the magic of the new styles and metres which Wyatt and Surrey had introduced, while Tottel did not hesitate to regularize even these where he felt that they fell short of contemporary standards.

The work was enormously popular and had run through nine editions by 1587. It taught succeeding publishers how to exploit the new market in poetry and established the miscellany as a popular form of publication for the next fifty years. The subsequent editors of the species changed their techniques to meet the demands of a changing public, and the tendency was, as always, to develop greater specialization. The Paradise of Dainty Devices, for example, which appeared in 1576, contains a much higher proportion of didactic verse and was clearly aimed at a less sophisticated audience than was Tottel's Miscellany. Clement Robinson's Handefull of Pleasant Delites, first printed in 1566 but surviving only in the edition of 1584, consists entirely of popular songs, while the famous Englands Helicon of 1600 is all pastoral.

As the Italian tales were translated in greater numbers, and the popular romances became more varied, the miscellanies had to take more pains to entertain, in a world where competition was becoming daily more acute; and the result can be seen in a collection such as The Gorgeous Gallery of Gallant Inventions in 1578, where the proportion of love poetry is higher and the amount of narrative verse greater than in any before.

The case of the living author who ventured to publish his work alone was rather different from that of the editor-publisher. The system of royalties was not yet in force and the poet was only paid what the printer would give him for his manuscript, so that the financial incentive to publish was not great. The ballad or hack writers like Elderton or Churchyard who wrote for a wide and semi-literate audience did contrive to make a living out of writing alone, but the gentleman poet found things more difficult. Apart from the fact that the audience for serious verse was inevitably smaller, it was not the thing for a gentleman to earn his living by his pen, and the great majority of XVIth-century poets wrote for fame or preferment, or to celebrate the house or the patron they served, rather than for profit.

Except in the case of the drama, the patron was for another century more important than the general public. Publishing must have seemed an adventurous proceeding, in the early days of printing, to a generation which had been accustomed to circulate its verses in manuscript among a relatively small group of interested readers. Now, for the first time, the poet's fancies were exposed to the eye of anyone who chose to buy them, and for this reason, perhaps, the early volumes were so often prefaced by a battery of apologies and dedications and protestations that the book was published without the poet's knowledge. Elizabethan poets were hyper-sensitive about criticism and often chose to publish under the anonymity which the miscellany provided.

The third quarter of the XVIth century saw a rapid increase in the publication of poetry by private authors, and since the standard was set by the publishers, the influence of the profitable miscellany form on such poetry is very apparent. This is especially so in the case of the little group of poets which centred on George Gascoigne. Gascoigne himself was a gentleman born who dissipated much of his inheritance in law-suits and was forced to serve as a soldier in the Low Countries; his friend, George Whetstone, followed a similar course as soldier and sailor, while his step-son, Breton, was impoverished through Gascoigne's marriage with his mother.

All three were Inns of Court or university men and thence gained their taste for letters, while the rather shiftless and impecunious nature of their lives caused them to consider literature more seriously as a living and to study the tastes of the publishers and the public with greater care. In consequence, Gascoigne Posies, first published in 1573, and Whetstone Rocke of Regard, which imitated it, both copied the methods of the miscellany very closely. The two collections are cast in a moral frame under cover of which they tell stories of love. In addition, there is a new element of satiric realism which became increasingly popular in both prose and verse during the next twenty years. Whetstone Invective against Dice is an Elizabethan rake's progress from dice and whores to moneylenders, and thence, inevitably, to gaol. It anticipates the Coney Catching pamphlets with which Greene so effectively caught the popular fancy a decade later. Gascoigne Voyage into Holland and his fine Dulce Bellum Inexpertis, in which he gave a vivid and cynical account of his experiences in the wars, introduce a new note of journalism which was later to set the style for Nashe Unfortunate Traveller or Dekker Wonderful Year.

Gascoigne and his group brought poetry back into contact with the everyday life of society from which it had been divorced since the days of Skelton, and they did this in response to pressure from the reading public. They represent the beginnings of literature as a serious profession, but it remained for the group of writers known as the University Wits to take the final step in the next decade and attempt to make a living by their pens alone.

This step was only possible because of the widening market for other forms of literature. There was no living from the sale of poetry alone, but the growing popularity of romances, pamphlets and, above all, plays, made it possible for the writer to pick up a living from these varied fields, and the University Wits were only incidentally poets. Lyly wrote Court entertainments and prose romances, of which Euphues is the most famous; Peele wrote plays and turned his hand to Lord Mayors' Pageants and accounts of Court functions. Greene was mainly known for his romances, though he wrote plays as well; Nashe was primarily a pamphleteer and journalist, Marlowe mainly a dramatist. All wrote poems on occasion, but none of them could have afforded to write only poetry, even if they had so desired. Lodge, the most prolific poet of the whole group, wrote romances and, later, practised as a physician.

The lives of the University Wits form a consistent pattern which is an inevitable result of the times. Their short-lived careers were violent, colourful and Bohemian, to the undoubted dismay of their parents, but this was so because the literary profession was very precarious and not yet respectable. The social and religious pressure which drove the critics to write defences of poetry drove the practising poets to flaunt their art all the more aggressively, and the eroticism of a poem such as *Hero and Leander* is self-conscious for this reason. The University Wits were a little premature in dispensing with patronage before the market for literature was ready to support them by the sale of their works; but this fact, by forcing them to attempt many different modes of writing to gain a living, enriched poetry greatly by bringing it into contact with other forms of literature.

The fact that the poets were also Romance-writers, dramatists, pamphleteers and social satirists is largely responsible for the sudden widening of the scope of poetry at the end of the century, and its extension into these new fields. The fact, too, that the printing press produced a larger and more rapid circulation of books led to a greater degree of cross-fertilization than ever before between the different types, and involved a swifter change of literary fashion. The Petrarchan sonnet, for example, did not come into quantity production until 1590, and by 1600 was already the object of parody. There is nothing comparable to this before the age of printing. By 1600, the Drama had established itself as the most profitable mode of writing, and increasing numbers of poets therefore joined the ranks of the dramatists.

The result was increasing literary specialization and a stricter cleavage between the different classes of writers. The professional poets were mainly dramatists and their work has the vivid popular quality which results from their inescapable contact with a mixed audience. The poets like Drayton and Daniel who could not turn their hand so easily to popular drama, still depended on the patron, and their writing tends to be more orthodox and literary in consequence. Finally, there is the gentleman amateur who, writing in his spare time and for his own amusement only, is free to experiment in techniques or to attack accepted standards without any fear for his livelihood. Sidney and Donne both belonged to this class and for this reason, perhaps, were the most startling innovators of their times. Their poetry shows, in its unselfconscious use of novelty, the effects of the freedom which they enjoyed, but suffers from the fact that they were not forced to come to terms with the main currents in the society to which they belonged. They and the sonneteers alike are academic in comparison with Spenser and Shakespeare.

## John Skelton

*JOHN SKELTON:* was not the only early Tudor poet, but he was the greatest. He deserves a chapter, both for his own intrinsic merits, and because he is so typical of the ear stages of the English Renaissance, when the poetry of the 15th century was outgrown but the new classical models had not yet made their impact. He was born about 1460, a year before Dunbar, and by 1490 was acknowledged as a scholar, "late created poet laureate".

The Laureateship in the 15Ith century was a degree in rhetoric awarded to a master of language and oratory, and with this qualification Skelton was accepted at the court of Henry Vllth as one of the little band of scholars and orators with which a Renaissance monarch was expected to surround himself. He was the tutor to the young Prince Henry for a time, and tells us proudly that "The honour of England I learned to spell" (*Against Garnesche*), but by 1504 he had left the Court and taken the rich living of Diss in Norfolk. By 1512 he was back again at Westminster as Orator Royal, celebrating English victories in verse and, for the next ten years, launching his great satires against Wolsey with whom, however, he seems to have made his peace in later years. He died in 1529, shortly before the Cardinal fell from power.

To the 15Ith century Skelton was known as a satirist and, even more, as a jester and buffoon. He was one of those characters to whom all the floating legends of his generation seemed to attach themselves, and the *Merry Tales of Skelton* with its accounts of insanitary jokes at the expense of friars and innkeepers was one of the most popular books of the century.

Most of the tales are probably apocryphal, although the

famous story of how Skelton outfaced his scandalized congregation by holding up his newborn child in the pulpit and challenging anyone there to produce a better has the ring of truth. Skelton certainly anticipated the Reformation in respect of the marriage of the Clergy, which was one reason for his popularity later on. But whatever the literal truth of these tales, there is in Skelton's poetry a strain of buffoonery which helps to explain the popular estimation of his character. A poet who could parody the service of the dead so gaily, as in *Philip Sparrow,* or write shocking epitaphs in rhyming Latin and English on a member of his congregation lately dead:

*Jam jacet hie stark dead*
*Never a tooth in his head.*
*Adieu, Jayberd, adieu...*
*I pray you all*
*And pray shall,*
*At this trental*
*On knees to fall*
*To the football;*
*With "Fill the black bowl*
*For the Jayberd's soul..."*
*With "Hey, ho, rumbelow!"*
*Rumpopulorum*
*Per omnia secula saeculorum! Amen*
*Requiem etc....*
*(A Devout Trental for old John Clarke.)*

a poet who could so enjoy his slanging match with Garnesche, or introduce the names of his enemies in cryptograms into the middle of serious poems, or invent the sophisticated riddles of which *Speak Parrot* is composed, must have been the sort of character around whom a legend will inevitably spring up.

Nevertheless, Skelton's jesting has more than a merely personal significance. It represents a reaction against the solemnity of much 15th-century verse, particularly that of Lydgate, and a turning towards Chaucer in the gayer, bawdier moods of the *Canterbury Tales.* The Scottish Chaucerians had already led the way and Dunbar, in particular, with his flyting and his earthy humour, has the closest affinity with Skelton. It is significant that Jane Scrope, the heroine of Philip Sparrow. prefers Chaucer to Lydgate and criticizes the latter on the grounds that some men find fault,

*And say he written too haut.*

Not that Skelton never uses Aureate Diction; there is plenty of it where the occasion demands, as in the early elegy on Northumberland or the more exalted parts of the *Garland of Laurel.* For Skelton, Aureate Diction still constituted the ideal of the high style, but on the whole he avoids situations in which it is necessary and turns for choice to whatever is colloquial and popular.

One of his favourite meters, for example, is Rhyme Royal, the meter of the *Clerkes Tale or The Fall of Princes,* yet, as used by Skelton, it has the dramatic fluency of the comic Interlude. It is used in the *Comely Coistrown* with a vigour, and in the *Bouge of Court* with a flexibility which had not been seen since Chaucer *Troilus and Criseyde.* The description of Riot beating time upon his tankard and bragging of his amorous conquests is very lively:

*Counter he could O Lux upon a pot,*
*An ostrich feather of a capon's tail*
*He set up freshly upon his hat aloft.*
*"What revel rout!" quod he an 'gan to rail*
*How oft he had hit Jennet on the tail,*
*Of Phyllis fetis, and little pretty Kate,*
*How oft he knockéd at her clicket-gate.*
*The colloquial euphemisms are anything but aureate.*

In a similar fashion, Skelton turns to the popular mediaeval song rather than to the courtly lyric, and his love poetry has a blunt realism which is unspoiled by the earlier conventions of Courtly Love or the later clichés of Petrarchism. Once again, Jane Scrope's comments on *Dame Gaynour"* and *La Belle Isold* show the devastating voice of realism and common sense which was rarely heard in the 15Ith century where love was the theme:

*Some say she was light*
*And made her husband knight*

*Of the common hall*
*That cuckolds men call....*

Skelton's treatment of love was realistic and only too human. His two beautiful lyrics, *Mannerly Margery* and *My Darling Dear, which Cornysshe,* the Court musician, set to music, treat sex with a frankness common in the Middle Ages but almost destroyed by the influence of Petrarch in the 15Ith century. *Mannerly Margery, Milk and Ale,* is a dialogue between a man and a maid in which the girl is won and left as in so many popular mediaeval songs. *My Darling Dear* corrects the picture with the tale of the wife who kisses her amorous husband to sleep and then runs off to herlover:

*My darling dear, my daisy flower,*
*Let me, quod he, lie in your lap,*
*Lie still, quod she, my paramour,*
*Lie still, hardely, and take a nap.*
*His head was heavy, such was his hap,*
*All drowsy dreaming, drowned in sleep,*
*That of his love he took no keep.*
*With hey lullay, lullay, like a child,*
*Thou sleepest too long, thou art beguiled....*

Dunbar wrote with the same spontaneity in his. *In secreit place this hyndir nycht,* but the note is not found again in serious verse until Donne, and then only with an intermixture of conscious wit which is itself a new form of convention.

All these are forms of reaction from the aureate and the courtly, a reaction which achieves its completest expression in the famous meter to which Skelton gave his name. The origin of the Skeltonic line has never been finally established; it has been identified with the half line of Anglo-Saxon verse, with the meter of mediaeval Latin poetry, with rhyming Latin prose and with old French. In any case the origin does not matter; what is important is that it provided Skelton with a medium both flexible and adaptable to a remarkable degree. At one extreme it is admirably suited for hurling abuse in pithy offensive doggerel, hammering away at a single rhyme sustained only by its own speed and impetus. At the other, it is capable in his hands of the most delicate expression of spontaneous feeling. Here, for example, is a part of Jane's description of her sparrow:

*Sometime he would gasp*
*When he saw a wasp;*
*A fly or a gnat,*
*He would fly at that;*
*And prettily he would pant*
*When he saw an ant.*
*Lord, how he would pry*
*After the butterfly!*
*Lord, how he would hop*
*After the gressop!*
*And when I said "Phip, Phip!"*
*Then he would leap and skip,*
*And take me by the lip....*
*(Philip Sparrow, p. 63.)*

As in form, so in idiom and allusion, Skelton turns wherever possible to the colloquial source. His poetry is full of popular euphemism, such as the example already quoted from the *Bouge of Court,* and proverbial sayings like "Dun is in the mire", or "Mock hath lost her shoe", or "By the right of a rame's horn". There is a wealth of traditional lore behind his poetry which gives it a provocatively allusive quality:

*But when the friar fell in the well,*
*He could not sing himself thereout*
*But by the help of Christian Clout.*
*(Colin Clout, pp. 275-6.)*

The very metaphors are often only half out of the Interlude, and one can see the popular Morality figure in process of shrinking into a figure of speech:

*Our sheep are shrewdly shorn,*
*And truth is all to-torn;*
*Wisdom is laughed to scorn,*
*Favel is false forsworn...*
*Havel and Harvey Hafter,*
*Jack Travel and Cole Crafter....*
*(Why come ye not to Court?, p. 311.)*

Characters very like these formed the actual cast of

*Magnificence.* His vocabulary supports this general picture—though caution is necessary here because a modern reader naturally notices the obsolete mediaeval words but takes for granted those still in use.

**Wyatt and Surrey**

THE names of Wyatt and Surrey have been coupled together ever since their verses appeared in *Tottel's Miscellany* in 1557. Puttenham refers to "Henry Earle of Surrey and Sir Thomas Wyat, betweene whom I find very little difference" (I, XXXI.), and the fact that the two have always been associated has to some extent obscured their individual merits. Until the XXth century, Surrey was considered the greater poet and Wyatt suffered in comparison; now the position is reversed and there is a danger that Surrey's qualities will be undervalued.

The two poets were men of very different backgrounds and characters, with almost a generation between them. Wyatt, born at Allington Castle in Kent in 1503, was one of the new men whose family had risen by supporting the Tudor cause in the later stages of the Wars of the Roses. His career as a diplomat in France, Italy and Spain had its vicissitudes, and he was in prison on more than one occasion; but Henry VIIIth had an unfailing eye for a good servant, and Wyatt retained the king's favour until his death in 1542.

His integrity and honesty shine through everything he wrote, whether it is a satire against court flattery, a sonnet on the fall of his patron Cromwell, or a song in praise of his favourite virtue, patience, of which, in his last years, he had both need and store. Surrey, in contrast, born in 1517, was a man of the old régime, the son of Thomas Howard, Duke of Norfolk, and that Countess of Surrey, who was the patroness of Skelton's later days.

The family made itself useful to Henry VIIIth by its military skill, and between campaigns played for power with its chief rivals, the Seymours, declining when Henry married Jane Seymour, rising with the fortunes of Catherine Howard, and suffering final eclipse in 1546 when Surrey himself was executed on a very thin charge of treason. By the violence of his temper and the pride of his blood Surrey was in continuous minor trouble. The traditions for which he stood were something of an anachronism in the new Tudor world, and his fate was probably inevitable. In view of the difference of age and career, it is unlikely that he knew Wyatt intimately, but he was an admirer of his poetry, as his epitaphs on the older poet show.

To the 15Ith century after them, Wyatt and Surrey appeared as the leaders of a new poetic movement, "the two chief lantornes of light to all others that have since employed their pennes upon English Poesie" (Puttenham I, XXXI. p. 62). They held this proud position because, in the words of Puttenham, having travailed into Italie, and there tasted the sweete and stately measures and stile of the Italian Poesie as novices newly crept out of the schooles of Dante Arioste and Petrarch, they greatly pollished our rude and homely maner of vulgar Poesie, from that it had been before, and for that cause may justly be sayd the first reformers of our English meetre and stile. (I, XXXI. p. 60.)

It will be seen that they were praised, first, for introducing the new Italian poetry into England, and, secondly, for reshaping meter and style. Let us consider their services to prosody first of all. There have been two main systems of prosody in the history of English poetry. The first one is the accentual system of Old English verse, in which the basic line consists of a regular number of accented syllables, often linked by alliteration and accompanied by an irregular number of unstressed syllables, so that the lines may differ in length but not in the number of stresses. The second system, first perfected by Chaucer and later developing into the accepted system of English prosody, is the foot and syllable system. Here, the basic line consists of a regular number of syllables and is divided up into feet, each containing stressed and unstressed syllables.

The lines are of the same length, but allow of much accentual variety by the interchange of equivalent feet within the basic line. As a result of the changes in pronunciation in the 15th century to which reference has already been made, the principles of Chaucer's prosody ceased to be recognized. It was no longer realized, for example, that verses of the same kind always had the same number of syllables, and the revival of alliterative and accentual verse, which had occurred in the 14th century in such poems as *Piers Plowman*, further confused the issue. As late as the 1580's, Chaucer's decasyllabic line, with its final "e" forgotten, could be mistaken for the irregular fourstress accentual line known as "Riding Ryme" because of its supposed affinity with the meter of Chaucer *Prologue*. Spenser used it in the *Shepheardes Calendar*, for example:

*Ah for pittie! will rancke Winters rage*
*These bitter blasts never ginne tasswage?*
*The kene cold blowes thrugh my beaten hyde*
*All as I were through the body gryde....*
*(Februarie.)*

So, too, Gascoigne in his *Certain Notes of Instruction* tried to scan Chaucer on the principles of the Latin hexameter, while, on the other side, Crowly, in the Preface to his 1550 edition of *Piers Plowman*, failed to realize the accentual nature of the meter and mistook it for a sort of rugged blank verse. The very principles of scansion had been lost, and the critics at the end of the 15Ith century who were labouriously establishing them again were all concerned with the most elementary mechanics of verse making. Webbe, Gascoigne and Puttenham alike found it necessary to deal with such matters as the need to keep the same number of syllables in each line, the nature of a foot, and so forth.

As usual, practice was ahead of theory, and 15th-century poets such as Lydgate and Hawes were already struggling to achieve regularity in a language whose accent and pronunciation was by no means fixed. In this process Wyatt was a great pioneer. Gascoigne's mistaken analysis of Chaucer's meters is very true when applied to Wyatt's verse, especially in the sonnets. "... although his lines are not always of one self same number of Syllables," he writes, "yet, beyng redde by one that hath understanding, the longest verse, and that which hath most Syllables in it, will fall (to the eare) correspondent unto that whiche hath fewest sillables in it; and likewise that whiche hath in it fewest syllables shal be founde yet to consist of woordes that have suche naturall sounde as may seeme equall in length to a verse which hath many moe sillables of lighter accentes."

The lines of his early sonnets often vary greatly in the number of their syllables, but by means of stress, elision and various kinds of poetic license already worked out in the previous century, the lines can usually be made to sound of the same length.

The final "e" is pronounced or omitted and final syllables such as "eth" elided as desired; long vowels and diphthongs can be pronounced as two syllables, and the basic meter becomes a Procrustean bed into which lines of almost any length can be tucked with a little vocal adjustment. A reader who is interested in this kind of groping after regularity should read aloud the sonnet beginning "Love and fortune and my mynde, remembre..." (No. 31).

By stressing the last syllable of "often" and "mesure", by sounding the final "e" of "beyonde" and "mynde", by eliding all the vowels in the phrase "dai*ly* yet *the* ill... ", the voice can feel its way to regularity. Possibly the association of poetry with music influenced Wyatt here, for song tends to prolong or suppress the sounds of its words according to its needs.

Writing of this kind is the result of applying the techniques of Lydgate to the new Renaissance forms of poetry; but Wyatt goes beyond it, and, in the later sonnets or the Terza Rima of the Satires, achieved a regularity entirely on modern lines.

*The flamyng sighes that boile within my brest*
*Sometyme breake forth, and they can well declare*
*The hartes unrest and how that it doth fare,*
*The payne thearof, the greef, and all the rest.*
*The watrid eyes from whence the teares do fall*
*Do feele some force or ells they wolde be drye.... (No. 175.)*

In this and many other examples, the words have their modern values and the lines are strictly decasyllabic; the secret of Chaucer's prosody had been rediscovered in the new language. Wyatt's greatest achievements in prosody, as in everything else, however, lie in the direction of the popular lyric. The early Tudor court saw a great burst of song, the influence of which has already been illustrated from the works of Skelton, and which drove the sober Hawes to complain of the new generation that

*They fayne no fables, pleasaunt and coverte,*
*But spend theyr tyme in vaynfull vanyte*
*Makynge balades of fervent amyte....*
*(Pastime of Pleasure, 1389.)*

These courtly lyrics are often in the short line meters which Wyatt used and mainly deal with the old commonplaces of love which had been the theme of lyric poetry since the time of the troubadours. Popular favourites such as "Pastime with good company" or "In faith ye be to blame" show clearly the source where Wyatt learnt his manner, and a lyric like the following can hardly be distinguished from the work of Wyatt himself:

*O Mestres, whye*
*Owtecaste am I*
*all utterly*
*from your pleasaunce?*
*Sythe ye and I*
*or thys truly,*
*famyliarly*
*have had pastaunce.*
*(Robbins, Secular Lyrics, No. 137.)*

If we compare it with a typical Wyatt lyric, the similarity in form and theme is very obvious.

*Wyth serving still*
*This have I wone,*
*For my godwill*
*To be undone;*
*And for redresse*
*Of all my payne*
*Disdaynefulnes*
*I have againe. (Wyatt, No. 157.)*

Wyatt improvises endlessly on these short line meters,

trying out new combinations of rhyme and modulating from one rhythm to another with an ease, which comes from practice in handling words and music together:

*Then why should I*
*Hold payne within my hert,*
*And may my tune apply*
*To ese me smart? (No. 84.)*

At times he experiments in combining lines of different lengths, as in the following poem where the lines are first lengthened and then shortened again:

*Ys it possyble*
*That so hye debate*
*So sharpe, so sore and off suche rate,*
*Shuld end so sone and was begone so late?*
*Is it possyble? (No. 111.)*

The stanza is itself, most appropriately, the epitome of the lovers' quarrel it describes, mounting up to a climax and as suddenly subsiding. Elsewhere he exploits the very uncertainty in the pronunciation of words which had proved such a stumbling-block to earlier poets. His poem on patience, for instance, begins by praising that virtue as the cure for all pains, and starts each line with an aggressive repetition of the word. But the last two lines of the poem turn round completely and show, with some pathos, how patience is at best a poor substitute for the pleasures of success:

*Patience of all my harme,*
*For fortune is my foo;*
*Patience must be the charme*
*To hele me of my woo:*
*Patience withoute offence*
*Is a painfull patience. (No. 39.)*

The changed pronunciation of "patience" to rhyme with "offence" corresponds to the change in attitude, and takes all the force out of the word and the virtue. Many illustrations could be given of this sensitive use of meter; and what distinguishes Wyatt from his contemporary—and, indeed, from most other 15Ith-century-lyricists is the subtle way in which he relates his rhythms to the specific situation with which he is dealing. To most modern readers, Surrey's contribution to prosody lies in his introduction of the decasyllabic blank verse line which he used in his translation of Books II and IV of the Aeneid. This, though a remarkable achievement, came before the times were ready for it, and the blank verse form, like Wyatt's sonnet, had to be rediscovered fifty years later by Peele and Marlowe, before it came into general use. His importance in. the history of prosody derives much more from the encouragement he gave to modern standards of regularity, at a time when poetry was in a state of confusion. He began where Wyatt left off in the sonnet, and any of Surrey's poems will pass muster for complete regularity of syllables. More than any other poet, he stabilized English prosody and used words with their fixed and modern accent, which is the reason why he was more highly rated than Wyatt for the next two centuries. That he sensed the needs of his age can be seen in his constant use of the line of fourteen syllables, alone or in conjunction with the line of twelve syllables, when it was known as "Poulter's Measure" because of the alleged habits of poulters "which giveth twelve for one dozen and fourteen for another". The fourteener and its combinations were old and famous measures which, when split up into Peter Quince's eight and six, formed the famous Ballad Meter. It was frequently the meter of the court lyric and appears in such popular poems as "Blow thy horn Hunter", which Cornysshe set to music, or the well-known "O Death! rocke me asleepe: bringe me to quiet reste". Occasionally Wyatt used it but generally broke it down into lines of shorter length with more frequent rhymes:

*O goodely hand,*
*Wherein doeth stand*
*Myne hert distrast in payne;*
*Faire hand, Alas,*
*In little spas*
*My lift that doeth restrayne. (No. 86.)*

Surrey used it much more frequently and always in its full extended form to give free play to the strong rhythmic swing of the line.

*In winters just returne, when Boreas gan his raigne,*
*And every tree unclothed fast, as nature taught them plaine,*
*In misty morning darke, as sheepe are then in holde,*
*I hyed me fast, it sat me on, my sheepe for to unfolde.*

Poulter's Measure is a monotonous meter with its regular caesura and unvaried iambic foot, often emphasized by the occurrence of alliteration on the stressed syllables; but its very monotony gave the poets just the help they needed to bring prosody back again on the proper Chaucerian lines where it has for the most part remained ever since.

Wyatt and Surrey rescued poetry from the uncertainty into which it had been thrown by the changes of language. In doing so, they sacrificed many of the fascinating possibilities inherent in the older prosody, and inaugurated a generation of crude and mechanical meters; but they laid down, nevertheless, the main lines of future development. Their services to poetic form were equally important, and, once more, Wyatt was the initiator, while Surrey was the more influential. On neither of them was the influence of the Classics strong. Two of Wyatt's satires were imitated from Horace, and have some of the grace and urbanity of their original; but even here, the echoes of Henryson and Chaucer are predominant, and Wyatt was always apt to revert to a mediaeval manner whatever form of poetry he might be writing. He writes, for example, a sonnet as Chaucer might have written it:

*You that in love finde lucke and habundance*
*And live in lust and joyful jolitie,*
*Arrise for shame! Do away your sluggardie!*
*Arrise, I say, do May some observance.... (No. 92.)*

It might be Pandarus waking Troilus up on a May morning. Again, he writes one of the fashionable French rondeaus, but addresses it in the style of Skelton to an amorous and elderly woman:

*Ye old mule, that thinck yourself so fayre,*
*Leve of with craft your beautie to repaire*
*For it is time withoute any fable:*
*No man setteth now by riding in your saddell;... (No. 35.)*

The French element in Wyatt's verse was inevitably strong

in view of the many links between the two courts during the reigns of the first two Tudors, and his epigrams, rondeaus, satires and psalms were the counterparts of what Marot and St. Gelais were doing in France at the same time. But Wyatt's really revolutionary achievement was to introduce the new Italian poetry, and in particular that of Petrarch, into England. The vogue of Petrarch's *Canzoniere* to Laura in the 15Ith century is one of the most extraordinary literary phenomena of all time, and it is not too much to say that the influence of Petrarch swung the bias of English poetry from the narrative to the lyric and amatory.

The reasons for this are varied. For one thing, he handed on the commonplaces of Courtly Love in a form acceptable to the Renaissance: he kept the agony and humility with which the lover served his lady, but replaced the achievement of the carnal end by a frustration which suited the Platonic idealism of the new age. Moreover, he analysed the moods and passions of love with a realism, which appealed to a century fascinated by the study of the human mind, and he did it, finally, on a scale and with an art which dazzled all who read him. Perhaps the brilliance of his style was the greatest factor in his popularity, for the 15Ith-century sonneteers who followed him imitated his conceits rather than his passion. The comparison of the lover to a ship at sea and of his wooing to a siege, the play of fancy around ice and fire, became the standard topics for love poetry, and even Wyatt turned mainly to the conceited sonnets for his models. He gives us the lover "burnyng a farr of and fresing nere" (No. 12), or assailed in his bark by "A rayn of teris, a clowde of derk disdain" (No. 28). He describes how his mistress' eyes strike and dazzle like lightning (No. 47) and he voices the paradoxes, which were to become so familiar as the century proceeded:

*I fynde no peace and all my warr is done;*
*I fete and hope, I burne and freise like yse;... (No. 26.)*

But Wyatt was never a "Petrarchan" and never became a slave to the conceit as did many of the later sonneteers. His progress in the sonnet resembled that in the roundel and epigram; in every case he began by close imitation of his original, but once having mastered the form, he used it for his own purposes. The later sonnets, for example, though often adaptations of the Italian, deal with such matters as his grief for the fall of Cromwell (No. 173) or his dislike of being in prison (No. 175). A great part of his love poetry is anti-Petrarchan in its sentiments and yet paradoxically comes nearer to the spirit of Petrarch than did much verse, which stayed closer to the Italian.

Wyatt's love affairs run in a convention different from Petrarch's; he is not content to love without reward but asks for a plain yes or no and wastes no time where there is no hope. Nevertheless, he shares with Petrarch a common passion and sincerity; he always gives the impression of describing real feelings and addressing them to a real woman, as Sidney and Donne do after him. His poems seem to burst into the middle of a conversation between two lovers, usually at a moment of some tension:

*What shulde I saye*
*Sins faithe is dedex*
*And truthe awaye*
*From you ys fled?*
*Shulde I be led*
*With doblenesse?*
*Naye, naye, mistresse! (No. 143.)*

Often the poem breaks into a lovers' quarrel and shows us the poet trying to explain away some unlucky remark he has made,

*Perdye I saide yt not*
*Nor never thought to do*
*As well as I ye wott*
*I have no powre therto;*
*And if I ded, the lott... (No. 134.)*

*or asking for forgiveness when the quarrel has gone too far;*

*And wylt thow leve me thus,*
*That hathe lovyd the so long,*
*In welthe and woo among?*
*And ys thy hart so strong*
*As for to leve me thus?*

*Say nay, say nay! (No. 113.)*

*Perhaps the finest of all his poems—and one to which the reader should turn—is the famous anthology piece*

*They fle from me that sometyme did me seke*
*With naked fote stalking in my chambre. (No. 37.)*

There is a note of real passion and pain as the poet remembers byegone favours shown to him and particularly "ons in special!", when his mistress came to him "in thyn arraye after a pleasaunt gyse" with her gown slipping from her shoulders, and softely saide, "dere hert, howe like you this?" The "armes long and small" with which she embraced him have just a hint of the long line of mistresses who adorn so much mediaeval poetry, but the omission of the rest of the formal description prevents the poem from becoming merely conventional. The strange lingering quality of the line It was no dreme: I lay brode waking expresses the shock and wonder of the moment so much more vividly than when Donne attempts the same thing with all the battery of his wit in *The Dreame* for example. And the sudden, contemptuous use of the word "new fangilnes" introduces a note of irony which is maintained in the bitter couplet with which the poem ends:

*But syns that I so kyndely ame served,*
*I would fain knowe what she hath deserved.*

It should be noticed that the poem is in Rhyme Royal, the stanza most closely associated with the aureate, but, as if to challenge the whole tradition, Wyatt writes in very colloquial language:

*That sometyme they put themselves in daunger*
*To take bred at my hand....*

Though not to be compared with Skelton in this respect, Wyatt is a colloquial poet, drawing much of his imagery from the ordinary terms of hawking, and using such popular idioms as "My shue ys trode awry" (No. 108), or "I put myself in prese" (No. 71), to mention only two. It must be realized that popular and courtly verse were not so rigidly distinguished from one another in Wyatt's day as they were by 1590, and that a song like his "Hey Robin, Jolly Robin", which was still being sung in Shakespeare's day, was at once courtly and popular. Wyatt makes great use of such features of popular song as the refrain, but develops it away from the simple repetition of a line of song into something full of meaning. The words "In eternum" which are used as a refrain to describe the quality of his love, take on a sombre menace when they are still used after the mistress has proved unfaithful: In eternum then from my herte I kest That I had furst determined for the best; Nowe in the place another thought doeth rest, In eternum. (No. 71.) The tendency of Wyatt's verse is away from the relatively simple verbal effects that are possible in song towards the richer, subtler qualities which are possible in verse designed to be read. The beautiful assonance of a's and o's which he achieves in his famous song to his lute does not need the help of music:

*Vengeance shall fall on thy disdain,*
*That makest but game on ernest pain:*
*Thinck not alone under the sonne*
*Unquyt to cause thy lovers plain,*
*Alltho my lute and I have done. (No. 66.)*

Surrey has nothing to compare with this; his love poetry has little of the individualized passion which marks that of Wyatt, and his pages abound in conventional lovers bemoaning their restless state or deploring the unkindness of their ladies; the conceits are more common, the verse more of an academic exercise in the Petrarchan mode. Surrey did more than anyone else to introduce Petrarchism, as it came to be understood in the second half of the 15Ith century. Yet he has other, more interesting qualities which, owing to his early death, were not able to mature. He has, for example, a genuine feeling for nature which is in advance of his period, and though he takes many, of his natural descriptions from Petrarch, yet he transforms them into English settings with touches of real observation:

*Somer is come, for every spray nowe springes;*
*The hart hath hong his olde hed on the pale:*
*The buck in brake his winter cote he flings;...*
*Winter is worne, that was the flowers bale.... (No. 2.)*

When he is not dealing with love he can write with the

personal sincerity which is found in Wyatt's satires, and his poem written while he was imprisoned at Windsor rivals Wyatt's account of his imprisonment at Allington. Surrey contrasts the present with the past, remembering the happy days of his youth at Windsor in company with the Duke of Richmond: he recalls the hunting, the tilting, and the tennis, played with one eye always "cast upp into the maydens towre" where the girls were watching the sports:

*The palme playe, where, dispoyled for the game,*
*With dased eyes oft we by gleames of love*
*Have mist the ball, and got sight of our dame,*
*To bayte her eyes, whiche kept the leddes above.*
*The graveld ground; with sleves tyed on the helme...*
*Where we have fought and chased oft with dartes.*
*With sylver dropps the meades yet spredd for rewthe,*
*In active games of nymblenes and strengthe.... (No. 31.)*

It is as fresh and vivid a picture of early Tudor life in the big house as one could desire. He can write dramatically, too, especially when he pictures the feelings of a woman whose husband is away on the high seas:

*I stand the bitter night*
*In my window, where I may see*
*Before the windes how the cloudes flee.*
*Lo, what a mariner love hath made me...*
*Thus is my wealth mingled with wo,*
*And of ech thought a dout doth growe;*
*Now he comes; will he come? alas, no no! (No. 21.)*

But this was a situation with which Surrey was familiar, having been refused permission to take his wife with him to the French wars.

There is also a suggestion of satire in Surrey's later verse which, if it had been allowed to develop, might have changed the whole character of his writing. His sonnet on the death of Wyatt, for example, hits at those hypocrites who, having worked for Wyatt's downfall, now "Yeld Cesars teres uppon Pompeius hedd" (No. 45), while his bitter poem on Sardanapalus describes epigrammatically how he

Murdred hymself to shew some manful! dede. (No. 40.)

His satire on the citizens of London, written in prison after his arrest for throwing stones at windows during a midnight frolic, is in a mock heroic strain which reveals more humour and maturity than the poet is usually given credit for. His future development might have been along interesting and unexpected lines.

Nevertheless, it was for none of these things that the 15Ith century revered Surrey. His fame did not rest on hints and promises of what might have been, but on a solid and invaluable achievement. For Surrey, more than any other single poet, brought about a revolution in poetry almost as momentous as that of Waller and Dryden a century later. He banished the aureate and the alliterative once and for all, and he established a standard of clear, controlled language which was what the century needed above all things. Read any aureate love lyric of the 15th century, and then turn to the clarity and precision of Surrey's six-line stanza

*When ragyng love, with extreme payne*
*Most cruelly distrains my hart;*
*When that my teares, as floudes of rayne,*
*Beare witnes of my wofull smart;*
*When sighes have wasted so my breath,*
*That I lye at the poynte of death:*
*I call to minde the navye greate,*
*That the Greekes brought to Troye towne;*
*And how the boysteous windes did beate*
*Their shyps, and rente their sayles adowne,*
*Till Agamemnons daughters blood*
*Appeasde the goddes, that them withstode.*
*And how that in those ten years warre,*
*Full many a bloudye dede was done,*
*And many a lord, that came full farre,*
*There caught his bane, alas! to some;*
*And many a good knight overronne;*
*Before the Grekes had Helene wonne.*
*Then thinke I thus: sithe suche repayre,*
*So longe time warre of valiant men,*
*Was all to winne a ladye fayre:*

*Shall I not learne to suffer then,*
*And thinke my life well spent, to be*
*Servyng a worthier wight than she?*
*Therefore I never will repent,*
*But paynes contented, stil endure:*
*For like as when, rough winter spent,*
*The pleasant spring straight draweth in ure,*
*So after ragyng stormes of care,*
*Joyful at length may be my fare. (No. 13.)*

I have quoted the whole of this lyric because its excellence lies not in individual lines but in the cumulative effect. In the whole thirty lines there are only three sentences, yet the poem unfolds itself with a clear and ordered logic. It has a form entirely appropriate to its content, and, while never pretending to more feeling than the occasion deserves, it treats a conventional theme with dignity and sincerity. It is a new form of art, urbane, controlled and self-conscious; and it embodies the qualities which the new poets, exploring their medium, most needed to cultivate. It has a classical restraint and clarity which the more exuberant taste of the Elizabethans tended to ignore and which does not really appear again until Ben Jonson came on the scene.

# Chapter 12

# Shorter Forms of Elizabethan Poetry

## Introduction

THE poetry of Skelton or Wyatt has an unmistakably individual flavour which is, for the most part, lacking among the Elizabethans. One always wonders whether a Wyatt love lyric is a record of a personal experience, but the average Elizabethan sonnet or lyric provokes no such conjecture and might be written by any one of a dozen different authors. One thinks of Elizabethan verse in terms of sonnets or pastorals rather than in terms of the writers who produced them, for the similarities between poems in the same category are greater than the differences; much of it has a curiously objective quality, as if it were written according to a recognized formula. This is not to say that Elizabethan poetry is shallow and insincere. The poet could write well without the spur of a personal love or grief. Peele's beautiful lyric, "His golden locks time hath to silver turned", was written as a purely formal compliment to Sir Henry Lee, on the occasion of his retirement in 1590 from the post of Queen's Champion, the Entertainment for which occasion Peele had been commissioned to write.

The source of this impersonal excellence lies partly in the glamour of the new verse forms, which fired the imagination of the poets and aroused them to a fever of emulation which was itself sufficient to provoke good verse. It lies even more in the Elizabethan capacity for sharing in generalized emotions and responding to traditional situations, by means of which they found deep satisfaction in the conventional poses of the love poem or elegy. This response to the great commonplaces is a sign of innocence, and is comparable, perhaps, to the Elizabethan taste for the wise saws and modern instances, which, however obvious they may seem, are nevertheless true. The Elizabethan sensibility was unspoiled, and the conventional themes could still be treated with freshness. For this reason, it is convenient to discuss Elizabethan poetry in terms of Kinds rather than authors; and, after a few general comments, I shall consider three of the more popular forms, namely, the pastoral, the sonnet and the lyric.

*Tottel's Miscellany* was the dominant influence on poetry for twenty years after its publication, and the attempts to master the lessons of Surrey's prosody and develop the Petrarchan conceit gave rise to much pedestrian verse. There was, however, a good deal of unobtrusive yet vital experiment within the frame-work of the fourteener, and though no major poets appeared, an increasing number of minor ones, writing indefatigably for the miscellanies, ensured that the lessons of the fourteener had been learnt and that poetry was ready to move on to a new flexibility. Gascoigne is the most notable poet of the period, and his moving Lullaby has justly found its way into the modern anthologies. Both for the variety and for the unacademic quality of his verse, he deserves more space than can be given to him here.

The publication of Spenser *Shepheardes Calendar* in 1579 is generally held to mark the beginning of the true Elizabethan poetic renaissance, but Sidney's eclogues and sonnets, written shortly afterwards though not published until 1591, should share the honour. The immediate inspiration of the new poetry was, as I have already indicated, the work of the Pléiade who had been experimenting in the incorporation of Italian and classical verse forms into the vernacular for the previous thirty years and who continued to do so until the beginning of the 15IIth century. Du Bellay had died in 1560, but Ronsard lived until 1585 and Desportes, the most prolific of the sonneteers, until 1606. Spenser and Sidney seem to have regarded themselves as the inheritors of the poetic mantle of the Pléiade in England, and to have undertaken the task of doing for English verse what Du Bellay and Ronsard had done for the French. They experimented in new verse forms and were consciously the leaders of a group of new poets which Harvey christened the Areopagus, although they were never so well established a body as the Pléiade.

Their early poetry was written according to the latest Renaissance theories, and their Manifesto, Sidney *Defence of Poesie*, defended the vernacular, surveyed the achievements of its literature, and, as Du Bellay had done before, pointed out the superiority of the Ancients.

Sidney, however, died with his works unpublished, and Spenser, having moved to Ireland in 1580, published nothing new for ten years, although the *Shepheardes Calendar* ran through several editions in the meantime. In their absence, the new movement was carried on by Lyly and Peele, the earliest of the University Wits, and developed by Greene, Lodge and Marlowe at the end of the decade. By 1590, the eclogue and sonnet were thoroughly established, while such new forms as the elegy, the madrigal, the Anacreontic and Pindaric had been introduced. English poetry was once more in the great European stream as it had not been since the time of Chaucer. There is scarcely a situation or conceit in the lyrical verse of the '90's which had not its counterpart in Italy or France.

Love was the main theme of the shorter forms of Elizabethan verse. The importance of love in Renaissance philosophy has already been indicated, and the vogue of Petrarch owes much to the spread of Neo-Platonic idealism. The European wave of Petrarchism reached England in the 1580's, when it began to sweep through sonnet, lyric and pastoral, bringing with it a flood of obdurate mistresses and protesting lovers who will never, never achieve a kiss. There are other strains in late Elizabethan love poetry, however, and among them, a rich and passionate sensuality that is deliberately anti-Petrarchan. The longer love poems of the '90's are sometimes Platonic, as Drayton *Endimion and Phoebe*, for example; but more often they are frankly sexual, and mock the usual Petrarchan convention by showing the maid passionately but vainly wooing the man. This is the theme of *Venus and Adonis* or Lodge's poem, Scillaes Metamorphosis, to name only two; the extremely provocative love scenes of Marlowe *Hero and Leander* are a far cry from the sonnet ladies on their platonic pedestals.

Though this note of deeper sensuousness in late Elizabethan verse derived in part from Italy, as the more licentious poetry of the Renaissance became better known, the influence of classical poetry was even more marked. The love poetry of the University Wits reads as if they were the first who turned to classical love poetry in the original and not merely to what had filtered through from the continent and the Middle Ages. The classical renaissance especially that of the Greek, reached England very late, and the spread of Greek studies was an important factor at the end of the century. Classical Greek was yet scarcely known, but later Greek literature, such as Longus' sophisticated and pornographic story of Daphnis and Chloe, set the fashion for the Arcadian Romance and provided some pretty models for lovemaking. In this connection, too, the *Greek Anthology* was very important.

This was a traditional collection of Greek poems, some of them extremely licentious, which had been published in Florence in 1494, to which was added a further number of late Greek poems discovered by the French printer Etienne, in 1552, and wrongly attributed to Anacreon. From here came the fashion for Anacreontic Odes with their gay, amorous philosophy and their conception of the god Cupid so different from that of the Middle Ages. The mediaeval god of love was a grown youth whose fierce darts could produce a tragedy on the scale of *Troilus and Criseyde*; the new god of the Anacreontics is the sportive little Cupid with his bow and arrows who played with Campaspe at cards for kisses and who shot his bolts at those who took pity on him. He can be seen at large in the lyrics of Lyly or in Sidney's sonnets, and he provided Elizabethan poetry with a great part of its conceits.

Of all classical models, however, Ovid was by far the most important and, after Petrarch, the greatest literary factor in the development of Elizabethan poetry. No longer moralized, as he had often been in the Middle Ages, he was enjoyed for his sophisticated sensuality; and the wider use of classical myth, together with such new forms as the love elegy and the heroic epistle, came from him. It is difficult to over-estimate the influence of the *Metamorphoses* on the later 15Ith century; its effects were felt far beyond the range of love poetry and left their mark, as we shall see later, on such essentially English poems as Drayton *Polyolbion*. It must not be forgotten, however, that there was already a great native tradition of frankly sexual verse which had found its last courtly expression in Skelton, before being relegated to the lower, unprinted levels of popular verse. Occasionally, in a form such as the lyric which built upon popular song, it rose to the surface, to produce such beautiful lyrics as that of Peele which echoes both the new pastoral and the old pagan song of the woman in love: Whenas the rye reach to the chin, And chopcherry, chopcherry ripe within, Strawberries swimming in the cream, And schoolboys playing in the stream; Then oh, then oh, my true Love said, She could not live a maid. (Ault, *Elizabethan Lyrics*.)

One further aspect of late Elizabethan verse which may be mentioned is its curious and deliberate artificiality. The sonneteers never tired of their make-believe wooing of impossibly obdurate mistresses, and the pastoral writers seemed to see life as a perpetual summer day in which there was nothing to do but woo, and play upon the pipes. This is a strange phenomenon in an age which was in so many ways hard-headed and earnest. One reason for it was undoubtedly the dazzling prestige of the new poetic models, and the kudos which attended their imitation. But a deeper reason lay in the triumphant majesty of the Virgin Queen herself. Elizabethan poetry was a poetry of the Court, and the Court revolved round its Queen in one long act of reverential ritual which, though based on make-believe, was not for that reason insincere. The Court and a large part of the nation revered the Queen as a symbol of national greatness and worshipped the myth which they themselves had created around her. To Raleigh she was Cynthia; to Spenser, Gloriana. On every progress she was welcomed by nymphs or woodmen who hailed her as their Goddess and queen; in every city pageant the virtues paid tribute to her, and Lyly could present before the Queen herself his play, Endimion, in which Leicester's courtship was thinly veiled under the fable of Endymion and the moon. It was all pretence; the Court knew only too well that she was an old woman, and, for that reason, cherished the myth the more passionately, as if in hope of prolonging the good days of which it was the expression.

The artificial conventions of verse were accepted because they corresponded to artificial, but not at all unworthy, conventions of life itself. They were involved in the very life and Idea of the courtier, and for this reason they remained fresh and spontaneous for two generations of poets. The growth of realism at the end of the century is a sign, on the one hand, that the great myth was at last cracking under the mounting pressure of political and religious problems, and, on the other, that the theatre had introduced a new and less courtly element into serious literature.

## The Pastoral

The eclogue or pastoral poem began with Theocritus as a relatively realistic picture of shepherd life, but was transformed by Vergil into a literary convention through which personal or social comments could be made. The Vergilian eclogue was revived and developed in Italy at the end of the 15th century, and the name of Battisti Spanguoli (more commonly known as Mantuan, after the place of his birth) was especially renowned in connection with the form and the satiric uses to which he put it. At the same time, the tradition of the Theocritan eclogue, enriched by the influence of later Greek poetry and the idyllic pastoral settings of *Daphnis and Chloe,* brought to the Renaissance a colourful and idealized picture of the shepherd life. With this mixed ancestry, the pastoral spread into every branch of Renaissance literature, reaching England in full force in 1579, although there had been earlier and less successful attempts at the form by Barclay, Googe and Turberville. In England, it quickly penetrated the lyric, the drama and the prose romance, to become one of the most pervasive conventions of later Elizabethan literature.

There are many reasons why the conception of the shepherd's life captured the imagination of the Renaissance. The ground was already well prepared; on the one hand, the prevalence of shepherds in the Bible and the image of Christ the shepherd made the conception familiar, and gave to the pastoral inevitable religious associations which appear both in *The Shepheardes Calendar* and *Lycidas*; at the other extreme, the unfading beauty of the mediaeval gardens of love is only another version of Arcadia, and the pastoral idyll carries on both the settings and the moral values of the *Romance of the Rose*. As a clearly recognized convention, the pastoral lent itself to a wide variety of purposes.

It could dally with the innocence of love or follow the more sexual models of the *Greek Anthology*; it could be used to pay a compliment to the Queen in the role of Diana or to attack abuses in Church and State. Both Sidney and Puttenham regarded it as a form of writing intended primarily "under the vaile of homely persons, and in rude speeches to insinuate and glaunce at greater matters". The majority of English poets used it without any allegorical purpose and expressed through their shepherdesses and swains a vision of the golden age where time stands still, beauty never fades, and there is neither ambition nor responsibility. The idyllic world of Marlowe "Come live with me" is the expression of an idealism which could never be satisfied, and for that reason the pastoral so easily slips into satire.

In a period of such rapid change as the 15Ith century, when the Court was increasing its power, London growing quickly and religion making ever-increasing demands on the individual, the simple shepherd's life stood as an escape from the new responsibilities and as a symbol of a less complicated, more spontaneous existence. One of the commonest pastoral themes is the contrast between court and country, the shepherd and the king, and in this mode it is the antithesis of the *Mirror for Magistrates*, the answer to human mortality and the penalties of ambition. It does not, in the 15Ith century, embody the desire to escape from the town to the country such as had emerged by the time of the Romantic revival; the picture it gave of country life was never for one moment mistaken for reality. The responsibilities and worries of "the head that wears a crown" are the source of its feeling, and it reflects in this the disquiet of a society consciously embarking on a new and more complicated stage of its evolution. Tennyson *English Idyls* come nearer to the pastoral than do the poems of Wordsworth.

It is impossible to deal with all the poets who wrote pastorals, nor is it necessary to do so, for pastoral poetry fell into well defined kinds, and it is difficult to distinguish the verses of one pastoral poet from those of another. Something, however, may be said about the eclogues, which Sidney inserted between the separate books of the *Arcadia,* and those of Spenser's collection, the *Shepheardes Calendar*, which really started the pastoral vogue in England. Sidney's poetry is, in some ways, the more interesting, for he never intended to publish it and it therefore exists in the experimental stage, whereas with Spenser we have the finished product.

It would appear from the eclogues that Sidney's interest at this stage was mainly in prosody and that he was primarily intent on introducing variety after a generation of Poulter's Measure and the "rym ram ruf by letter" of the followers of Surrey. De Baïf had been experimenting with classic meters in France, and the four pleasantly flippant letters, which passed between Spenser and his Cambridge friend, Gabriel Harvey, show that Spenser was interested in the possibilities of these meters, though he quickly abandoned them. Sidney, on the other hand, tried them out side by side with more orthodox methods to test their possibilities, and, having discovered their inadequacy by practical means, abandoned them for the sonnet form.

In the eclogues, he tried Elegiacs, Sapphics, "Exameter verses", Anacreontics and many others, giving a little diagram of the accents in each case to assist the reader, and demonstrating clearly, in spite of one or two successes, that the English language does not lend itself to classical meters. Sidney's experiments along more orthodox lines are staggering in their variety and show the influence of the Pléiade. He tried combinations of blank verse and rhyme, interlocking stanzas and echo patterns, fantastic compound rhymes such as "garrison" and "tarry soon" which remind one of Gilbert and Sullivan, rhymes which occur in the middle of the line instead of at the end, and occasional excursions back into the fourteener or Rhyme Royal. Most of the verse in Sidney's Eclogues is too consciously experimental to be good, but he gave a spring-cleaning to English poetry which helped to liberate it from the old meters and made possible the new and subtler developments of the next decade.

The *Shepheardes Calendar* was published anonymously in 1579, with a dedicatory epistle and notes by a certain E. K. whose identity has never been finally established. In form it consists of twelve eclogues spoken by a variety of shepherds whose pastoral names in some cases cover real people. E. K. tells us that "the Authour selfe is shadowed" under the name of Colin, just as Sidney included himself in his own eclogues under the name of Philisides, and Drayton by the name of Rowland. Such pseudonyms were common currency in the restricted literary circles of Elizabethan London, and the pastoral is often more topical than appears on the surface. The twelve eclogues correspond to the twelve months of the shepherds' year, and already, the architectonic bent of Spenser's mind is shown by his welding the poems together into a single unit.

The January eclogue, for example, is a winter's tale in which the unhappy lover "compareth his carefull case to the sadde season of the yeare, to the frostie ground, to the frosen trees...."; March, as the beginning of the spring, is cheerful and full of love; April, a compliment to the Queen and full of spring flowers; May, an attack on Catholic superstition which arises from the sight of people going a-maying. And so it goes on through the heat of the summer until autumn comes and with it a more sober song. October is a complaint of the unhappy lot of the poet, November a lament for the death of a lady, and the year concludes with the meditations of an old shepherd looking back over his life from its spring to its fall:

Winter is come, that blowes the bitter blaste, And after Winter dreerie death doth hast.

E. K. further tells us in the "Generall argument of the whole booke" that there are three kinds of eclogues in the Calendar, namely plaintive, recreative "such as al those be, which containe matter of love, or commendation of special personages", and lastly, moral, "which for the most part be mixed with some Satyrical bitternesse". Of the plaintive eclogues, January and June are the complaints of unhappy lovers, and the last two, as we have seen, are laments for death and age. Of the recreative, March is a comic tale out of Greek poetry of a shepherd who hunts Cupid with bolts and stones in mistake for a bird; April is a song in commendation of Eliza, and August, a singing match between two shepherds on the lines of Theocritus.

The moral eclogues deal with secular and religious themes. May, July and October are in the manner of Barnabe Googe whose "eglogs", imitated from Mantuan, had been printed in 1563. They show Spenser's uncompromising Protestantism by their attack on the opulence of Rome, the prevalence of false pastors, and the Catholics who still lurk in the new church like wolves in sheep's clothing. These three types of eclogue are interwoven so as to give variety to the pattern and to avoid the monotony which is the weakness of so many Elizabethan collections of pastoral poetry.

E.K. also congratulates his author, in a passage already quoted, on his choice of an English rather than an "Inkehorne" vocabulary. Spenser, in his desire to rescue many good old words from the disrepute into which they were falling, uses such archaisms as tottie, yode, swinke, corbe, lorrel and bouze (the last two both favourites with Skelton); and E. K. praises his "Dewe observing of Decorum" in their use, thinking, no doubt, that a vocabulary of archaic or dialect words is appropriate for upland shepherds. There was nothing new in the principle of pastoral rudeness which had been accepted from the time of Horace. What is important about the *Shepheardes Calendar* is the thorough manner and intense care for detail with which Spenser applied the theories of Decorum.

For example, the archaism of the language differs according to the type of eclogue. In the plaintive ones which usually deal with love at a relatively courtly level, the language, though obsolete, is genteel and literary, and the archaism consists of adding the prefix "y" to past participles as in ylost, yclad and so forth, or in the use of such well-known Chaucerian words as couth or soote. Satire, in contrast, was traditionally rough, and when pastoral, doubly so, especially when associated with such uncouth figures of satire as Piers Plowman and Colin Clout. In consequence, Spenser uses language which is very much more colloquial and rough for his religious eclogues, and makes his shepherds talk in dialect or homely proverb:

But they that shooten neerest the pricke Sayne, other the fat from their beards doen lick. (*September*.) There is little rhetoric in these poems in the "low" style, whereas the love eclogues show all the rhetorical virtuosity which the sonnet was to exhibit in the next decade, and they draw many an admiring comment for this quality from E. K. in his notes.

With complete consistency, Spenser chooses his meters to match. February, May and September all use Riding Rhyme with its Chaucerian associations and its alliterative echoes of Langland; while July, which is consciously rustic, employs the fourteener with alliteration, already beginning to go out of date. To match the general archaism, words of French origin are often revived in their mediaeval pronunciation, such as "jouysance" to rhyme with dance, in May, and "flowres" with "colowres" in February, though this pronunciation was obsolete by Spenser's time. The less rustic eclogues, on the contrary, have meters appropriate to their kinds, and experiment in the complex modes of Sidney and the Pléiade. Colin Clout's love lament in June has a most complicated eight-line stanza on the very difficult rhyming pattern of *ababbaba*, for example, while the beautiful April song to the Queen anticipates the rhythms of the airs at the end of the century:

Bring hether the Pincke and purple Cullambine, With Gelliflowres: Bring Coronations and Sops in wine, Worne of Paramoures: Strowe me the ground with Daffadowndillies. At times Spenser seems to be reaching towards the meter of the *Faerie Queene*, as in the haunting lines of Cuddie's lament for the death of patronage in the October eclogue:

But ah! Maecenas is yclad in claye, And great Augustus long ygoe is dead, And all the worthies liggen wrapt in leade That matter made for Poets on to play.

In a mixed eclogue such as that of August, which begins with rustic rhymes by Willie and Perigot but ends with a song by Colin himself, one can see how deliberately Spenser suits his meter and style to a low and high occasion respectively, and how brilliantly he combines alternate lines of Riding Rhyme with those of the true decasyllabic stamp, as a final gesture to both levels:

O Colin, Colin! the shepheards joye, How I admire ech turning of thy verse! And Cuddie, fresh Cuddie, the liefest boye, How dolefully his doole thou didst rehearse!

The extent to which Decorum is a controlling principle of the poem can be seen in the November eclogue, which is an imitation of Marot's poem upon the death of the French Queen. In acknowledgement of this fact, Spenser makes use of rhymes of French origin, jouisance, sovenaunce, advaunce, which take us back almost to the aureate style.

I have examined the *Shepheardes Calendar* in detail because it shows in the poet's first serious work so many of the qualities which went to make the *Faerie Queene*. In particular, it anticipates the later poem in its attempt to integrate so much of the floating material of poetry which was available at the time. Its main sources are Mantuan and Marot, with Vergil and Theocritus in the background, but it is typical that Spenser acknowledges only the influence of Chaucer, although the actual debt to Chaucer is slight:

The God of shepheards, Tityrus, is dead, Who taught me homely, as I can, to make; (*June*.)

The blend of old and new language and meter, of eclogue and satiric fable in the *Shepheardes Calendar*, exemplifies the attempt which Spenser made again and again to fuse the classical and the English traditions, the Renaissance and the Middle Ages. He is at once the most revolutionary and the most traditional of poets. Sidney, "Of pastorall, the lively springing sappe" as Drayton called him, and Spenser between them set the fashion for the eclogue, and by 1590, it had become as obligatory for a young poet to write his pastorals as to try his hand at a sonnet cycle. No other Elizabethan poet, however, used the pastoral as seriously as Spenser had done in the satirical eclogues of the *Shepheardes Calendar* or as he was to do in the VIth book of the *Faerie Queene.*

The best collection of pastorals outside Spenser's works is Drayton's *Idea, the Shepheards Garland,* published in 1593 and directly inspired by the *Shepheardes Calendar* which had by then reached its fourth edition. Drayton acknowledges the debt when, in the Third Eclogue, Perkin incites Rowland to awake his "drowsie Muse" and supply the place of "learned Collin" who "is to fayrie gone a Pilgrimage". Drayton writes no satire, but uses the convention to pay formal and sincere tributes to Sidney and to his sister, the Countess of Pembroke, that "cleere bell of Rhetoricke, ringing peales of love", as he describes her in a fine phrase.

He gives a beautiful picture of the Golden Age in the eighth eclogue and follows it up by a genuinely English pastoral to Dowsabell which possibly owes something to Greene's merry milkmaid of Fressingfield in his play, *James IVth.* Her skin as soft as Lemster wooll, As white as snow on peakish hull, or Swanne that swims in Trent.

The native local colour and detail is a pleasant change after Arcadia, and one finds that as the pastoral becomes acclimatized, the scenes and occupations it depicts become more and more English. Barnefield's Daphnis tempts his Ganymede with "a pie-bald Curre to hunt the Hare", although the *Affectionate Shepheard* as a whole, for all its local colour, is an obvious imitation and expansion of Marlowe's "Come live with me".

Breton's charming collection, *The Passionate Shepheard,* printed in 1604, is full of vignettes of English country life: Or to heare the Partridge call, Till she have her covye all; Or to see the subtill fox How the villaine flies the box; After feeding on his pray, How he closely sneakes away, Through the hedge and downe the furrow, Till he gets into his burrowe... And the little blacke-haired coney On a banke for sunny place, With her fore feet wash her face.... (*Pastoral* 3.)

The many references to fields and hedges in the pastoral support C. S. Lewis' conjecture that the enclosing of land had both improved the English landscape and drawn attention to its beauty. Whatever the reason, the pastoral utters more than conventional praise for the country-side, and is the father of such works as the *Compleat Angler*.

But the pastoral began to decay even at the height of its popularity, and by 1600, two tendencies were already apparent, both ultimately destructive of the convention. On the one hand, the fatal voice of realism was making itself heard in *As you like it* or Raleigh's famous reply to "Come live with me and be my love". On the other, the simple conventions of the traditional pastoral were giving way to something more sophisticated, and the whole genre was beginning to become remote, like the romantic plays of Beaumont and Fletcher. Drayton's exquisite *Muses Elizium* in 1630 is a land of elves and fairies, and the shepherd swains have become shadowy and etherealized. *Lycidas* is the last example of the serious Renaissance pastoral; by the 15IIIth century, it has declined into decorative idyll or rustic realism. Johnson's attack on *Lycidas* reveals how the pastoral had ceased to be an acceptable convention for the expression of serious ideas.

## The Sonnet

The term "Sonnet" was used very loosely in the 15Ith century to denote any short love poem. The Quatorzaine was, as we have seen, introduced into England by Wyatt and developed by Surrey who first devised the form of three quatrains and a final couplet, which was to become the characteristic Elizabethan type. These early sonnets, however, had little influence, and only a handful of fresh ones were written from the time of Tottel to that of Sidney.

The art of sonnet writing seems to have been rediscovered, like so many other things, from the Pléide, and the great outburst of English sonnet writing did not begin until the '80's.

The first systematic collection of sonnets to be published in England was Thomas Watson *Passionate Centurie of Love,* a most unpassionate and academic set of imitations from the French and Italian, which appeared in 1582. But it was Sidney *Astrophel and Stella,* written between 1580 and 1584 and circulated in manuscript until its publication in 1591, which really introduced the vogue for sonneteering. It was followed by a flood of sonnet cycles, of which the best are Daniel *Delia* and Constable *Diana* in 1592; Fletcher *Licia* and Barnes' *Parthenophil and Parthenope* in 1593; Drayton *Ideas Mirror* in the next year, and Spenser *Amoretti* in 1595.

The sonnet was essentially the verse form of the gentleman amateur. It was the fashionable thing, which the Berownes of the '90's wrote to their mistresses or circulated amongst their friends, and its witty affectation comes from their efforts to outdo one another in the ingenuity of their conceits. The author of *Zepheria* varies the old image of the ship-wrecked heart by writing of The *naufrage* of my poor afflicted bark and in this, he speaks with the authentic voice of the young Inns of Court man, fresh from the university and primed with that knowledge of the tongues which Sir Andrew Aguecheek coveted so greatly.

The original source of all sonnet cycles was, of course, Petrarch, but no English sonneteer brought to his theme the sincerity, the psychological insight and the sustained feeling which the master had shown. The majority of sonnet writers were more impressed by Petrarch's conceits than by his passion, and the form held no very serious place in the poetical hierarchy. The terms most commonly applied to the cycles were "conceitful sonnets" and "witty amorous toys", appropriate in a young man, but something to be left behind as one grew to poetic maturity.

This is not, of course, to say that the Elizabethan sonnet was a mere literary exercise—although, while the craze was on, many sonnets were no more than this, and one wonders whether Percy wrote his pedestrian sequence to *Coelia* in 1594 for any other reason than that Barnes had dedicated his *Parthenophil* to him in the previous year. But the fact that many great as well as little poets tried their hand at the sonnet suggests that it met some genuine need of the times, and we can understand that need better if we turn to the most sympathetic and revealing portrait of the sonnet lover which has come down to us, namely Shakespeare's Orsino.

The delicate allusive satire of Shakespeare's portrait suggests that Orsino was a familiar figure at Court. He is not in love with Olivia, but he enjoys following the code which is laid down for the young man of fashion: For such as I am all true lovers are (*Twelfth Night,* II, IV. 17.) He languishes at a distance, cherishes his amorous melancholy with the help of song, and is self-consciously changeable in his behaviour among friends, since it is a point of honour with the lover to be constant only in his thoughts of his mistress.

His relationship with Olivia is a prolonged self-dramatization in which he plays the role of the lover with a passionate intensity which he mistakes for love itself. That such behaviour was expected from the young lover is proved by the many debates on love between youth and age in Elizabethan literature. Even Polonius in his youth suffered much extremity for love, and Shakespeare gently satirized the whole convention in his portrait of the shepherd Silvius. The code of formalized wooing made a profound appeal to an educated and leisured class, conscious of its own elegance and desirous of avoiding all trace of barbarism.

It is the complement to the violence and daring of the age, the ladies' faces which accompany the fierce dragons' spleens. It is a part of the Idea of the gentleman which the sonnet expresses directly through its situations, and indirectly through its polished, sophisticated style. For this reason, even the poorest cycles treat the stock Petrarchan situations with a conviction which is unmistakably real, though it may have little to do with love. There is in all of them a prodigality of language and invention which the conventional nature of the sonnet themes encouraged by freeing the poet from the labour of creating his own situations.

For this reason, the sonnet was a most important factor in the evolution of Elizabethan verse, for it enabled the writer to try out his figures and tropes with an irresponsibility impossible in a more serious context. The sonnet, more than any other form of poetry, was the testing ground for the newly revived classical rhetoric and the means by which it was subdued to the purposes of poetry. The "Conceit", for example, so often referred to in connection with the sonnet, is any rhetorical figure fully worked out, and a reader who dips into the sonnets with his Puttenham beside him will see that the majority of them are organized around one basic figure of periphrasis or metaphor into which all minor figures are incorporated.

In particular, the sonnet is important as the origin of a number of techniques for which Donne is usually given the credit. We have seen how logic was reabsorbed by rhetoric in the 15Ith century, and the sonnet was the principal means by which it was established in poetry as well.

Spenser habitually begins his sonnets with a dilemma such as "Is it her nature, or is it her will..." or "Shall I then silent be, or shall I speake ?..." (XLIII) and solves it by a process of argument in which logic is put to strange uses. Many sonnets consist of a complete proof of something inherently nonsensical, as if one should prove by Euclidean geometry that the square of the hypotenuse is not equal to the sum of the squares on the other two sides. In this way, Sidney proves "That I love not, without I leave to love" , or argues that the double negative, "No, no" of his mistress' refusal is grammatically an affirmative (LXIII). With even greater virtuosity, Constable, being told that it is an impossibility for his Diana ever to love him, tells her to relent, since "Gods only do impossibilities", and thus "A goddess thou shalt prove; and happy I" (*Dianà*, I, IV). Or Fletcher improves upon the old ice and fire conceit by begging that he and his Licia may die upon the same day, for if he dies first, the heat of his love will dry up the Styx as Charon rows him across, while if she dies first, her frigidity will freeze it; together they will effect a thaw (*Licia,* XLI-XLII). It is a parody of argument.

Logic has broken loose from scholasticism and become entirely secularized for anyone to play with. The sonnet shows the exuberance of release and anticipates the poetry of Donne with its tough, logical wit. The sonnet convention also encouraged much flippant experiment in metaphor which again anticipated the methods of the Metaphysicals.

All forms of metaphor are common in the sonnet, and the allegory, a metaphor extended throughout a whole sentence, "as, for example if we should call the common wealth, a shippe; the Prince a Pilot, the Counsellors mariners, the stormes warres..." (Puttenham, III, 15iii. p. 187), frequently filled the whole fourteen lines. Metaphor, as the rhetoricians conceived it, was a very deliberate figure of speech springing out of a real analogy between the objects compared, and ranking, for this reason, as one of the figures by which logic effected its definitions.

The main function of metaphor—as its name, the Figure of Transport, implies—was to establish accurate relationships between different objects and hence to place a particular thing in a more general category. When Shelley compares the grief of the lonely heart to "sad dirges, like the wind through a ruined cell", he is not seeking to establish a precise analogy between an empty heart and a hollow cave so much as to present a roughly analogous object, which shall convey an appropriate emotion in an intenser form. When, however, Sidney compares himself ridden by love to the horse which he is riding, he establishes a most accurate and logical series of analogies between himself and the animal.

The reins and the bit which control the horse's motions are, in him, the reverent thoughts which govern his passion; the curb is his fear,... but with gilt bosse above Of hope, which makes it seeme faire to the eye.

Love's whip is Sidney's own will, the saddle, fancy, the girths which hold it in place, memories, and by this means, love "spurres with sharpe desires my heart" (XLIX). The whole edifice of the allegory is built up from the first premise in a series of logical steps which maintain a careful parallel between subject and image at every level. Good Elizabethan metaphor always makes one ask what is the connecting link between the image and the object, and in recognizing the logic of the connection one also sees the defining force of the metaphor. Barnefield's description of a woman's painted face as

*Il-worshipt Idoll, false Imagerie,*
*Ensign of vice, to thine own selfe a lier,*
*Silent Inchaunter, mindes Anatomie,*
*Sly Bawd to Lust, Pander to Infamie....*
*(Complaint of Chastitie.)*

is extremely illuminating when the several images are weighed, and the same is true of Donne's famous comparison of lovers to compasses, a symbol so apt as to be capable of almost infinite expansion.

As in the case of logic, so the peculiar irresponsibility of the sonnet encouraged the poets to parody metaphor as well, and they delight in establishing purely factitious analogies in which the most heterogeneous objects are yoked by violence together. In this way, Barnes writes twelve sonnets comparing the progress of his love to the sun in each of the twelve signs of the Zodiac in turn, or toys with the conventional comparison of his "stonyhearted" mistress to a rock, only to reject it on the grounds that a rock gives back an echo which agrees with the last words of the speaker, whereas her words never agree with his.

Constable even manages to compare his iron-hearted mistress to Mahomet's coffin suspended in mid-air, because his eyes, "love's strange exhaling adaments", have raised her "to my heart's temple's height" (Diana, IV, IV). The sonnet writers show a particular virtuosity in linking the two sides of a comparison by the use of common terms and cementing the relationship by means of a pun. In this way, Barnes compares his mistress' face to a calendar, which shows, in the variety of its expressions, all the days of the year. The Sundays are her smiles, the working days her frowns, numbering "six to one more than the rest", and in conclusion, he looks forward to his Leap year

*When all my cares I overleap and feast*
*With her fruition.... (Parth., LXX14.)*

The audacious pun on "leap" brings the two sides of the comparison together with a snap and anticipates Tourneur's famous silk-worm "undoing herself", or Donne's medical voyage over his own sick body—"Per fretum febris, by these streits to die". In a similar fashion, Donne learned from the sonnet his favourite trick of arguing from one metaphor to a totally new one. Constable, for instance, begins a sonnet by comparing his mistress' hand to a bow

*From whence at me five ivory arrows fly;*
*So with five wounds at once I wounded lie.*

St. Francis suffered a like fate without dying and was made a saint for it, and the lover can therefore lay claim to sainthood on the same grounds; but if he is a saint, then the bow which shot the arrows is a religious relic, and that is why he wishes to kiss his lady's glove,

*This arrow's quiver and this relic's shrine.*
*(Diana, II, IX.)*

The delightful argument in a circle resembles the process by which Donne argues from tears to worlds and from worlds to tides in his Valediction; *of weeping*, for example, and illustrates yet again the debt of the Metaphysicals to the sonnet writers. The Elizabethans had no illusions about the value of what they were doing, and rightly classed such writing in the category of witty toys, a category into which the bulk of Donne Songs and Sonets also fell. We are in greater danger than they were of taking them too seriously. Such seriousness as most of the sonnets possess arises mainly from a reverence for style in language and in living rather than from any serious experience of love. Nevertheless, the greater sonnet writers were inevitably stirred into profounder feelings by the sonnet themes. Drayton, for example, was perhaps the most polished rhetorician of them all, and his poems to Idea are always enjoyable for the vitality and competence of their technique. Yet at his best, as in the passion of "How many Paltry, foolish, painted things...", or the tortured concentration of

*You not alone, when You are still alone,*
*O God, from You, that I could private be....*

(*Ibid.*, Sonnet 11.) he gives an extraordinarily powerful interpretation of the moods of love. His famous and dramatic sonnet "Since there's no helpe Come let us kisse and part"

(*Ibid.*, Sonnet 61), is too well known to need comment. In the same way, Daniel's sonnets, while, always unexceptionably smooth and sugared, are full of a compassionate and mellow awareness of the passing of youth which gives to the best of them a ripeness only excelled by the sonnets of Shakespeare:

*When thou surcharg'd with burthen of thy yeeres,*
*Shalt bend thy wrinkles homeward to the earth;*
*When tyme hath made a pasport for thy feares,*
*Dated in age the Kalends of our death.*
*But ah no more, thys hath beene often tolde,*
*And women grieve to thinke they must be old.*
*(Delia, XLII.)*

It is only to be expected that the two greatest poets of the period—always excepting Shakespeare—should write the two greatest sonnet cycles; and Spenser and Sidney, though using all the current conceits, yet managed in their different ways to express deep feeling through them. Both their sequences are genuinely concerned with love and do not merely use it as an excuse for fine writing. In Colin Clouts come home again Spenser sneered at the fashion of courtly sonneteering, so full of fine gestures and so devoid of real affection:

*For all the walls and windows there are writ*
*All full of love, and love, and love my deare.*

His Amoretti was published together with the Epithalamion in 1595, and the two have been traditionally held to record his wooing of Elizabeth Boyle and its joyful culmination in his marriage to her. Unlike the other sonnet cycles, the Amoretti expresses an idealized conception of love and the belief that marriage is its proper channel. Spenser's mistress is "The glorious image of the Makers beautie" , and he prays:

*Let not one sparke of filthy lustfull fyre*
*Breake out, that may her sacred peace molest; (LXXXIII)*

There are, of course, difficulties and misunderstandings, moods of great happiness and moods of melancholy to balance them, as in the beautiful seventy-fifth sonnet:

*One day I wrote her name upon the strand;*
*But came the waves, and washed it away;*

As in no other cycle, the impression of the poet's own personality comes through the sonnets, and we can hear the note of his tolerant laughter at the whole convention of the conceit, even as he uses it himself. This appears in his mock-heroic address to one of his sonnets, which the lady has burned,

*Innocent paper; whom too cruell hand*

Did make the matter to avenge her yre: (XLVIII.) or in the Easterday prayer which he utters with apparent sincerity,

*And grant that we, for whom thou diddest dye,*
*Being with thy deare blood clene washt from sin,*

May live for ever in felicity only to twist it unexpectedly into a bit of special pleading with his mistress

*So let us love, deare love, lyke as we ought:*
*Love is the lesson which the Lord us taught." (L15III.)*

The Amoretti has more humour and maturity than any other cycle; it is not for nothing that Spenser wrote the sonnets relatively late in his career and at the very height of his powers.

The greatest of all the sonnet cycles, apart from Shakespeare's, and that which most nearly approximates to Petrarch Rime, is Sidney Astrophel and Stella, star and star lover, the first cycle to be written. Like the Amoretti, Sidney's sonnets have been traditionally associated with a particular woman, Penelope Devereux who became Lady Rich; and the fact that several of the sonnets making vicious puns on the name Rich were suppressed in the early editions of the sequence gives colour to the tradition.

Like Spenser, too, Sidney had no patience with the conventional conceited love poem and in the Defence he criticizes the whole genre for its flagrant insincerity: "many of such writings, as come under the banner of unresistible love, if I were a mistress, would never perswade mee they were in love". The sonnets themselves are full of sneers at

*You that old Petrarchs long deceased woes*
*With new borne sighes, and wit disguised sing;*

The first sonnet of the cycle sets the key to the whole, describing in excessively formal rhetoric Astrophel's desire to write a love poem and his search for an appropriate style:

*Loving in trueth, and fayne my love in verse to show,*
*That the deere Shee, might take some pleasure of my paine:*

Pleasure might cause her reade, reading might make her know, Knowledge might pittie winne, and pittie grace obtaine. I sought fit wordes, to paint the blackest face of woe but concluding abruptly with the simple advice

*Foole saide My muse to mee, looke in thy heart and write.*

The story is told through the sonnets and through a number of longer songs inserted at intervals after the manner of Petrarch—though these songs were not inserted in their proper places in the 1591 edition, possibly to conceal the identity of the persons involved.

The story, which is more elabourate than in any other cycle, is one of passionate wooing, of a woman who loves yet will not break her faith with her husband or injure the career of her lover, and of a lover torn between his desire and his reason.

The songs describe in several different forms an occasion on which Astrophel comes to Stella but is repulsed: in one form, the scene is at her house:

*Your faire Mother is a bed,*
*Candles out, and curtaines spred;*
*She thinkes you doo letters write:*
*Write, but first let me endite.*
*Take mee to thee, and thee to mee:*
*No no no no, my Deare let be.*
*(Collected Works, Vol. II, p. 287.)*

In another, the incident takes place underneath her window, and on a third occasion, in a grove. The inclusion of these songs at their proper places in the sequence heightens immeasurably the dramatic realism of the whole, and makes more comprehensible the magnificent sonnets of renunciation which, though not published as a part of Astrophel and Stella, would seem to be its natural conclusion:

*Leave me o love, which reachest but to dust,*
*And thou my mind aspire to higher things:*
*Grow rich in that which never taketh rust:*
*What ever fades, but fading pleasure brings....*

*Then farewell world, thy uttermost I see,*
*Eternall Love maintaine thy life in me. (Ibid., p. 322.)*

In such a setting the conventional conceit has no place, and Sidney, though admiring witty logic as much as anyone and inheriting a great body of traditional conceits, always attempts to relate them to real life.

The imagery of the sonnets is drawn from the social background of the times rather than from the usual school of Cupid; and accountancy, bankruptcy or horse riding all pay their tribute. Kisses are called

*Nest of young joyes, Scholemaster of delight...*

Breakfast of love and sleep, although it was a well-worn subject for Petrarchan poetry, is described by Sidney in imagery of fresh social content which reveals the essentially realistic bent of the poet's mind:

*Come Sleepe, O Sleepe, the certaine knot of peace,*
*The bathing place of wits, the balme of woe*
*The poore mans wealth, the prysoners release*
*The indifferent Judge betweene the hie and low.... (XXXIX.)*

The sonnet has something of the quality of Macbeth's more famous speech on the same subject, which appears to echo it; life keeps breaking in, and Sidney sees his love affair against the wider background of Elizabethan wars and politics. In Sonnet XXX, for example, he runs over all the things which ought to occupy his mind:

*Whether the Turkish new Moone minded be*
*To fill her hornes uppon the Christian coast,*
*How Polands king mindes without leave of hoast*
*To warme with ill made fire cold Muscovie....*

and yet, with all these to think about, he still thinks of Stella. The hackneyed Petrarchism is given new life and brought up to date. Cupid ceases to be the conventional little boy with bow and arrows and becomes a foot-pad:

*See there that boy, that murthering boy I say,*
*Who like a thiefe hid in a bush doth lye,*
*Tyll blooddy bullet get him wrongfull pray...*
*Stella is not the usual naked goddess but*
*Sweete garden Nymph which keepes the Cherry tree.*

Inevitably Sidney attempts to introduce a freer movement into the sonnet and to capture the human voice in a manner which takes us back to Wyatt or forward to Donne. In Sonnet XLVII, for example, Astrophel determines to break off his fruitless wooing and regain his liberty, but his resolution vanishes on the sudden appearance of Stella:

*Vertue awake, beautie but beautie is:*
*I may, I must, I can, I will, I doe*
*Leave following that which it is gaine to misse,*
*Let her goe: soft, but there she comes, goe to...*

The pompous insincerity of the first line is followed by the mounting amplification of "I may, I must..." in which Astrophel nerves himself to make his protest; but the braggadocio of "Let her goe" is followed by the very human collapse when Stella appears. It is rhetoric, but rhetoric treated with humour and sympathy to convey a sequence of real emotions, and it anticipates the technique of the drama by ten years.

It is not, of course, suggested that Astrophel and Stella and the Amoretti are strictly autobiographical. The time had not yet come for the sonnet to be treated as the medium for personal confession. It is more likely that these two cycles, starting from personal situations, developed them dramatically so as to incorporate as many as possible of the features expected in love poetry, just as the initial love of Petrarch for his Laura fired his imagination and stimulated his poetry long after she was dead and he was married elsewhere.

From its earliest days, the 15Ith-century love poem had contained dramatic elements, dealing with generic lovers in a variety of stock situations rather than telling the histories of the poets themselves. The real parallel to an Elizabethan sonnet sequence is Maud rather than The House of Life; it is enough if the poet gives the illusion of life without telling a true story.

The sonnet is the most mediaeval form of Elizabethan love poetry in that it carries on, however flippantly, the traditional adoration of the lady. Its popularity sprang, to some extent, from its blend of traditional material and new art. It is a thin little trickle after the great river of mediaeval Courtly Love, but, with the stricter canalization of Renaissance poetry into the Kinds, it was only one form of love poetry out of many, and the whole range makes a formidable total. In any case, it was a less esoteric form than it might appear now, for it had connections in a number of other contexts, and should be read in conjunction with, for example, the Emblem books which were so popular throughout Europe in the last quarter of the 15Ith century.

The Emblem pictures of hearts being broken or burned or pierced by robust little Cupids are the pictorial equivalent of the sonnet conceit; Vaenius draws a Cupid burning a lover's heart in a furnace or hammering it on an anvil, and a hundred sonnets reproduce the conceit in the form of a metaphor:

*My Hart the Anvile where my thoughts doe beate...*
*Love is the fuell which maintaines the fire....*
*(Drayton, Ideas Mirrour, Amour 44.)*

In addition, the two commonest metaphors of the sonnet, namely, the comparison of the lover to a storm-tossed ship, and of the lady to a besieged fort, are entirely traditional, and have a long history of religious and secular symbol behind them. Drayton's lament for his "poore soule, the Barke of sorrow":

*See how her sayles be rent, her tacklings worne,*
*Her Cable broke, her surest Anchor lost....*
*(Ibid., Amour 34.)*
*or Spenser's*
*Retourne agayne, my forces late dismayd,*

.Unto the siege by you abandoned quite have their counterparts in the mediaeval Homily and Morality play, in the Faerie Queene, in the sermons of Donne and in the religious poetry of the Metaphysicals. One thinks of Donne's "Batter my heart, three person'd God" or Herbert's "Sick-tossed vessel, dashing on each shelf...". The materials of poetry from the Middle Ages through to the Augustans are homogeneous to a remarkable degree, and the sonnet, together with other forms, was enriched and made more subtle in its effects by the echoes and associations, often incongruous, which must have accompanied it for a contemporary reader. It is, in fact, a more traditional form of verse in style and content than we are apt to think it.

## The Lyric

The Elizabethan lyric was still close enough to oral verse to inherit the traditional association of poetry with music. The relationship was, indeed, revived and intensified in the 15Ith century, partly on account of the revival of the classical lyric which took its name from the lyre to which it had been sung, and partly owing to the break up of the religious foundations and the dispersal of their musicians and singing men who carried their art into secular life and helped to raise the general level of musical skill as the century proceeded. The Elizabethan and the Jacobean years are the great age of English music.

It formed an important part of education, and the Elizabethan gentleman was expected to be proficient both in song and with the lute, while an apprentice found a good voice and the ability to read music a sure way to advancement. It was an age when every barber's shop had a lute hanging on the walls for the delectation of the customers and when lute strings were favourite gifts to ladies. Madrigal music was habitually printed with the separate parts along the four sides of the sheet, so that the family could sit round the table and sing, and the singing journeymen in Dekker Shoe-Maker's Holiday, or the shepherdesses who sing Autolycus' ballads at sight give a true picture of the general level of skill and interest. By 1610, the names of Byrd, Morley, Dowland, John Daniel, Campion and Weelkes, to mention only a few of the great galaxy, were famous throughout Europe for their madrigals and airs.

For this reason, the lyric is the most ubiquitous of Elizabethan verse forms, penetrating to all social levels and assimilating all the different modes of pastoral, sonnet, elegy or hymn into itself. At the beginning of the century, lyric verse was fairly homogeneous, and Wyatt and Surrey could use the popular ballad meter for their courtly verses; but as the century progressed, the courtly lyric became more courtly under the influence of new Italian models, the popular lyric more popular and less reputable through its participation in the religious controversies of the reigns of Mary and Elizabeth. The decline in prestige of the Fourteener from *Tottel's Miscellany* to Peter Quince's play of *Pyramus and Thisbe* is a symptom of the process, and by 1590, the courtly and popular lyrics were as clearly distinguished as highbrow and jazz today.

It is necessary, therefore, to consider the lyric at different social levels. In the first place, the traditional oral ballad was still a living thing, though its days were numbered. A popular writer like Deloney included many old ballads in the text of his novels, and his own poems in the Garland of Goodwill show that he was still attempting to write in the traditional form. Many of them are narratives with instructions attached to them such as "To be sung in the old ancient sort, or else to the tune of Labandalashot". The same tradition is still at work, on a higher level, in Raleigh's "As you came from the Holy Land" or Drayton's fine ballad of Agincourt.

In the 15Ith century, however, a new type of ballad emerged with the advent of printing, namely the broadsheet that is the printed ballad of the kind that Autolycus was selling. As it was designed to be sold, it tended to be topical in its appeal, and in drawing its materials from the more sensational incidents of the time, it fulfilled some of the functions of the modern cheap press. Autolycus' ballad about the usurer's wife who was brought to bed of twenty money-bags can be paralleled in Elderton's account of the monstrous child born at Stony Stratford or the accounts of the last confessions of such notable murderers as Mrs. Anne Saunders. Some of Elderton's ballads are lively and amusing, and their circulation must have been enormous; but, as a whole, the standard of verse was not high, and the upper levels of the literary profession united in sneering at the "pot-house poets" and the "red-nosed ballet-mongers".

Not all broadsheets were news ballads, and many were plain love-songs such as Mopsa and Dorcas sang in the *Winter's*

*Tale*. Clement Robinson's attractive miscellany, A *Handefull of Pleasant Delites*, first published in 1566, consists entirely of such songs to which the tunes are indicated, and it is noticeable that their meters are far more flexible and interesting than those of contemporary verse written in less close conjunction with music. At a time when writers were struggling for regularity with the mechanical help of Poulter's Measure, Robinson's lyrics, sustained by the movement of their tunes, can change their rhythm and vary their meter with the greatest confidence. The influence of the tune is obvious in a complex stanza such as the following, for example, which varies its rhythm twice in a few lines:

*Now Ladies, be merie*
*Because you are werie;*
*leave work I say, and get you home;*
*Your businesse is slacking,*
*Your lover is packing;*
*Your answer hath cut off his comb.*
*How then?*
*The fault was in him, sir,*
*He wooed it so trim, sir,*
*Alas! poore seelie fellow,*
*Make much of thy pillow*
*Make much of thy pillow. (H of P.D., p. 15.)*

Even the ballad meter itself is capable of taking on a new lilt when written to the tune of "Lustie Gallant".

*Fain would I have a pretie thing,*
*to give unto my Ladie.*
*I name no thing, nor I meane no thing,*
*but as pretie a thing as may bee. (Ibid., p 74.)*

The livelier rhythms come in from the popular dances, the Almans, Brawles, Galliards and Canaries which go with the tunes, and it is interesting to note that popular song has a range of rhythms which are all its own and scarcely ever appear in the more courtly lyric of the period. Tunes in triplet measures are very common in the popular song, corresponding, perhaps, to the hop and skip of a popular dance. Turkey Loney, Packington's Pound, Cock Lorrel and

Light o' Love, to name only a few of the more famous tunes of the century, are written in the rhythm of "The bonnets of bonny Dundee", and this results in a verse meter based on the anapaestic foot of two short syllables and one long, such as Byron used in his poem "The Assyrian came down like a wolf on the fold", to quote a familiar example. Verses such as the following occur very frequently in the Broadsheets:

*If ever I marry, I'll marry a maid,*
*To marry a widow I'm sore afraid*

*sung to Turkey Loney; or the famous ballad of Mary Ambree:*

*When Captains Courageous, whom death could not daunt,*

Had roundly besieged the city of Gaunt or Desdemona's Willow Song. The only other context in which such meters appear in any quantity is the *Five Hundred points of Good Husbandrie* by Thomas Tusser, who used them to describe the whole farming year:

*Wife, into thy garden and set me a plot,*
*With strawberry rootes, of the best to be got. (September.)*

*or*

*Good bread and good drinke, a good fier in the hall,*
*Brawne, pudding and souse and good mustard withall. (December.)*

Tusser himself had been a singing boy in an ecclesiastical foundation which was dissolved in 1549. He carried his musical training over into his farming and wrote what was possibly the most popular book of verse in the 15Ith century. These anapestic meters stayed below the level of serious verse until in the 15IIIth century, when low life became the fashion, they rose to the surface and achieved respectability in *The Beggar's Opera*.

The popular ballad was there throughout the whole of the 15Ith century, but the courtly lyric decayed in the troubled years after the death of Wyatt and only came to its own again in the general poetic renaissance of the '80's. A chronological collection such as Ault *Elizabethan Lyrics* shows how dramatically the quality and quantity of lyric verse increased with the advent of Spenser, Sidney and the University Wits. The new song contained both the Petrarchan and the passionate strains, and put a rich sensuous vitality into the old icon:

*Have you seen but a bright lillie grow,*
*Before rude hands have touch'd it?*
*Have you mark'd but the fall o' the snow*
*Before the soyle hath smutch'd it?*
*Have you felt the wooll o' the Bever?*
*Or*
*Swans Downe ever?*
*Or*
*have smelt o' the bud o' the Briar?*
*Or*
*the Nard i' the fire?*
*Or*
*have tasted the bag o' the Bee?*
*O so white! O so soft! O so sweet is she!*
*(Ben Jonson, Her Triumph. The Underwood, II, 4.)*

It has a fresh sense of the country which is in part a development out of the mediaeval spring song but in part, also, an indication of a new interest in the English landscape. Flowers and country matters are the source of most of its settings and images.

The sources of the new poetry have been discussed earlier, but with the lyric, there is something else to consider, namely, the influence of the Italian madrigal and air which affected English music during the last quarter of the century, although Byrd and Dowland did not begin composing them in England until the last decade. The madrigal was essentially a musical technique and had little direct influence on poetry. It is a contrapuntal exercise for a number of voices in which no one melodic line is dominant. The general tone of the poem sets the mood of the music, but as the words are worked over in rotation by the different voices, the original metrical patterns are lost, and verse written for the madrigal has few recognizable characteristics. In subject, it was mainly Petrarchan, since the musical form was evolved in conjunction with the revival of Petrarch's poetry in Italy, round about 1530. But the range of its poetry covers verses from the Bible,

English hexameters, stanzas from the *Mirror* or the *Faerie Queene*, sets of hunting calls, and in one case, as a joke, a verse made up of the little prose tags with which the madrigalists concluded their compositions:

*Here is an end of all the songs*
*That are in number but four parts....*
*(Fellowes, English Madrigal Verse, p. 108.)*

The only essentials are that the verse must be short so that it is not too lengthy when extended by the fugal methods of the music, and that it must contain no subtleties of thought, language or emotion, since these would inevitably be lost under the music.

There can be no great continuity of thought or image, since the separate phrases of the poem are taken out of their context and repeated by the different voices. The madrigal was nevertheless important for its indirect effects on verse, since, at a time when poets were obsessed by meter, whether the old fourteener or the new classical, it directed attention away from meter towards the fundamental rhythm. The handling of the same set of words in different rhythms within a single Madrigal encouraged variety and helped to loosen up meters in general. The rhythmic flexibility of later Elizabethan verse owes much to the labours of the musicians.

The air, in contrast, had an immediate effect on verse form. It was a tune sung to the accompaniment of a lute or of other voices, and it only differed from the popular song in that it used the new Italian tunes and rhythms. It was more literary than the madrigal, and words and tune were more precisely matched to each other. "I have chiefely aymed to couple my Words and Notes lovingly together," wrote Campion in the Preface to his *Two Bookes of Ayres* of which he was both poet and composer, and, for this reason, poetry written for the air reflects the inevitable demands which music makes on it. Like the popular ballad, it tends to consist of longer units than the madrigal, and to contain more drama and narrative. It can even employ elabourate rhetoric, especially figures such as Gradation which mark the beginnings of sentences in correspondence with the musical phrases:

*Love, the delight of all well-thinking minds,*
*Delight, the fruit of virtue dearly loved,*
*Virtue.... (Cavendish Ayres, vii. Fellowes, p. 377.)*

It usually has a very definite stanza form to correspond to the repeated pattern of the tune, and, in the best songs, the stanzas echo each other precisely, word for word, in emotion and movement as they do, for example, in Shakespeare *"Come away, come away death"*, or John Dowland *"Come away, come, sweet love"* (Fellowes, p. 413). This leads to the cultivation of a most delicate sensitivity to the values of words, and the maintenance of the same emotional pattern in different verses, by which a good lyric is bound into a perfect formal harmony of echoes and analogies. By this means, the air can capture a moment of emotion with unrivalled force, but for the same reason, it suffers from rigidity when it tries to express any development in emotion or idea. The air, written to an unchanging tune, cannot cope with any sudden change of mood or unexpected departure from the main pattern.

Above all, the air has the most subtle and flexible rhythms, from the fact that the tunes were composed for particular words, or vice versa. Dowland's beautiful lyric is only one example of the control which results from the wedding of words and music:

*Weep you no more, sad fountains;*
*What need you flow so fast?*
*Look how the snowy mountains*
*Heaven's sun doth gently waste.*
*But my sun's heavenly eyes*
*View not your weeping,*
*That now lies sleeping*
*Softly, now softly lies*
*Sleeping.*
*(John Dowland. The Third and Last*
*Booke of Songs or Aires, 15. Fellowes,)*

The music enables the poet to modulate through a series of changing rhythms, and the diminishing lines are sustained by the lengthening quantities of single words which only music can indicate. The lyrics of Dowland or Campion and the rest as we see them in print are pale reflections of what they can be when music smoothes off the angularities and clothes their naked skeletons. Consider, for example, John Attey's dramatic and *passionate air:*

*On a time the amorous Silvy*
*Said to her shepherd: Sweet, how do ye?*
*Kiss me this once and then God be wi' ye,*
*My sweetest dear;*
*Kiss me this once and God be wi' ye,*
*For now the morning draweth near....*
*(First Booke of Ayres. Fellowes,)*

The tune begins rather hesitantly, and wanders off into another key with "Sweet, how do ye?", as the shepherdess sees with dismay her partner sleeping and the dawn coming. With "Kiss me this once", the tune moves with a stronger, more confident rhythm, carried on by the sudden flood of her passion, and "My sweetest dear" is extended into the length of a full line with a languishing run of notes on "sweetest" to convey the prolonged kiss. The kiss rouses the lover, for the last two lines move with joyful vigour, and the hesitation of the opening moments is completely gone. The slightly halting rhythm of "and then God be wi ye" is smoothed out by the omission of "then", and the last line becomes a triumphant cadenza in which "for now the morning" is repeated. It is difficult to describe the effect without the music, but the tune adds another dimension to the poem and increases immeasurably its dramatic and emotional force.

I have dealt only with the lyric in conjunction with music, since this was the main 15Ith-century type; but it is important to realize that the advent of printing encouraged the development of the lyric designed to be read, which can be seen emerging from the time of Tottel onwards. The needs and natures of the two kinds are essentially different. It has been seen that the song has great flexibility of rhythm and intensity of emotion, but that it is limited when it comes to express complex ideas or feelings.

The lyric for reading, on the other hand, is relatively pedestrian in its rhythms and more dependent on meter, but has an unlimited capacity for handling complexity of idea, mood and language. Whereas the song is public, declamatory and, therefore, impersonal, the read lyric can be introspective, and personal; the lyric expressing private emotions and personal confessions, as the Romantics conceived of it, for example, is essentially a form for reading. We can see signs of this new lyric in *Tottels Miscellany,* in a number of poems which make a more ambitious use of rhetoric than is suited to song. The sonnet, of course, did much to establish the lyrical poem for reading, and many of them, though lyrical in quality, yet preclude the accompaniment of music by the lack of stanzaic repetition in their form and the complexity of their conceits. By the end of the century, the proper Decorums of sung and read lyric were established; a miscellany such as *Englands Helicon,* with its simplicity of theme and language, clearly belongs to the former class, while another, the *Phoenix Nest,* which contains so much of the complicated sonnet rhetoric, is predominantly in the latter.

The distinction was most clearly established by Donne whose complex imagery and subtle logic would be obscured by the accompaniment of a tune. The sudden and surprising changes of mood and direction which are characteristic of his verse can only be done once without becoming mechanical, but a recurring tune would demand their recurrence in every verse. The arguments of such poems as *A Valediction; of weeping* or *Lovers infinitenesse,* which begin tentatively in the first and end triumphantly in the last verse, would be unsuitable to a tune incapable of a like development; the air was unfitted to cope with poetry which rose to a single, final climax. Donne learnt a great deal from the air, but the resemblance of his lyrics to contemporary song is only superficial, and he found another principle than music on which to base his astonishingly flexible meters. Not the tune but the human voice, especially the human voice in argument, is the basis of Donne's patterns, and his variety of line and pace is designed to emphasize the salient words in his argument:

*On a round ball*
*A workman that hath copies by, can lay*

*An Europe, Afrique, and an Asia,*
*And quickly make that, which was nothing, All.*
*(Valediction; of Weeping.)*

His repetition of a complex stanza is a triumph of intellectual discipline, and shows a capacity to develop an argument in a continuous pattern, rather than to echo mood and phrase through a series of verses. A reader should compare Donne's poem, *Lovers infinitenesse,* with what appears to be the same poem written in the form of a song, possibly by Donne himself, and called *Love's Exchange* (Donne, I, p. 449). The former poem is an unbroken sequence of argument, in which, since the subject is Donne's desire for the whole of his Mistress' love, the predominant rhyme, and that on which it begins and ends, is the word "All". *Love's exchange* on the other hand, though using many of the same arguments and phrases, is thoroughly disjointed. The rigid stanza destroys the continuity, and the alternation of long and short lines kills the decision of statement. It is the clearest illustration of the real difference between the two kinds of lyric, and an object lesson in the dangers of confusing them.

## Chapter 13

# Historical Poetry

The literary judgments of posterity rarely coincide with those of a poet's own time, and we still sing and read the songs and sonnets, which the Elizabethans valued as trifles, whereas the historical poems, which they took far more seriously, are nowadays virtually ignored. Yet history was one of the main subjects of Elizabethan verse, and the composition of serious historical poems by Daniel, Drayton and Spenser, the vogue of the historical play, and the effusions of Warner or Deloney at a lower level, all testify to the enormous popularity of the historical mode. The taste for history was a symptom of the Renaissance nationalism which showed itself elsewhere, as we have seen, in the patriotic development of the vernacular. There was a sudden growth of historical consciousness with the accession of the Tudors which found its expression in the great chroniclers and antiquarians of the century, of whom Hall and Holinshed, Leland, Camden, Stow, and the Italian Polydore Vergil, official historian to the Court of Henry VIIth, are the most famous. The 15Ith century is a period of map-making, county histories and regional surveys, and Stow's *London* or Harrison's *Description of England* are typical examples of a very large field.

In a period so avid for moral instruction as we have seen the 15Ith century to be, the approach to history was naturally didactic, and Sidney only placed history lower than poetry as a teacher of morals because the facts of life are not always as edifying as they ought to be. But when the truths of history are combined with and modified by the powers of divine poetry then indeed the most moving form of persuasion results, and this was what the Elizabethans understood by a heroic poem, and the reason why they rated it so highly. Spenser's *Faerie Queene* has an essentially moral aim, "to fashion a gentleman or noble person in vertuous and gentle discipline", and its method is to take a great national hero and use him as an allegory. Shakespeare, Drayton and Daniel chose to teach rather by example than by allegory, but they too held up the figures of English history as noble models of what to emulate or grim warnings of what to avoid.

The study of English history included everything from the ancient Britons to the reign of Elizabeth, but two periods attracted special attention. The first was naturally the Wars of the Roses, still almost a living memory and acting as a terrible warning to a nation not yet wholly unified and often on the verge of renewed civil war. Henry VIIth and the Tudor line after him made all the political capital they could out of the union of the white rose and the red, which had inaugurated an age of peace after "York and Lancaster's long jars". After 1570, when patriotism rose under the stimulus of a Spanish and Papal threat, there was an acute sense of the blessings of unity and an overwhelming fear of internal dissension, which formed the driving force behind Shakespeare's history plays. For the same reason, the reign of Edward II was a favourite with the writers because, like that of Richard II, it ended in the deposition of the king.

The second period of special interest to English patriotism was that which covered the fabulous descent of the ancient British kings from Aeneas of Troy. Geoffrey of Monmouth had first propagated the legend, which had been elabourated after him and was very hotly debated and sincerely accepted by many 15Ith-century historians. According to the legend, Aeneas, after escaping from Troy, had made his way to Italy where he had founded Rome. His grandson Brute, led by divine guidance, went to Greece where he collected the remnants of the Trojans still in captivity there, and from thence sailed to Britain, landing at Totnes in Devonshire. From him came the line of British kings which included such illustrious figures as Lud, Lear, Gorboduc and Cymbeline and which reached its peak of greatness under King Arthur. The royal line resisted and survived the Roman Conquest but finally succumbed before the Saxons; and Cadwallader, the last of the British kings, was driven into exile in Brittany. Merlin, however, had prophesied that the British kings would eventually come back to their kingdom, and Arthur himself return to the throne "when unto a first Succeeds a second she". The fulfilment of the prophecy came with the Tudors whose ancestor, Owen Glendower, was held to be a descendant of the ancient line, so that Elizabeth, succeeding Mary, was virtually an incarnation of the great Arthur himself.

This again was a flattering and useful legend which the Tudors assiduously fostered, and even King James was included in the pattern, as a descendant of Fleance who married into the British line after his escape from Macbeth. It was pleasant to believe that London had originally been Troy Novant, the third Troy founded by the illustrious family of Priam, with Rome, of course, as the second; and for this reason Welsh and Arthurian lore played a very large part in 15Ith-century literature, although there were sceptics like Polydore Vergil who, being an Italian, had no patriotic incentive to believe in it. Even more than the classics, the tales of King Arthur formed the real mythology of the Elizabethan age.

The first poetry to deal with historical themes in a really ambitious way was the Mirror for Magistrates. This gigantic compendium began very humbly with a suppressed edition in 1555, but came out successfully in 1559 and from that time grew like a snowball through successive editions throughout the remainder of the century. The preface to the reader in the edition of 1559 tells how the printer had intended to publish Lydgate Fall of Princes but was patriotically offended because the old poet had ignored so many tragedies out of English history. A group of seven well-known scholars, therefore, headed by William Baldwin, a translator and philosopher, undertook to supply the deficiency and, by working through the chronicles, to produce a further series of falls of great men which should bring Lydgate up to date. Each of the seven chose a number of figures from English history and, in each case, wrote a poem in which the character concerned told his own story and complained of his unhappy lot. The seven composers then assembled and, with Baldwin in the chair, read out their poems and discussed them afterwards.

The poems were tragedies in the Chaucerian sense, that is, accounts of how a great person falls into misery; but whereas Lydgate had designed his tragedies to illustrate the fickleness of fortune, the writers of the Mirror had a more practical intention, and one more in keeping with the times. The term "Mirror" meant the essential type or example, something approximating to the Platonic Idea, while a Magistrate, as Baldwin explained in his preface, was anyone in a position of authority. The Mirror was conceived as a pattern for statesmen, a series of political examples which should teach their own age to avoid the mistakes of the previous one, at a time when the country needed all the political guidance it could get. The seven therefore turned to the Wars of the Roses as a period particularly rich in historical lessons, and chose those figures which drove home a point most forcibly rather than those which were the most illustrious. On occasion, they took advantage of poetic licence to tamper with the facts where a small adjustment made the example more telling.

The series begins with the complaint of Robert Tresilian, the Lord Chief Justice of Richard II, whose Tragedy illustrates the evils of "misconstruyng the lawes and expounding them to serve the Princes affections". Richard II is held up as a "Kyng that ruled all by lust", Lord Clyfford as an illustration of the way in which political revenge recoils back upon the instigator. Throughout the whole, the Tudor doctrine of Divine Right is emphasized, and Jack Cade's rebellion, for example, is quoted to prove that

*Whan we presume our princes to resist*
*We war with God, against his glory to,*
*That placeth in his office whom he list.*

The fact that the king may be a bad king like Richard II, or the rebellion be a successful one like that of Bolingbroke, makes no difference. We cannot know God's purposes, and he may have sent a bad king to try the people's patience or to test the virtue of the ruler himself. The subject is not concerned with the ultimate ends but only with the rightness or wrongness of his immediate actions. Good is good and bad, bad, irrespective of the consequences, and no one is justified in committing an evil deed for a good purpose. The tragedy of Thomas Montague, Earl of Salisbury who was slain "in the middes of his glory" was intended to teach the very un-Machiavellian moral that

*God hateth rigour though it furder right,*
*For sinne is sinne, however it be used....*

The first edition of the Mirror is of a competent standard throughout, but contains two especially remarkable contributions, one by Thomas Sackville, part author of the play Gorboduc which resembles the Mirror in its political intention, and one by John Dolman. Sackville famous Induction and his Tragedy of Buckingham are such outstanding achievements that Baldwin included them although they did not fit into his general scheme. Sackville seems to have intended to write a Mirror of his own on the lines of Lydgate Fall, and his Induction was to have formed the framework for his collection. It begins with a brilliant evocation of the tragic atmosphere: it is a winter's evening, Hawthorne had lost his motley liverye,

The naked twigges were shivering all for colde when the poet meets an old withered woman who is Sorrow, a personification conceived very much in the Senecan manner in endeles tormentes payned,

*Among the furies of the infernall lake.*

She takes him down to a Hades, which is a superb fusion of Senecan, Vergilian and mediaeval elements, and the whole description owes its peculiar richness to the strains of different civilizations which meet and are harmonized within it. The accompanying tragedy of Buckingham is in the same sombre vein, and if Sackville had completed his design, the poem would have been very different from the Mirror as it exists, less political in intention, but more profoundly tragic. Sackville was, moreover, a remarkable prosodist who achieved by unobtrusive subtlety the regularity, which the writers of the contemporary fourteener sought with so much labour. He replaces the mute "e", for example, by an extra adjective, turning Chaucer's "fresshe floures" into "soote fresh flowers"; and he solves the problem of changing accents by a simple inversion, as when he converts Wyatt's "sodayn pale colour" with its stress on the last syllable to "her colour pale".

In contrast, Dolman, the writer of the twenty-first tragedy of the Lord Hastings, gains his effects by cultivating the very robustiousness of the old style which Sackville avoids. His description of the sea, with its puns and its vocabulary out of the Senecan translations, is uncommonly lively:

*The restless tyde, to bare the empty baye,*
*With waltryng waves roames wamblyng forth. Away*
*The mery maryner hayles. The braggyng boye,*
*To masts hye top up hyes. In signe of joye*
*The wavering flagge is vaunsd. The suttle seas*
*Theyr swellyng ceasse....*

His account of life on board ship has the compressed simile and abrupt syntax, which takes one forward to the verse of Donne or Chapman:

*In pryson pent, whose woddye walles to passe*
*Of no less peryll than the dying was;*
*With the Oceane moated, battered with the waves*
*(As chaynd at Oares the wretched Galley slaves*
*At mercy sit of Sea and enemyes shott,*
*And shonne with death what they with flyght may not)...*

The poem is full of moments of humour and scraps of vivid conversation which bring Richard Crookback with his "goggle eye" suddenly to life. Sackville and Dolman, indeed, epitomize the two main lines of 15Ith-century verse, the linef Imitation that goes through to Milton, and that of colloquialism, which finds its culmination in Donne.

The later editions of the Mirror produced by Higgins and Blenerhasset complete the story of British history from the arrival of Brute to the Norman Conquest. The serious political aim is, however, abandoned and the tragedies abound in such curious moral lessons as that which concludes the history of Kimarus who was eaten by wolves:

*By this appeares that time in Britayne were*
*Aboundant store of wolves and vices rife.*
*(Lenvoy. Parts added to the Mirror.)*

The quality of his verse forces us to believe Higgins' confession that "I have not spent in poetrye my dayes", though Blenerhasset is more competent. As late as 1600, new tragedies were still being added to the Mirror, but by that time history was thoroughly established as the theme for serious drama and poetry, and the future of the historical mode had passed from the hands of the compilers to those of individual writers.

The truest historian of all the Elizabethan poets was Samuel Daniel who himself began a prose history of the Wars of the Roses. His Defence of Rhyme, which came out in 1602 in answer to Campion's eulogy of classical meters, is not merely a discussion of literary techniques; it is a denial of the supremacy of the classics and a defence of English poetry based on a truly historical perspective with regard to the achievements of the Middle Ages. "And is it not a most apparent ignorance, both of the succession of learning in Europe, and the generall course of things," he asks, "to say, that all lay pittifully deformed in those lackelearning times from the declining of the Romane Empire, till the light of the Latine tongue was revived by Rewcline, Erasmus and Moore". He quotes mediaeval architecture and philosophy to prove that "The distribution of giftes are universal!" (p. 143), and argues in words which anticipate those of Shakespeare's Cloten, that "All our understandings are not to be built by the square of Greece or Italie. We are the children of nature as well as they". The study of the chronicles seems to have bred a tolerance for the Middle Ages which is in contrast to the contempt which Bacon and the new scientists felt for them.

Daniel most considerable historical poem is his Civil Wars between the two houses of Lancaster and Yorke, the first four books of which were printed in 1595 and a second four added by 1609, when the poem stopped at the reign of Edward III. The aims of the poem were first to show that the Wars of the Roses were an inevitable result of Bolingbroke's deposition of Richard II, and secondly to contrast "the deformities of civile

Dissension" with the blessings of Elizabethan peace. Daniel never allows himself to be distracted from these aims; in his determination to "tell the worst of every raigne", he refuses to be drawn into an account of the victories of Henry V, and he resists the temptation to use fine language since, as he says, "I versifie the troth, not poetize". His interest is in the motives rather than the actions of his characters, and he analyses with great shrewdness the selfish calculation which led to the shifting loyalties of the times.

The poem conveys well the sense of instability which accompanies usurpation; Henry IV and his son are never sure of themselves and are hampered by never being able to take their royal right for granted. The civil wars develop with inevitable logic out of the initial act as each injustice provokes a greater one, and Daniel supports Divine Right on the grounds of political expediency if nothing else. The Civile Wars was not a popular poem in an age which liked colour and fine language, but Daniel hit the public taste much better in his Complaynt of Rosamond, an important and influential poem which was printed in 1592. In form, it is an orthodox Complaint in the style of the Mirror, the tragedy of the fair Rosamond who became the mistress of the aged Henry II and was finally poisoned by his jealous queen.

Its importance lies in the fact that it exploits history for other than historical purposes. The fact that it deals with historical characters is only incidental, for it is primarily a love story told in appropriately conceited language, and in crossing the historical "Complaint" with the traditional lament of the forsaken woman, Daniel created what was virtually a new "Kind" of poetry. The Complaynt is dramatically effective; Rosamond is a living and pathetic figure with her guilty conscience and her joyless relationship with an old man. History is made an effective teacher of private as well as public morality.

The most voluminous writer of historical poetry was Michael Drayton, whose favourite period was the reign of Edward II, and who never tired of revising and rewriting his poems through edition after edition until the final version of most of them appeared in 1619. His first batch of historical poetry, written between 1593 and 1596, shows the same deliberate exploitation of history as we have seen in Rosamond. His poems Peirs Gaveston, Matilda, The Tragical Legend of Robert, Duke of Normandy and the longer Mortimeriados, The Lamentable civil wars of Edward the second and the Barrons, all reveal by their very extensive rhetoric, their amorous laments, their emphasis on character and dramatic situation, their experiments in form, that Drayton had found in history a new and popular subject capable of serving almost any literary purpose. The plundering of history was most successful in Drayton deservedly popular collection, Englands Heroicall Epistles, which first came out in 1597 and passed through countless editions before 1619.

The work, which is modelled on Ovid Heroides, consists of pairs of love-letters supposedly written between famous lovers of English history. Drayton begins the series with letters between Rosamond and Henry II, and King John and Matilda, from whence he moves on to the Wars of the Roses, with Queen Isabel and Richard II and with Edward IV and Jane Shore, for example. He finishes up in the Tudors with Surrey and his Geraldine and the ill-fated couple, Lady Jane Grey and her husband, Guildford Dudley. The combination of a new poetical form, a strong love interest and a glimpse into the private lives of great ones proved as irresistible to the public then as it would now, but the poems are worth reading for their own sakes.

The letters really answer each other, and the pairs of lovers are selected with skill and treated with variety. Thus Rosamond is clearly an honest and well-meaning woman and King Henry achieves real pathos when he complains that the whole nation expects his favours but that he alone is denied the right to ask for favours in return. In contrast, King John, pursuing the chaste Matilda, is drawn as a cynical lecher who under-estimates the passionate virtue of his mistress and, when she retreats into a nunnery to escape him, woos her with sonnet conceits which are little short of blasphemy in the circumstances: Holy Matilda, Thou the Saint of mine,

*Ile be thy servant, and my Bed thy Shrine.*
*When I doe offer, be thy Brest the Altar,*
*And when I pray, thy Mouth shall be my Psalter....*

His flippant suggestion that even the Phoenix is chaste only because she is alone, and had our Mother Nature made them Two, They would have done as Doves and Sparrowes doe; shows a real misconception on his part of Matilda's character. In contrast again, Jane Shore is a pretty picture of hypocrisy, the seemingly virtuous wife who is in reality only too anxious to be seduced by her king, while Geraldine is a young and modest virgin, Lady Jane Grey a pathetic child writing under the shadow of the scaffold.

The characterization is vivid, and the poems have the precision of Browning's dramatic monologues Drayton's strong historical imagination enables him to create characters who are genuinely involved in the minor events of history which surround them, and whose reactions, in consequence, have a verisimilitude which rivals that of the drama. The verse has a springy regularity very different from that of contemporary satire, and often anticipates the movement of the later Augustan couplet:

*But if that Love, Prince Edward doth require,*
*Equall his Vertues, and my chaste desire;*
*If it be such as we may justly vaunt,*
*A Prince may sue for, and a Lady graunt...*
*That Faith I send, which I from you receive:*
*The rest unto your Princely Thoughts I leave.*
*(Alice Countesse of Salisburie.)*

By 1605, however, a curious change has come over Drayton's attitude to history. His revised version of the Mortimeriados, which he brought out in 1603 under the title of the Baron's Warres, is a reversion to the manner of Daniel Civile Wars, with much of the dramatic material omitted and a closer adherence to the chronicle materials. The same is true of his Legends of Robert of Normandy, Matilda and Gaveston which are revised versions of his earlier poems and have a new one, that of the Great Cromwell, added to them. Drayton is at pains to describe the four as "Legends", which he defines as a "species of an Epick or Heroic Poeme" in the manner of the individual books of the *Faerie Queene*. The best of them is the legend of Cromwell which contains a new critical attitude to the reign of Henry VIII, and one which was impossible while Elizabeth was still on the throne. Drayton was perhaps the first man to laugh at the great king for having six wives. All four of the poems, however, show a more serious attitude to history, a more sober use of rhetoric and a closer approximation to the original ideals of the Mirror.

The reason for the change lay in the ending of a great era and the dawn of a new, less certain one with the accession of James. Drayton is not the only writer to sense the loss of unity and to deplore the decline of the old heroic patriotism in the new century. He is never tired of criticizing the new Iron Age, which has replaced the old one of gold, and he can see in the new dispensation only a growing passion for money, a loss of social responsibility on the part of citizen and landlord alike, and an increasing effeminacy at court. Poetry itself is becoming harsh gibberish, making a "viler noyse, than carts upon the stones" (Polyolbion, XXI. 174), or debased by the popular press. Drayton satire, The Moone-Calfe, written about 1607, is one of the most bitter attacks of the period, and although much of the acid may be attributed to personal disappointment, the poem clearly reflects a widespread disenchantment and a general feeling of disintegration.

For this reason, the old historical parables took on new vitality, and in his latest historical verse, the Miseries of Queene Margarite and the Battaile of Agincourt printed in 1627, Drayton turned back to point the old morals once again. The two are companion pieces, the one a picture of the miseries of civil war, and the other, of the glories of patriotic unity. Written as they were with the next bout of civil war almost in sight, they form a grim and prophetic warning to the times. The Battaile of Agincourt is a deeply felt account of a great national triumph. Drayton knows as well as anyone that war is cruel, and that the motives behind Henry Vth's attack on France were largely unworthy ones. He shows the Church fostering the campaign to divert the King's attention from reform, and the

Commons rising to the bait hysterically. He makes no secret of the fact that many of the English ports only sent ships in the hope of gaining further trade out of the expedition, and that the soldiers quarrelled over the amount of the ransoms on the very field of battle. And yet, in the blazons of all the troops and the ships which assemble from all parts of England, and in the unfolding of the great plan of battle which finally routs the French, there is the purest heroism, as patriotism transcends all personal motives in the heat of the fight. The poem is full of vivid and unforgettable scenes such as the description of the French horses galloping away with their rears stuck full of English arrows:

*Upon the Horses as in Chase they flye,*
*Arrowes so thick, in such aboundance light,*
*That their broad buttocks men like Butts might see,*
*Whereat for pastime Bow-men shooting be. (1493.)*

It is in the light of this that we must read Drayton great *Polyolbion,* that "Topo-chrono-graphicall Poeme", as Wither christened it in his prefatory verses to the second part. Begun early in the century, the first part was published in 1612 with explanatory notes by the antiquary John Selden, to be followed by the second part in 1622. The poem, which drew its materials largely from Camden *Britannia,* consists of a trip round Britain and Wales in company with the Muse. Rivers play an especially prominent part in Drayton's topography; every stream is a nymph or a swain, and every confluence a marriage in the manner of Spenser's wedding of the Thames and Medway, though without the symbolic significance which he attached to it. The lovely Bry in Somerset, for example, sets his affection on "beauteous Avalon" and cannot be seduced from it:

*Though many a plump-thighed moore and ful-flanck't marsh do prove*
*To force his chaste desires, so dainty of his love.*

The woods are full of satyrs, and every fountain is a nymph metamorphosed. The poem is a rich example of Elizabethan myth-making which is only excelled by Spenser; in it the *Metamorphoses* has become acclimatized to England;

the maps which accompany the Songs are dotted with naiads, while Neptune and his herds sport themselves in the British seas. There are some fine topographical descriptions in the poem, especially of country which Drayton himself knew well. The Peak with its frowning cliffs and gloomy caverns is described with something of the Gothic fervour of the Romantics, and Drayton does full justice to the bird-song of the Forest of Arden, or the rich flocks of the Cotswolds, or Lincolnshire with its fishermen on stilts and its "foule woosie" marshes. There are famous anthology descriptions of hawking or coursing the hare, or hunting the stag; yet the poem as a whole is far less descriptive than historical. Drayton has something of Kipling's feeling for England; it has been fought over and conquered by many races and every one of them has left something precious and enduring behind. The frontispiece to the poem shows Britannia in the centre with her horn of plenty, while at the four corners are the figures of Brute, Julius Caesar. Horsa and Henry VIIth. It is with the deeds of the kings and their subjects that the poem is really concerned. There are lists of great soldiers and seamen, catalogues of English battles and English saints, blazons of all the counties, tales of Robin Hood or Guy of Warwick and the rolls of all the British and Saxon kings

As in the *Battaile of Agincourt*, the intention is plain. In an age which exports all its own produce in exchange for foreign goods, and chops down its own forests to feed the forges and the "smokie citties", Drayton is reminding his countrymen of their glorious heritage, and of the greatness which has been and might be again. *Polyolbion* is the true epic of the Elizabethan age, and Drayton speaks with the voice of Shakespeare's dying John of Gaunt. It is the voice of a man out of sympathy with the new modern world of the 15IIth century and looking back nostalgically to the age of "globe-engirdling Drake".

Drayton was the last of the Elizabethan historical poets; already, by the time of *Polyolbion*, the taste had changed, and Donne was complaining of the mendacity of "Hollensheads or Halls or Stowes". Drayton himself, in his Preface to Part II of the poem, denounced those "outlandish, unnaturall English" who can find "nothing in this Island worthy studying for". One reason for the neglect, had he but known it, was the influence of such men as Selden who wrote the historical notes for him. For Selden, with his passionate curiosity into the origins of things, quietly yet systematically undermines the authority of the myths which he is elucidating. He is a man of the new science, sceptical of the Arthurian fable and suggesting that the bones of the old giants are perhaps only the bones of animals after all. He allows poetry a liberty to play with myths which he will not allow to history, and in doing so, he relegates it to the level of a polite entertainment, the relaxation of an idle hour but unworthy the serious attention of a man of science. Ben Jonson praised him truly when he wrote

*What fables have you vext! what truth redeem'd!*
*Antiquities search'd! Opinions dis-esteem'd.*
*(Epistle to Selden.)*

A further reason for the decay of historical verse was the intensification of religious feeling. The man of the 15IIt century was more concerned to save his soul than to preserve national unity. As Spenser *Faerie Queene* with its all-embracing analysis of personal and social morality was naturally couched in terms of the Arthurian legends, so was it equally inevitable that Milton should abandon an Arthurian epic for one based on the Bible.

# Chapter 14

# Spenser's Faerie Queene

The poetry of the late 15Ith century was divided against itself with more than usual ferocity. Plato and Lucretius, Petrarch and Ovid challenged each other within the same poetic kinds and, in the case of *Hero and Leander* which was begun by Marlowe and finished by Chapman, within the same poem. In a wider conflict, Petrarch and Ovid alike were ranged against the Puritan, and even Sidney renounced the love of Astrophel in his later sonnets; "Leave me, O Love, that leadeth but to dust" was, by 1590, no longer the academic protestation which it had been in the earlier miscellanies. There was scarcely a popular ballad or madrigal in the period which had not its moralized counterpart or a pastoral idyll which was not balanced by a piece of satiric realism from Marston or Hall. Some of this contradiction may be attributed to the conception of the Kinds which, as it divided poetry into mutually exclusive categories, encouraged poets to be eclectic. Breton, for example, and Drayton, in his early days, tried their hand at every mode—love, morality, idyll and satire—without apparently caring whether this procedure involved any inconsistency or not.

They were all different poetic exercises to be attempted, and the question of beliefs did not enter into the matter. Nevertheless, the diversity of modes corresponded increasingly to a diversity of opinions, and Daniel, in his *Musophilus*, saw his age as one of confused greatness in which the different excellencies cancelled each other out:

*All that which might have many ages grac'd,*
*Is borne in one, to make one cloid with all;*

*That goodnes seems, goodnes to have defac't,*
*And virtue hath to virtue given the fall.*

In this situation, the *Faerie Queene* was the one great force of integration in poetry, touching Elizabethan life at the greatest number of points, and bringing into an ordered harmony the opposing strains of love and religion, body and soul, real life and romantic ideal. For Spenser, the active life was the theatre in which this integration had to be achieved, and the Red Cross Knight, though he saw the Holy City afar off from the hill of Contemplation, had yet to go back into the world and finish his quest. For this reason, Milton rated Spenser as a better teacher than Scotus or Aquinas, for bringing his Knight through the Cave of Mammon and the Bower of Bliss.

The first three books of the *Faerie Queene*, together with the explanatory letter to Raleigh, were first published in 1590 and republished in a slightly amended form, together with the second three books, in 1596. That the work was begun much earlier is proved, however, by references to it in letters which passed between Spenser and Harvey as far back as 1580, when Spenser was still in London under the patronage of Leicester. It was not until 1589, when Raleigh, a great Irish landlord as well as the Queen's favourite, visited Spenser at Kilcolman, that the poem was brought to the point of printing. Spenser accompanied Raleigh to England, arranged for the publication, and, after several trips backwards and forwards between London and Ireland, returned home finally in 1591, richer by a pension of £50, but disappointed in his experiences of the Court as we can see from the account he gave in *Colin Clouts come home again*.

The remaining three books may have already been under way, since they contain references to Spenser's early days in Ireland when he was Lord Grey's secretary. In any case, they were completed by 1595, as we can see from the reference to them in Sonnet LXXX of the *Amoretti*. After this period, conditions in Ireland grew rapidly worse, and Tyrone's rebellion drove Spenser out of his lands to England, in 1598, where he died early in the following year. The two cantos of

Book VII on Constancy, commonly known as the *Mutability Cantos*, together with two verses of a further one, were published in 1609, when the complete *Faerie Queene* was brought out in folio.

The precise order of composition is not known in a work which was so long a-growing, but it has been argued that it began with Books III and IV as a romance in the manner of Ariosto, that the theme of Gloriana with her Order of Maidenhead came next, and that Arthur and the twelve moral virtues were added last of all. All that we know for certain is that the final scheme had been worked out by 1590 when it was outlined in the letter to Raleigh, and we may take the letter, therefore, as a convenient starting point. The author's letter, "Expounding his whole intention", begins by describing the poem as "a continued Allegory or darke conceit", the aim of which is "to fashion a gentleman or noble person in vertuous and gentle discipline".

This is a typically Renaissance intention and links the poem with such works as *The Courtier* and *The Governour*. Spenser goes on to say that he chose Arthur as his hero, following the example of Homer, Vergil, Ariosto and Tasso who took great national figures as their heroes; and that he proposes to embody in him the "twelve private morall vertues, as Aristotle hath devised", though these private virtues will also be personified by the twelve knights who are to be the heroes of the twelve separate books. The centre of the whole scheme is Gloriana, the "Faerie Queene", by whom he means Glory in general, and Queen Elizabeth in particular.

On the one hand, Arthur, having seen her in a vision, is seeking her in deed, human virtue seeking glory and perfection; on the other, as all virtue flows from perfection, the twelve virtuous knights take their quests from her court. Since, however, the book explaining the origin of the quests is not yet written, Spenser tells his reader of the twelveday feast at the Court of the Faerie Queene, and how the quests originated, which leads him to explain why he began his story in the middle of the adventure instead of at the beginning. The historian must describe affairs "orderly as they were donne", he says, but a poet "thrusteth into the middest" to gain a more striking literary effect. The echoes of Sidney *Defence of Poesie* are obvious throughout the letter, and Spenser may have talked the matter over with him when he was still in London.

The letter to Raleigh was a very topical document, dealing with contemporary problems of literary theory. The heroic poem was one of the great preoccupations of the Renaissance, the acknowledged crown of poetic achievement and the patriotic ambition of every serious poet. As we have seen, it was closely linked to history, and, as already attempted in Italy and France, it paid a compliment to the ancestors of the poet's monarch or patron, as Ariosto had paid tribute to the d'Este family in his *Orlando*. The main lines of the heroic poem were already there for Spenser to follow, although there was still much discussion about the details. One school preferred the Vergilian form with its single hero and single great action; but Ariosto's picaresque romance with its multiplicity of heroes and ever-changing scenes was challenging the classical type, and Spenser seems to have tried to combine the two. The twelve separate heroes, and the rapid change from one thread of the story to another which is so marked a feature of Books III and IV, clearly derive from Ariosto, and Spenser, like the Italian poet, is clearly amused by the game of narrative hide and seek which the method encourages:

*Now turne againe my teme, thou jolly swayne,*
*Backe to the furrow which I lately left,*
*I lately left a furrow one or twayne,*
*Unploughed, the which my coulter hath not cleft....*
*(F. Q., VI, IX. I.)*

The introduction of Arthur into each book, on the other hand, is an attempt to unify the whole poem around a single figure, in the manner of the ancients. The initial plunge into the middle of the action is modelled, too, on the classical epic; but in spite of these devices, Spenser's poem resembles the *Orlando* far more than the *Aeneid*. In its attempt at a compromise, it is a typical poem of the English Renaissance, and its composition at that period was as inevitable as that of the sonnet or the pastoral. The allegorical form of the *Faerie Queene,* though not surprising in a poem of the Renaissance, was derived from older sources. Spenser had behind him a great tradition of allegorical verse which included the *Romance of the Rose, Piers Plowman,* many of Lydgate poems, the Morality play and, in the 15Ith century itself, Hawe *Pastime of Pleasure* or the more recent allegorical trifles of Breton.

The Middle Ages and the Renaissance alike habitually thought in terms of allegory, and moralized Ovid, Vergil and Ariosto, or searched the classical myths for their moral and scientific meanings, as Boccaccio had done in his *Genealogia* and Bacon was to do in *The Wisdom of the Ancients.* The great tradition of scriptural allegory, which went back to the early Christian fathers, was by no means dead in Spenser's day. The fourfold interpretation of the Bible, which was the standard form of mediaeval exegesis, was based on the assumption that the Scriptures concealed within their literal story moral, allegorical and anagogical truths; and although the simultaneous existence of so many levels of meaning had been denied by the reformed Church, yet the Protestants allowed the Bible to contain allegorical meanings, provided that it was not literally true at the same time.

There were many who, like Bale, regarded the Bible stories as extended metaphors by means of which esoteric truths were expressed; and the preachers of Spenser's day habitually drew on the scriptures for their own metaphors and parables. More than ever before, myth was becoming established as a form of conscious literary allegory. The Neo-Platonists, with their heightened consciousness of the divine Ideas in the material creation, inevitably turned to symbolism, and the movement gave a real, if temporary stimulus to the allegorical approach. As a result of their mediaeval and Renaissance heritage, the Elizabethans had a peculiar aptitude for finding sermons in stones and books in the running brooks, which shows itself in emblem, metaphor or literary interpretation alike. When the Queen visited Elvetham, she was met by a number of virgins who were busily removing blocks from the road in front of her, which blocks, we are told, had been placed there by the person of Envy. It is against a background of this kind that we must read the *Faerie Queene*.

15Ith-century allegory was, however, a very fluid thing, and one must be careful of trying to interpret it too rigidly. The *Faerie Queene* is an almost continuous allegory, but the reader must approach it with what Dr. Tillyard has happily called "a kind of sustained tact", and be capable of adjusting himself continually to the ever-changing assumptions of the poem. The characters continually change their allegorical meanings, or carry two or three meanings simultaneously, as the scriptures had been made to do. Artegall, for example, can be interpreted in a literal, a moral and an allegorical sense at once—as the ancestor of the Tudors, as the knight of Justice and as Lord Grey liberating Irena. Duessa, through whom the Red Cross Knight falls into temptation, is deceit and Roman Catholicism and the Scarlet woman all in one, and, at her trial by Mercilla in Book V, she was sufficiently like Mary, Queen of Scots, to evoke an angry protest from King James. Arthur represents a different virtue in each book, while the Queen performs a number of different roles and exists in a variety of embodiments.

She is, of course, Gloriana; but she is also Belphoebe in respect of her virginity, and Mercilla in respect of her mercy. It is always unsafe to try to limit the interpretation of the *Faerie Queene* to any one level. Book I is both a moral and a historical allegory, symbolizing, on the one hand, the pursuit of holiness by the true faith and the good life in conjunction, and on the other, the defeat of Roman Catholicism by the Protestant Church. The two meanings are simultaneous, but the relative emphasis changes from episode to episode. Consider, for example, the account of Una's visit to the cottage of Corceco, blind devotion, in the third canto of the first book. The general allegory is that of faith, separated from the good life, falling into superstition; but the lion who defends Una by despoiling Corceca's daughter, Abbessa, and killing Kirkrapine, her lover, introduces a stronger element of historical allegory. The Abbessa episode is clearly the destruction of the monasteries by Henry VIII, the Defender of the Faith; but Kirkrapine, who robs "The Holy Saints of their rich vestments", would seem to be the Puritan attack on ritual and vestment, so that the lion who kills him is now the Church of Elizabeth. Two simultaneous and contradictory political allegories exist, therefore, in the same episode; a little later, the lion is killed by San Loy and, losing his specific historical meanings, becomes in more general terms law and order destroyed by lawlessness. Such patches of local allegory occur frequently within the larger pattern, but except inthe fifth book, where the historical allusions are generally more precise, it is difficult to be sure of the exact historical reference.

The choice of an Arthurian setting for the poem was an obvious one, in view of the seriousness with which the ancestry of the Tudors was taken. The marriage of Arthur to Gloriana with which the poem must have culminated, had Spenser completed his design, symbolized a very real belief in the return of Arthur to his kingdom. The introduction of the land of Faerie, however, forms an interesting and original variation on the wellknown theme. Fays with magic shallops and knights with magic swords are a commonplace of the Arthurian legends, but Spenser wove his fairy lore systematically into the texture of his allegory. Gloriana, at the centre of the poem, exists in dual form; she is the Faerie Queene symbolizing Glory, and she is the Elizabeth of history. The roles of the mortal and elfin races are carefully distinguished. When Arthur and Guyon are in the House of Alma, they read their respective genealogies, Arthur, a chronicle of Briton kings; Guyon, the rolls of Elfin emperors. The Chronicle gives the familiar list, from Brutus to Uther Pendragon; Guyon's roll, on the other hand, begins with Prometheus who created man, and works down through seven hundred generations of Elfin heroes, all of them mighty conquerors, magicians or giantkillers, to Elficleos, Oberon and Tanaquil, who are clearly Henry VII, Henry VIII and Elizabeth.

The two lines both unite in Elizabeth, but are kept distinct throughout the poem; and the distinction seems to be that the Britons are historical, the Fairies, purely allegorical. Arthur and Britomart are mortals who come to Fairyland seeking glory, but Guyon, Calidore, Satyrane, Amoret, Belphoebe and the rest are fairies, being purely allegorical figures who embody virtues which help in the quest for glory. Their ancestors are the mythical heroes of civilization like Prometheus, Hercules, Bacchus and Osiris, who gave divine gifts to mankind, and their glorious consummation is Gloriana. There is, however, a further class, the changelings, of whom Artegall and St. George are the examples. Both are mortals who were carried off to Fairyland in their infancy and have been brought up as fairies.

The explanation of this is possibly that both, though historical figures, were yet of such eminence that they have passed into legend and have joined the ranks of the Elfin heroes. Arthur himself was too firmly rooted in history to be treated as anything but a human being, but St. George's story fits him for the category, although it is difficult to see why Artegall should be a changeling whereas Britomart, whose position is precisely similar, should not. Presumably Spenser considered justice a more heroic virtue than chastity, even though Britomart does unhorse Artegall. In the temple of Isis we are told that justice descended from Osiris and that Artegall is his prototype (V, VII. XXII).

It has often been pointed out that Spenser's main type of allegory resembles that of the *Romance of the Rose* rather than that of the *Pilgrims Progress*. Bunyan's allegory is of people; he shows a Christian faced by certain temptations and overcoming or being overcome by them. Spenser, in contrast, draws qualities, holiness, temperance or chastity, and his allegory is intellectual rather than dramatic. Christian, falling into the sin of despair, is knocked down by a giant who beats him with his club and locks him in his dungeon, and one is given a vivid sense of the hopelessness which despair entails. But when Red Cross is overcome by despair in Book I, canto IX of the *Faerie Queene*, the qualities of the sin itself and not the feelings produced by it are described. The power of despair is expressed through the arguments which he uses and which are the quintessential arguments on which despair is founded. He offers death as the only escape from the miseries and sins of life which go on increasing the longer we live, and when

Red Cross replies that it is sinful to shorten our lives, he counters that all must die, and who is to say that suicide is not our appointed fate; if we are to die anyway, better to do it willingly than under duress. The intellectual persuasiveness of his arguments is very strong in the context and, as in Tennyson's *Two Voices*, could tempt a reader to fall, where as Bunyan's Despair could only act as a deterrent. In a similar fashion, Bunyan's description of death expresses the sense of darkness and heart-fear which assails Christian when he faces it, whereas Spenser's picture in the Mutability Cantos is an intellectual analysis of death in his true quality

*Death with most grim and griesly visage seene,*
*Yet is he nought but parting of the breath;*
*Ne ought to see, but like a shade to weene,*
*Unbodied, unsoul'd, unheard, unseene.... (VII, VII. XLVI.)*

For this reason, temptations in the Faerie Queene are not drawn as tempting but appear in their true, repulsive nature. The House of Pride into which Red Cross enters in Book I, canto IV, is shown in all its hollowness and not as it would appear to a proud man: it is made of bricks without mortar, and its walls, though high, are thin and coated with golden foil in front but all in ruins behind. Its foundations are of sand, and the clock on top points the period of its glory.

Similarly the Cave of Mammon into which Guyon is drawn contains none of the tempting glamour of riches; and the temptations of the five senses, the "monstrous rablement" who besiege the Castle of Alma, would not attract any sensualist. Such allegory, although intellectual, is not impersonal, for it has behind it the whole force of Spenser's moral passion which, according to Shaw, is the strongest passion of all. When Duessa is stripped by Arthur, she. is not simply a deceitful woman being exposed; she is the quality of deceit itself which, as it is uncompromisingly evil, is pictured in extremely repulsive terms:

*Her crafty head was altogether bald,*
*And, as in hate of honourable eld,*
*Was overgrowne with scurfe and filthy scald;*
*Her teeth out of her rotten gummes were feld,*

*And her sowre breath abhominably smeld.... (I, VIII. XLVII.)*
*Spenser's exposure of evil has a passionately*
*ruthless quality which is essentially emotional.*

An abstract virtue cannot weaken or be tempted, and when Spenser wishes to portray temptation, therefore, he is forced to personify the temptation itself. Guyon, for example, worn out by the strain of too much austerity, relaxes by a fountain, and in this state is seized by Pyrocles and Cymocles who strip him of his armour (II, VIII. 15). He has already parted from the Palmer, Reason, when he went aboard the boat of idle mirth and, in fact, ceases to be temperate. But the quality of temperance itself cannot be intemperate, and Spenser, therefore, sends Guyon into a deep trance, while his place is taken by Pyrocles and Cymocles, two extremes of intemperance on whom reason can make no impression. The role of Temperance is now taken over by Arthur who conquers the two; but it is noteworthy that Spenser makes the knights of Intemperance stronger for the qualities which Temperance possessed and which they, in replacing him, have inherited, just as Satan was all the more capable of evil for having been an angel. When the two unruly passions have been quelled, Guyon wakes out of his trance and is himself again.

Allegory of this kind demands a sustained intellectual effort and an unflagging sense of moral values, both of which are present in the Faerie Queene to an unrivalled degree. The ceaseless analysis and precise definition of virtue and vice which Spenser's type of allegory inevitably fosters give the poem an affinity, at one level, with such treatises of moral philosophy as the Nicomachean Ethics; and Spenser undoubtedly conceived of his poem as such a treatise presented in the most attractive and persuasive colours possible. The general treatment of the separate virtues is, indeed, Aristotelian, consisting of the analysis of excesses and deficiencies in relation to a virtuous mean; but the virtues themselves spring from a mixture of classical and Christian sources. It is typical of Spenser's desire for integration that he should begin with the main Christian virtue and pass on immediately to the main classical one, temperance. The ethical nature of the Faerie Queene can best be illustrated by Spenser's treatment of the group of passions, which were a main preoccupation of his age, namely, those related to sex. In the first place, they are treated in relation to each of the main virtues of the poem. Love and lust are shown to be respectively the chief source and the chief enemy not merely of chastity but of holiness, courtesy and the rest. The fourth book dealing with concord, for example, is composed of a pattern of happy marriages and bitter quarrels, and as everyone unites in the quest for the true Florimell, so they all fight over the false one. Within this framework, the individual varieties of passion are precisely drawn and evaluated with reference to four central figures who act as the norm of morality. These are Belphoebe, the personification of virginity; Amoret, of physical love; Britomart, of chastity, and Florimell, of female modesty which is perpetually in flight and which draws all men irresistibly after it. Since Spenser is so firm a believer in marriage, chastity is the most important virtue of his sexual code, and Britomart is drawn in loving detail. She is the embodiment of sane, natural desire, neither inhibited nor overdone. She looks into the magic mirror to see who will be her husband out of normal curiosity,

*Not that she lusted after any one,*
*For she was pure from blame of sinfull blott;*
*Yet wist her life at last must lincke in that same knot,*
*(III, II. XXIII.)*

*but she is in no way lacking in natural desires, as her pursuit of Artegall shows.*

Around these figures are grouped a number of excesses and perversions. Lust is the general enemy of all four, and therefore appears in many forms, whether as the lustful forester who pursues Florimell in the first canto of Book III, or as the loathsome personification with his great empurpled nose and nether lip "like a wide deepe poke" who runs off with the halfwilling Amoret in Book IV, canto VII. He is blind in his passion and cannot distinguish between the old woman and the young Aemylia in the darkness of his cave, and he can only be killed by the completely virgin Belphoebe. The different types of lust are carefully analysed by Spenser and embodied in a variety of characters. There is first the chaste lust which can exist in marriage itself and which Amoret exemplifies when she is carried off by Busyrane.

There is the more heinous kind of unchaste lust, which is expressed in the pruriency of Acrasia and her Bower of Bliss in the second book; beyond this are the incestuous and bestial passions of the monstrous brother and sister, Argante and Ollyphant (III, VII. XLVIII).

Chastity is drawn in its deficiency and its excess. The adultery of Paridell and Hellenore, with its echoes of Paris and Helen (III. X) exemplifies the former, as do the casual love affairs of Blandamour. The excess of chastity is pictured in Malbecco, who begins as a jealous husband and ends by being metamorphosed into jealousy itself. His desire to take Hellenore back, even after she has become the common mistress of the satyrs, is not intended to show a more than human charity on his part, but to indicate a fidelity which is itself a form of excess, since its object is an ignoble one (III. X). In the same way, the varieties of virginity are analysed, and Briana (VI. I), Columbell (III. VII) or Mirabella, the stock mistress of the sonnet (VI. VII), are different embodiments of the right thing for the wrong reason. Sonnet material forms an amusing background to much of Spenser's allegory and gives him, so to speak, an additional language with which to make his points.

The false Florimell, for example, that unwholesome imitation of the true who feigns modesty to draw men's eyes to her, is manufactured by the witch out of all the materials to which the sonneteers compared their mistresses; snow, virgin wax, burning lamps, golden wires (III, VIII. VI). The complexity of Spenser's allegory of love is greater than that of mediaeval allegory, and however different was the aim and technique of the Faerie Queene it resembles Elizabethan drama in its delineation of different human attitudes. The new psychological interests of the period are apparent beneath its allegory.

Next to love, justice, embodied in the adventures of

Artegall, receives the fullest analysis. It is shown to be opposed to the communism of the giant with the scales, and to the suffragettism of Radigund, the latter an especially serious issue at a time when three ruling monarchs were queens. That Spenser considers justice to be more important than mercy is implied by the condemnation of Duessa and the punishment which Artegall suffers for his gentleness towards Radigund. That justice is dependent on the law which, by its pitiless rigidity, often seems to deny the principles it is defending, is apparent from the history of Talus, the unsleeping iron man.

He alone can break down the walls of Munera's castle against which the strong lance of justice is by itself impotent, and though merciless and often opposed to equity, he is yet necessary in a world of fallen men. For this reason, we are told, Astraea left him behind on earth when she was driven back to heaven by human wickedness. As with justice, so with the other virtues; each sets out in company with the quality on which it is most dependent, and is faced with the temptations, which enable it to define itself most fully.

I have dealt at some length with the method of Spenser's allegory, because the moral aspect of the poem was that to which Spenser's contemporaries attached the greatest importance, and it is one, which we are still prone to neglect. The Faerie Queene is not, of course, exclusively allegorical, although it is almost always didactic, and Books III and IV, in particular, teach by example as much as by the sort of allegory, which has been described.

Each book, however, builds up to one or two great allegorical pieces, the one a pageant of virtue, the other of vice. Such are the Palace of Pride and the House of Holiness in the first book, the House of Alma and the Bower of Bliss in the second, the Castle of Busyrane and the Garden of Adonis in the next, the Temples of Venus and Isis in the fourth and fifth respectively.

It is noteworthy that these set pieces are almost all traditional in character; temples, castles and gardens are the commonplaces of both religious and love poetry throughout the Middle Ages, and their appearance as the high spots of

Spenser's allegory illustrates yet again his power of absorbing traditional material and putting it to new uses. It is significant, too, that perhaps the finest of all the set pieces, the vision of the Graces dancing in a ring in the sixth book, is an essentially classical scene. Spenser's great and catholic genius integrates and reconciles everything.

Spenser's religion is an attempt to reconcile the conflicting philosophies of his age. On the one hand, he wishes to accept the neo-Platonic idealism, which recognizes the immanence of God in the material world and sees the eternal everywhere within the temporal. On the other hand, as a Protestant with Calvinist sympathies, he is very conscious of the fallen nature of man and the transience of earthly things. Astraea has fled to heaven, the Blatant Beast will break his chains and Duessa will return even though Una has married St. George. The Mutability Cantos give a melancholy picture of a universe subject to change and decay, as the great pageant of birth and death unrolls itself.

Spenser vacillates between the two conceptions and never wholly succeeds in reconciling them. The idealized picture of the human body in the House of Alma, for example, is not entirely compatible with Venus' lament in the Garden of Adonis for her perfect flowers which have been sullied by the "sinfull mire" of the world, and beaten down by time's "flaggy winges".

The Faerie Queene is primarily an ethical poem and, on this level, shows no acute conflict between Christianity and Platonism, since both are united in an endeavour to lift mankind above his merely carnal nature. The metaphysical problem, however, presents more difficulties, and Spenser attempts to solve it by arguing that Mutability is not as black as she has been painted, and that sin, though real, is by no means inevitable. In the Garden of Adonis, he tells us, the perfect forms of all things to be created exist in unfading beauty, until the earthly Venus sends them forth to unite with first matter in the act of creation.

*Chaos, which supplyes*
*The substaunces of natures fruitfull progenyes.* (III, VI. XX151.)

*The temporal world thus owes its existence and continuity to the perpetual imposition of form on first matter:*

*All things from thence doe their first being fetch,*
*And borrow matter whereof they are made;*
*Which, whereas forme and feature it does ketch*
*Becomes a body.... (III, VI. XX15IL.)*

Under the pressure of time, the individual combinations of form and matter break up and revert to their separate elements. First matter, being indestructible, sinks back into the "wide wombe of the world" from whence it rose, until its turn comes again to take on new form; the forms, for their part, fade and return to the Garden of Adonis where, being replanted, they grow afresh and are used over again in the course of nature.

So, like a wheele, arownd they ronne from old to new. (III, VI. XXXIII.)

In this way, the endless process of creation and decay goes on, as form stoops to matter and matter takes on form after form, driven by the mutual love which God has placed. within them. The union of Venus, the creative power of nature, with Adonis, "the Father of all formes" (XLVIII), is Spenser's symbol for the mechanics of creation.

Mutability itself thus becomes the agent of a fuller creation, and the medium by which First Matter achieves a richer association with form. Form is eterne in mutability And by succession made perpetual and it is on these grounds that Nature refutes the boast of omnipotence which Mutability makes in the Mutability Cantos:

*I well consider all that ye have said,*
*And find that all things stedfastnesse do hate*
*And changed be yet, being rightly wayd*
*They are not changed from their first estate;*
*But by their change their being do dilate,*
*And turning to themselves at length againe*
*Do worke their own perfection so by fate. (VII, vii. LVIII.)*

But more than this, mutability is the only means by which degenerate man can gain a glimpse of his maker. With the Fall, man lost his power to look on the naked glory of God, but he can still understand something of it when the divine form is reduced to the level of human comprehension under the veil of mutable matter:

*But we, fraile wights, whose sight cannot sustaine*
*The Suns bright beames when he on us doth shyne,*
*But that their points rebutted back againe*
*Are duld, how can we see with feeble eyne*
*The glory of that Majiestie Divine....*
*The meanes, therefore, which unto us is lent*
*Him to behold, is on his workes to looke....*
(*Hymne of Heavenly Beautie.*)

This, of course, is supremely true of the central mystery of Christianity, and Spenser sees in the Incarnation the true harmony of Christianity and Neo-Platonism. God revealed himself to man most fully through an imperfect and corruptible body, and the temporal nature of the world became the very means by which humanity can raise itself to the eternal and undo the damage of the Fall.

For this reason, Spenser believes that the world is intrinsically good, and the symbol he chooses in Book VI for supreme perfection is that of naked maidens dancing without shame. He takes unbounded satisfaction in the human body and all its workings; the House of Alma is a wonderful piece of mechanism, whether it be the two gates "placed seemly well", or the porch "fayrely wroght", the cook Concoction, "full of comely guyse", or even the admirable arrangements of the "Port Esquiline":

*Which goodly order and great workmans skill*
*Whenas those knights beheld, with rare delight*
And gazing wonder they their mindes did fill.... (II, IX. XXXIII.)

But the House of Alma is the body used with temperance, and the world and the flesh are only good as they are wisely used. Virtue, to Spenser, is that which struggles to attain the divine form within the material cover; vice, that which stays content with the fleshly exterior. To help us in our pursuit of virtue we have Reason and Grace. Vice inevitably results when the eye of reason is "with rage yblent", as when Red Cross abandoned Una in the second canto of his book, or when Guyon stepped into Phaedria's little shallop, leaving the Palmer Reason behind (II, VI. XIX.). Grace is even more important and can rescue man from evils which reason is impotent to resist.

It is symbolized by the shield of Arthur which dazzles Orgoglio, or the miraculous well of life into which Red Cross falls during his fight with the dragon, or the guardian angel who comes to the rescue of Guyon when he leaves the Cave of Mammon. With the help of these two, the Christian may keep the divine ideas in sight and by so doing, reproduce, as far as our earthly nature will allow, the divine virtues at the level of the world. Earthly virtue is the shadow of heavenly; justice follows the pattern set by Astraea, concord is the image of divine harmony, and the graces of courtesy are taught by the example of the eternal Graces whose dancing Calidore saw for a brief while

*Therefore they alwaies smoothly seeme to smile,*
*That we likewise should mylde and gentle be:*
*And also naked are, that without guile*
*Or false dissemblaunce all them*
*plaine may see... (VI, X. X14.)*

As Christ is the incarnation of God, so the Christian virtues of faith, hope and love embody the qualities of the Trinity at the human level and show the way to salvation. The vices are the opposite of this, blinding the eye of reason and obscuring the divine image. Intemperance, hypocrisy, discord and injustice never see further than the material advantage and lack the essential idealism.

Once again, Spenser's treatment of love best illustrates his conception of virtue and vice. Divine love, as we have seen, exists in two aspects, namely, the contemplative and the procreative. God first contemplated his own perfections, we are told, and then reproduced them in his creation. Human love, therefore, must exist in these two modes, the earthly forms of which are contemplative virginity and procreative womanhood, symbolized in the Faerie Queene by the two divinely created sisters, Belphoebe and Amoret. Belphoebe was brought up by the virgin Diana, and Amoret was reared by Venus in the fruitful Garden of Adonis; both are necessary. The idealism of Belphoebe is implicit in her nature, but it is equally essential, though not always present, in physical love. Carnal desire is only justified when its aim is not solely pleasure but the propagation of God's image and the fulfillment of his commandment to be fruitful and multiply (III, VI. XX14.). Human passion, therefore, must be informed with *this idealism:*

*But man that breathes a more immortall mynd,*
*Not for lusts sake, but for eternitie,*
*Seekes to enlarge his lasting progenie:*
*For, having yet in his deducted spright*
*Some sparks remaining of that heavenly fyre,*
*He is enlumind with that goodly light,*
*Unto like goodly semblant to aspyre....*
*(Hymne in honour of Love.)*

The perfect form of physical love is naturally marriage, since it is a holy sacrament and the convenient medium of procreation. In its natural harmony it is the symbol of divine concord, and it is significant that Spenser makes Scudamour's seizure of Amoret in the Temple of Venus one of the central allegories of Book IV. Britomart, Amoret and Pastorella are all embodiments of this virtuous and idealistic love, but even marriage is no guarantee that it will remain idealistic, and in the seizure of Amoret by lust, Spenser utters a stern and traditional warning against a sin which can exist within the confines of chaste matrimony. Provided, however, that the fundamental idealism is retained, sexual pleasure is good and holy; in the Garden of Adonis where "Frankly each Paramor his leman knowes", it is the child of Cupid and Psyche, Pleasure, that doth both gods and men aggrate.... (III, VI. L.)

The greatest enemy of virtuous love, therefore, is lust, the pursuit of pleasure for its own sake, and Spenser finds its chief embodiment in the code of Courtly Love which, as it aims at purely carnal satisfaction, is a denial of nature. Britomart has two brushes with Courtly Love. The first is in The Castle Joyeux, which is owned by the Lady of Delight and manned by the specifically courtly temptations, Gardante, Parlante, Jocante and the rest (III, I. XLV). To underline his disapproval of it all, Spenser describes Britomart by the very significant image of a "vermeil rose"—not, however, a rose which is doomed to be plucked, as in the mediaeval allegory, but one whose thorns repell the lustful intruder (XLVI).

The second much fuller episode is Britomart's rescue of Amoret who has fallen into the grip of lust on her wedding day, and is now tormented by the carnal desires of which Busyrane is the embodiment. Spenser identifies Amoret's sufferings with those, which afflict the lovers in the courtly tradition. The House of Busyrane where she is imprisoned contains all the properties of the mediaeval temples of love, the altar to Cupid, the tapestries showing his victories and, in the masque which passes in the night, all the personified fears and griefs which accompanied the god in his mediaeval and Petrarchan triumphs.

The torment of Cupid's service is shown in the sufferings of Amoret whose heart Busyrane has torn from her breast. Chastity restores it to its proper place, not, however, by killing the enchanter, but by making him forswear his irreligious practices. The cure for lust is not asceticism but holy love.

The Busyrane episode is concerned mainly with the carnal aspect of Courtly love, but Spenser deals at equal length with another manifestation of it and of lust in general, namely, sterility. This finds its fullest expression in Acrasia's Bower of Bliss which is, of course, the Elizabethan "Waste Land". Sterility, as a denial of fruitfulness, is always branded as unnatural in the full Elizabethan sense of the word, something which denies the laws by which the universe exists. We see our first glimpse of the Bower in Book II, canto V, when Cymocles lies "all carelessly displaid" on a bed of lilies, while wanton damsels sport around him; and as they expose themselves to his gaze, he cherishes and savours his desire, preferring to gloat over the lustful images in his mind rather than make love in the natural way:

*His wandring thought in deepe desire does steepe,*
*And his frayle eye with spoyle of beauty feedes:*

*Sometimes he falsely faines himselfe to sleepe,*
*Whiles through their lids his wanton eies do peepe... (II, V. XX14.)*
*It is an epicurean refinement of lust which even*
*original sin can hardly explain.*

When Guyon visits the Bower in canto XII, he experiences the same deliberate carnal provocation from the nymphs who hide their lower limbs in the water only to make them more tempting, and who offer wine to stimulate desire. The treatment of the theme in this canto is, however, allegorical, and is based on the contrast which Spenser draws throughout between art and nature. As C. S. Lewis has shown so well in his *Allegory of Love,* nothing in the Bower of Bliss is natural; the flowers are painted, the ivy around the fountain is artificial, the grapes which hang in the porch are either of gold, "So made by art to beautify the rest", or else are compared by Spenser not to living things but to the finest precious stones:

*Some as the Rubine laughing sweetely red,*
*Some like faire Emeraudes, not yet well ripened.(II, xii. LIV.)*

It is a fitting place for Acrasia's sterile passion, the fruit of artificial stimulation rather than natural desire; and Spenser contrasts it very deliberately with the Isle of Venus where Scudamour finds Amoret in the tenth canto of Book Four. The island is equally luxurious, but everything is natural:

*Delightfull bowres, to solace lovers trew;*
*False Labyrinthes, fond runners eyes to daze;*
*All which by nature made did nature selfe amaze (IV, X. X14.)*
*Here, as in the garden of Adonis, love is naked and frank;*
*it does not need to be arayd or rather disarayd,*
*All in a vele of silke and silver thin,*

That hid no whit her alabaster skin....as it is in the case of Acrasia. The one love is natural, fruitful, idealistic; the other sterile and entirely carnal.

Spenser's symbolic use of art and nature is very apt in the circumstances. By nature was understood the creative power of God which imposed form on first matter; and true art, by embodying the artist's perception of form, was in itself a parallel act of creation which transcended the world of matter. Art without nature, however, was that which Plato banished from his Republic, an imitation of an imitation; a painted bunch of grapes twice removed from the truth. As such, it is an accurate symbol of that love which remains at the carnal level and never penetrates to the divine purpose.

The Faerie Queene, therefore, justifies human love by a blend of Platonic idealism and Christian marriage, which reconciles original sin with Platonism, and Courtly Love with religion. Spenser's conception of Courtesy in Book VI retains the valour, constancy and care for the lady's reputation which belonged to the mediaeval conception of that virtue; but they are now all harnessed to the cause of honest marriage in place of the adultery and bold bawdry which Ascham had complained of.

Living by this code, man may regain his lost place a little lower than the angels, and the great gap in nature created by the Fall may be filled, the hierarchy of existence from highest to lowest be restored in its completeness.

The full allegory of the Faerie Queene is thus four-fold, like that of the scriptures. Above the literal and the moral is the allegoric meaning which teaches the hero the way to earthly glory; but beyond that is the anagogic, which shows how the virtuous soul may attain heavenly knowledge and perfection:

*Beginning then below, with th' easie view*
*Of this base world, subject to fleshly eye;*
*From thence to mount aloft, by order dew,*
*To contemplation of th'immortal sky....*
(*Hymne of Heavenly Beautie.*)

The poem has a cyclic quality which reminds one of the beautiful "Circle of Love" so commonly described by the Platonists. As Arthur seeks Gloriana, so the virtues go forth from her, and the circle will be completed when all meet at the Court of Faerie. For Spenser, Queen Elizabeth was not only the fountain of earthly glory, but the symbol of divine, the Empress of Cleopolis. It is Contemplation who says of her,

*For she is hevenly borne, and heaven may justly vaunt:*

Something has been lost since the Middle Ages, something which both Chaucer and Skelton possessed, an acceptance of the earthy body in all its coarseness and all its humour. Forms of idealism change, but the body remains the same, and Spenser has suffered from the vicissitudes of fashion. The Faerie Queene, moreover, is conceived in terms of aristocracy; its aim is to fashion a *gentleman* or *noble person*, and Spenser believes that the man of noble blood has a natural advantage in the practice of Courtesy, though he implies nothing of the kind in respect of the other virtues. It must be remembered, however, that Spenser was trying to show the "Idea" of a gentleman, and felt, quite rightly, that such an all-round pattern of perfection was more likely to be found in the court than the cottage.

Jane Austen would have agreed about the Graces, although, like Spenser, she would have found low birth and poverty no bar to the achievement of the remaining and possibly more important virtues. We should be careful not to confuse Spenser's medium with his ideas; he may be describing knights, but he deals in men. Justice is perhaps an aristocratic virtue since, in one aspect, it concerns the administration of the law; but holiness, temperance, chastity and friendship are the monopoly of no class, and even courtesy is found at home amongst the humble shepherds.

The style of the Faerie Queene has been condemned for diffuseness and compared unfavourably with the pithy colloquial diction of Donne. Such a criticism is based on a misapprehension concerning the nature of poetry which the Elizabethans themselves would never have been guilty of. The Faerie Queene and the Songs and Sonets are different Kinds of poetry, as different from each other as Astrophel and Stella and Paradise Lost; and what is appropriate to a love poem would destroy the effect of an heroic allegory. Spenser, like Yeats, uses simple language to express very complex symbols which are only comprehensible at all because they are described in vivid, pictorial terms. Complex ideas need clear and simple language for their expression; and Elizabethan love poetry can only afford to use so many verbal fireworks because it is dealing with relatively simple ideas. It is significant that when Donne treats of ideas, he produces something very like the Spenserian symbol:

*On a huge hill,*
*Cragged, and steep, Truth stands, and hee that will*
Reach her, about must, and about must goe.... (Satyre III.)

Much of the ingenuity of the sonnet and metaphysical conceit can, indeed, be found in Spenser's allegories that are only extended metaphors of an especially pictorial kind. Red Cross' Christian armour, for example, which is already dinted at the beginning of his quest, and which becomes so hot as to be unwearable when breathed on by the dragon of sin, shows the same logical development of an initial comparison as we find in rhetorical allegory. The comparison of greediness to a great whirlpool

*That deepe engorgeth all this worldes pray;*
*Which having swallowd up excessively,*
*He soone in vomit up againe doth lay,*
*And belcheth forth his superfluity.... (II, XII. III.)*

is as unexpected and as accurate as Donne's image of the compasses.

Having accepted the fundamental Decorums of the Kind of poem he is writing, Spenser exploits them to the full. The imagery is everywhere most carefully matched to its object and springs logically out of the context in which it occurs. Images of Chaos and storm are common in the fourth book, for example, because Chaos is the ultimate cause of human discord, and storm is its parallel manifestation in the macrocosm:

*As when Dan Aeolus, in great displeasure...*
*Sends forth the winds out of his hidden threasure.*
*And all the world confound with wide uprore*
*As if instead thereof they Chaos would restore. (IV, IX. XXIII.)*

The same combination is very common in King Lear. Throughout the poem, the imagery performs the double function of describing incidents and simultaneously defining their moral implications. Radigund, burning with wanton love for Artegall, is described in a contemptuous bovine image which indicates the animalism of her feelings:

*Which long concealing in her covert brest*
*She chaw'd the cud of lover's carefull plight. (V, V. X15II.)*

The single image used to describe Acrasia as she bends over her lover, "greedily depasturing delight", is as forceful in its implications as Polonius' loosing of Ophelia to Hamlet. Often the poetry is enriched by the deliberate use of literary echoes, as when Despair adds weight to his assault on Red Cross by couching his arguments in terms of an image which had, for centuries, been the traditional expression of temptation:

*But all in vaine: no fort can be so strong,*
*Ne fleshly brest can armed be so sownd,*
*But will at last be wonne with battrie long,... (I, IX. XI.)*

Occasionally there are images of startling boldness, as in the challenging description of Serena lying naked upon the altar:

*Her paps, which like white silken pillowes were*
*For love in soft delight thereon to rest....*
*Her goodly thighes, whose glorie did appeare*
*Like a triumphal Arch, and thereupon*
The spoiles of Princes hang'd which were in battel won.
(VI, VII. XLII.)

Spenser is here vindicating the goodness of the human body and its functions in face of the unwholesome lust of the savages, and Donne could go no further in implication.

In spite of its enormous length, the Faerie Queene shows a ceaseless attention to detail and an unfailing observance of rhetorical decorum. The fight between St. George and the Dragon is a highly-wrought piece in the grand style, very vivid, and culminating in an impressive series of Anaphoras to mark the fall:

*So downe he fell, and forth his life did breath...*
*So downe he fell, that th'earth him underneath*
*Did grone.... (I, XI. LIV.)*

But if the formal rhetoric is pushed a little too far, or made a trifle too elabourate for the occasion, a sense of artificiality is produced. The artificiality of the Bower of Bliss is underlined by the conceited style in which it is described:

*No tree whose braunches did not bravely spring;*
*No braunch whereon a fine bird did not sitt;*

*No bird but did her shrill notes sweetely sing;*
*No song but did containe a lovely ditt*
*Trees, braunches, birds, and songs were framed fitt*
*For to allure fraile mind to careless ease.... (II, VI. XIII.)*

The overlaboured lines match the overloaded trees to produce an effect of cloying richness. By a similar device, the use of excessive alliteration, Braggadocio is held up to ridicule:

*But minds of mortall men are muchell mard*
And mov'd amisse with massy mucks unmeet regard. (III, X. XXXI.)

The Elizabethan poet was not expected to write as well as he could all the time, but to match his style to his occasion; and a stupid person or a low occasion demanded a corresponding style.

In this sense, all Elizabethan poetry is fundamentally dramatic, and the facility of the later drama was greatly assisted by the conventions of non-dramatic poetry. Often the language of the poem drops into simple realism; the knights are always "letting fly" or "letting drive" at each other, or "falling to" their food, and the moral is often pointed in the most homely proverb.

The ordinary level of the verse is economical, swift and vigorous, and there is no better narrative poet in the language than Spenser. Normally it has an unobtrusive narrative efficiency, which should be judged as one would judge the less spectacular passages of Malory, for example; but at the least necessity, the poetry rises to the occasion, and we have the lingering cadences of the Syren's song:

*O! turne thy rudder hitherward awhile*
*Here may thy storme-bett vessell safely ryde,*
*This is the Port of rest from troublous toyle,*
*The worldes sweet In from paine and wearisome turmoyle.*
*(II, XII. XXXII.)*

*and, at the other extreme, the vigorous description of Guyon's boat as the Palmer rows it over the ivory sea:*

*So forth they rowed; and that Ferryman*
*With his stiffe oares did brush the sea so strong,*
*That the hoare waters from his frigot ran,*

*And the light bubles daunced all along,*
*Whiles the salt brine out of the billowes*
*sprong.... (II, XII. X.)*

Spenser has a particular gift for writing light and tripping verse which makes effective use of reiterated "t"s; Phaedria's "little skippet floting", or Amoret's flight from lust,

*Full fast she flies, and farre afore him goes,*
*Ne feeles the thornes and thickets pricke her tender toes.*

*have an amusing delicacy of touch.*

Perhaps the most astonishing quality of the Faerie Queene is its allusiveness. There is no other poem in the language, which incorporates so much material from so many different sources, and yet subdues all to the harmony of a single great design. In this, it is a product and a symbol of its age, when so many different civilizations met, and when the Court itself, for a brief moment, held in suspension the opposing elements, which were to fly apart in the next century.

The ancient world, the Middle Ages, the Renaissance; the classics, the Bible, The Romance of the Rose or the poetry of Chaucer and Ariosto; the British Isles and the New World; ancient myth and modern history—all meet and are harmonized within the Faerie Queene. Classical myths are everywhere, but handled with a boldness, which quite transforms them from their original nature.

The tale of Antaeus, for instance, unexpectedly provides Spenser with the material for his allegory of sickness attacking the human body, which is contained in the battle of Arthur and Maleger (II, XI). The mediaeval courtly tradition appears, as we have seen, in the Grail setting of the House of Busyrane with its surrounding wall of fire, or in the numerous gardens of the Rose. Christian symbol is introduced on countless occasions—in the pageant of the seven deadly sins within the Palace of Pride; in Speranza, clad in blue and bearing of a silver anchor on her arm; in the symbolic triplicity St. George's three-day battle with the dragon, or the three-inone of Priamond and his two brothers in Book IV. Traditional folk elements are there in the girdle of Florimell which only chaste women can wear, or in the variety of shapes to which Guile changes himself when grasped by the Law (V, IX. 15II). The episode calls to mind such ballads as Tam Lin, and occasional lines show that Spenser made use of the ballad tradition too:

*He tooke her up forby the lilly hand. (V, XI. 15II.)*

Contemporary history adds its quota of allusions and topical references, especially in Book V, which ranges abroad into the Low Countries, or gives a picture of the monopolists and usurers at home. Even the New World makes its contribution in the account of Marinell's rich strand, covered with "pearles and pretious stones of great assay", which echoes many a traveller's tale (II, IV. 15III). The very knights and jousts which form the basis of the poem were common both to the popular romances and to the exquisite but academic chivalry which the Tudors revived in their courtly tourneys and passages of arms.

The fusion of all these materials gives an unrivalled richness to the texture of the poem which we may illustrate, in conclusion, from a short but famous sequence, Guyon's journey to the Bower of Bliss in the last canto of the second book. The voyage is, of course, based on that of Odysseus, and the separate adventures are made to carry the moral allegory with astonishing felicity. Guyon and the Palmer first pass between the Gulf of Greediness and the Rock of Vile Reproach, the latter so sinister and haunting, with its yelling Meawes, with Seagulles hoars and bace, And Cormoyraunts, with birds of ravenous race,

*Which still sat waiting on that wastfull clift*
*For spoile of wretches, whose unhappy cace,*
*After lost credit and consumed thrift.... (II, XII. VIII.)*

When it is remembered that Cormoyraunt was a name commonly applied by the Elizabethans to usurers and profiteers, it can be seen how complex the allegory has already become, and how many are its levels. Next they pass the quicksands of Unthriftyhood where they see the wreck of a richly loaded ship; and the introduction of so universal a symbol reminds us that Guyon himself is making his own hazardous voyage over the sea of life. From here they come to the terrible and very topical sea-monsters, "Spring-headed

Hydres; and Sea-shouldring whales", creatures about which any Elizabethan seaman would have a tale to tell.

These are symbolic of the perils which beset man on his voyage, and all of them are put to flight when the Palmer strikes the sea with his "vertuous staffe", as Christ had done on another occasion (X15I). At this juncture they are tempted in their five senses by the five Syrens, but, leaving these behind, pass into the dark fog of fears, and hear the roaring of the wild beasts, symbolic of their own unruly animal passions. At last they reach land, as Odysseus came to Circe's island, and they too are offered the drink which turns men into monsters. The fusion of allegory and romance is so complete and the verse moves in so many dimensions that the complexity of the Metaphysicals is thin in comparison.

Behind it all, and giving fire to the abstractions of which the poem is composed, is a purely personal emotion. When we reach the very centre of the poem, we find not a philosophical belief or a moral abstraction, but a living woman. There in the middle of the ring of nymphs are the three Graces, and in the centre of them, as in the centre of a garland, is

*Another Damzell, as a precious gemme*
*Amidst a ring most richly well enchased.... (VI, X. XII.)*

It is Elizabeth Boyle, the poet's betrothed, the object of his marriage song; and the whole pageant of virtue and beauty moves around her. It is an astonishing idealism. In it the adoration of every sonnet mistress and pastoral Phyllis finds its final expression and its cause.

## Donne and the Elizabethans

THERE is a tendency to think of Donne as the great iconoclast who, single-handed, overthrew the tyranny of Petrarch and replaced the outworn conventions of Elizabethan poetry by a new strain of realism. Donne is technically an Elizabethan; he began writing his *Songs and Sonets,* his *Elegies* and his *Satires* as early as 1593, so that his early verse was contemporaneous with the sonnets, lyrics and pastorals which have been discussed elsewhere, and he led the field in satire, which was not produced in quantity until the appearance of the first three books of Hall *Virgidemiarum* in 1597. In this concluding chapter, therefore, I shall attempt to relate Donne to the main stream of Elizabethan poetry, and to define what is new and what traditional in his verse.

Elizabethan poetry was a highly formal art: that is to say, it expressed its meaning through accepted conventions and formal poses. If a poet wrote about love, he did it in the Petrarchan or the anti-Petrarchan modes; if he wished to describe a wooing or to attack the Court, he would do it through the mouths of shepherds and shepherdesses. For this purpose, the Kinds offered him a set of recognized patterns corresponding to any aspect of human experience with which he might wish to deal, just as rhetoric offered him a formal diction with which to express anything he wanted to say. There is the closest affinity in function and purpose between rhetoric and the Kinds.

There were both advantages and disadvantages in writing in this way. On the one hand, poetry gained in intensity from the exclusion of all irrelevant matter; young love is more idyllic and passion more undilutedly passionate in the Elizabethan lyric than in any other form of verse. On the other hand, the complexity of Elizabethan poetry suffered through the separation of modes of feeling which, in real life, usually accompany one another. In the *Canterbury Tales,* for example, high, low, comic and serious matters and styles rub shoulders as freely as the Knight and the Franklin with the Miller and Reeve.

The poetry of 1590, in contrast, is divided both horizontally and vertically into separate strata. Horizontally, the Kinds are distinct from one another, each with its appropriate range of imagery, meter and diction, and its accepted rules according to the best literary models; vertically, there are rigid class-distinctions between the Court poet and the ballad-maker which can be seen in the different treatments afforded to such common legends as that of Jane Shore or Fair Rosamond by Drayton and Deloney, for instance.

The treatment of humour is a case in point; laughter is a universal phenomenon in real life, but one rarely meets with it in the sonnet or the lyric. Instead, we can see it becoming a Kind of its own, to be treated in mock heroic, with deliberately fantastic rhyme and indecorous classical allusion. Ben Jonson handles his *Famous Voyage* in this way, surrounding his very funny account of the two young gentlemen who went on a tour of the London sewers with all the trappings appropriate to the Odyssey. Elizabethan poetry possesses, though it is not necessarily weakened by, the "dissociation of sensibility" which Mr. Eliot, in his famous essay on the Metaphysical poets, deplored in Victorian poetry.

By 1590, there were already signs of a change, though the revolution was very gradual and never completed. *Englands Helicon,* the most typical collection of Elizabethan poems, did not appear until 1600; and all the Elizabethan forms continued to be written far into the 15IIth century. It was apparent by 1600, however, that the Elizabethan conventions were no longer adequate for the needs of the new generation of poets, and that once the old symbols had ceased to be the conductors of emotion, they began to appear artificial.

The conventional themes upon which the poets had once been content to improvise their own variations were becoming hackneyed, and a new sensitivity to plagiarism showed itself. There was a mounting chorus of protestation against verse which "doth but champe that which another chewd", and a demand that the poets should stop being literary and deal with life once more. It is really the perennial "back to nature" movement which always appears when any set of artistic conventions is growing out of date, and it can be seen in Sidney's "Looke in thy heart and write", or Shakespeare's "My Mistress' eyes are nothing like the sun", or Drayton's not entirely truthful declaration that he is no "pickpurse of another's wit". It is most explicit in Hall *Toothlesse satyrs* of 1597, which open with a comprehensive attack on the Kinds. The pastoral (Spenser always excluded), the erotic love poem, the *Mirror* complaint "of some dreerie fates of lucklesse peeres", the sonnets to the poet's "durtie ill fac'd bride", are all held up to lively ridicule. Marston *Scourge of Villanie* followed suit in 1599 by mocking the poets who "invocate some lose-legd dame", or who invoke "good Colin Clout" in their pastorals. The sonnet always came in for the most scathing attack, because it dealt with a part of human experience in which everyone shared; its conventions were therefore most obviously artificial, whereas those of the pastoral, for example, were so removed from real life anyway that they never challenged comparison with reality.

The attack on poetic attitudes was inevitably accompanied by an attack on the poetic styles which went with them. In particular, the indiscriminate use of classical myth came under fire, partly because the myths were hackneyed, and partly because their celestial rapes and seductions were proving offensive to Puritan ears.

Marston attacked them on the same grounds as Ascham had denounced the bold bawdry of the Arthurian tales; and there was a considerable anti-classical movement at the end of the century which had already shown itself in Astrophel and Stella, but which came out more strongly in Donne's avoidance of classical reference or in Daniel's defence of the Middle Ages.

The changes in literary taste arose in part from the fact that the novelty was inevitably wearing off the new poetic forms, but even more from the fact that the times were changing too. The end of a great century and a great reign, the growing political tension over such issues as monopolies, the increasing problems presented by Puritanism and the Counter-Reformation all were reasons to induce a more sober frame of mind and a greater desire to see and present things as they really are.

On a more literary level, the drama was, by its very nature, introducing a greater realism into the artistic treatment of human behaviour. The new taste in poetry was, therefore, for something more literal in method, less rhetorical in language and more contemporary in idiom. "More matter with less art" would make a good motto for the whole period.

As one would expect, the new manifested itself, at first, in terms of the old, and, instead of an attack on the fundamental conception of the Kinds, one sees the creation of new Kinds more congenial to the changed sensibility. One example of this is the verse epistle as written by Donne, Daniel or Jonson, which is often no more than a personal letter couched in simple, manly verse such as Philocosmus, the new man of business and science, considered appropriate for poetry, when he argued the matter with Musophilus. Another new Kind is the long, serious philosophic poem, such as Sir John Davies' poem on human knowledge, *Nosce Teipsum*, where the style is plain and the emphasis is on content. Most important of all is the emergence of the formal satire which began with Lodge and reached its peak in Hall and Marston, before the great bonfire of satires which the Archbishop of Canterbury ordered in 1599 put an end to satire for the time being.

Hall and Marston had a considerable touch of the Puritan in their make-up—Hall, indeed, was at Emmanuel College, the headquarters of the Cambridge Puritanism, which had left its mark on Spenser twenty years earlier. In their efforts to bring poetry into direct contact with life, they give us brilliant pictures of contemporary figures.

The upstart gentleman buying himself a noble pedigree and claiming as his ancestors any old "rainbeat" statues he can find in his local churchyard. The young Inns-of-Court lawyer going home to pontificate over his father's tenants; the rack-renting landlord battening on his abbey lands, without which, "Who now's a monke, had been a Mendicant"; the effeminate courtier; the monopolist, and the rest of the figures who also came under the lash of Ben Jonson's plays or Dekker's pamphlets. Both poets are a little self-conscious as satirists, and are apt to take the sting out of their attacks by directing them against such shadowy generalizations as Labeo or Curio, a device, which Skelton would have scorned.

Nevertheless, we must remember that satire was a dangerous thing at the end of the 15Ith century, and that many a good writer went to jail for it. These new Kinds have in common a more literal type of statement and a plainer style than that of most previous verse. Ben Jonson's terse and masculine style established the main line, which the 15IIth century was to follow, and the new Science was already making itself felt in the avoidance of conceited language and the desire to let facts speak for themselves.

In this development, Donne is the most interesting because the most transitional figure. His basic forms and techniques are all Elizabethan, yet, after his death, Carew could praise him for purging the Muses' garden of its "Pedantique weedes", and banishing from nobler poems the "traine of gods and goddesses" who had been borrowed from the *Metamorphoses*. Donne began writing as an Elizabethan love poet, and his *Songs and Sonets* and his *Elegies* show a familiarity with all the contemporary fashions. On occasion, he wrote in the Petrarchan vein, mainly to express a genuine if unwillingly platonic relationship between himself and such patrons as Mrs. Herbert or the Countess of Bedford whose social superiority put them out of his reach.

However, he was an anti-Petrarchan, mocking the sonnet writer's constancy to their mistresses, and challenging their Platonism in his frank delight in physical love. He is by far the greatest of the Ovidean imitators, and his Elegies place him alongside Marlowe and the University Wits. They are all repretentative of one of the periodical swings from the romantic to the sexual within the great tradition of English love poetry; she Wife of Bath had stood for the same values against the Knight and the Squire in earlier days. It is significant, however, that Donne followed the *Amores* rather than the *Metamorphoses,* and whereas the University Wits had declared their sexual philosophy through such classic myths as that of Hero and Leander, Donne presented the same values in terms of contemporary life.

His kinship with the sonneteers has already been noticed. His play of logic and his use of the extended metaphor, though handled with greater brilliance, are fundamentally the techniques of Sidney and Constable. Donne's method was not to reject the conceit, as Drayton did in his revisions of *Idea,* but to revitalize it by making it express new experience. The *Songs and Sonets* are at once more conceited and more profoundly concerned with love than any but the greatest sonnet cycles. The common images of the sonnet can all be found in Donne's poetry, but put to different uses. The fourteenth *Holy Sonnet*, for example, "Batter my heart, three person'd God", restores the popular image of the besieged fort from the amorous to the religious context:

*I, like an usurpt towne, to another due,*
*Labour to admit you, but, Oh, to no end....*

The fort had traditionally been used in connection with religion, but never with such patent sexual associations as it carries here. Donne enjoys shocking his reader by the conflicting suggestions of his image, and yet this mixture of Kinds is appropriate in the mouth of a lover who has become religious but still finds his greatest temptations in his physical nature. Such imagery is essentially personal and indicates an element in Donne's verse, which is lacking in Elizabethan poetry as a whole.

The prevalence of the word "I" in Donne's poetry has often been noted, and the aggressiveness of "I hate extremes" or "I hate dead names" is something new in poetry. What is happening—and a most important thing it is—is the re-emergence of the personal lyric, the short confessional poem whose aim is not to conform to a Kind but to express frankly the poet's own feelings. It records private experiences by whatever form of imagery can do so with the greatest accuracy, and, for this reason, the personal lyric cuts across the accepted hierarchies of Decorum and leads ultimately to such hybrids as the *Prelude*, a personal epic which represents a combination quite unthinkable under the rules of 15Ith-century Decorum.

Most of the common sonnet conceits are given life in this way. The pun, which Barnes used with such exuberant flippancy, ceases to be a form of verbal juggling and, in Donne's poetry, carries a double load of meaning. The play on straits and streights in the *Hymne to God my God in my sicknesse*, or the sombre puns upon his own name in the *Hymne to God the Father*, are cases in point:

*When thou hast done, thou hast not done,*
*For, I have more.*

Paradox, too, was a favourite device of Sidney, and its

establishment, the sole function of many a sonnet. With Donne it is always a provocative vehicle of meaning, as, for example, in the eighteenth of the, *Holy Sonnets*, "Show me deare Christ, thy spouse so bright and clear". Beginning with the traditional description of the Church as the bride of Christ, Donne develops the metaphor to its logical conclusion and gains an ironical effect from the contrast between the Church and the image by which he describes it.

The Church is certainly "trew, and pleasing" to Christ "When she is embrac'd and open to most men", but the same can hardly be said of a wife to her husband; and the last lines of the poem express a great commonplace in a manner which is at once novel and perhaps slightly mocking. The rather contemptuous list of possible spouses, the flippant comparison of himself to an adventuring knight, and the final highly equivocal image make one wonder whether Donne thinks that there is such a thing as a true and only Church. At a deeper level, paradox is a fundamental constituent of Donne's religion, and occurs repeatedly in his poems. There is the virgin-mother who is "At once receiver and the legacie" in *The Annunciation and Passion*, or the ingenious puns on sun and son, and the corresponding play with west and east, in the poem *Riding Westward* written on Good Friday:

*This day, when my Soules forme bends towards the East.*
*There I should see a Sunne, by rising set,*
*And by that setting endlesse day beget....*

Such conceits spring out of Donne's profound sense of the fundamental Christian paradox that death touches the Resurrection,

*Therefore that he may raise the Lord throws down.*
*(Hymne to God my God, in my sicknesse.)*
*The whole force of the Christian mystery is behind them.*

The personal element in Donne's poetry shades into the dramatic, and it is often impossible in the love poetry to tell when he is recording his own experience and when describing creatures of his imagination, though the religiously poems are more obviously autobiographical. Donne's greatest achievement was to develop the dramatic impulse in non-dramatic poetry, and what Sidney had begun in *Astrophel and Stella* he carried on to perfection. The conflict which he felt in himself between God and the Devil is full of dramatic potentialities, and the *Holy Sonnets* often Faustean dramas in miniature:

*I dare not move my dimme eyes any way,*
*Despaire behind, and death before doth cast*
*Such terrour....*

The Satires are essentially dramatic, gaining their effect, for the most part, by vivid picture and snatches of conversation, and even when Donne deals with abstractions, he clothes them in concrete forms such as the unlovely collection of girls which he uses to personify the varying Churches in the third satire:

*Religion, plaine, simple, sullen, yong,*
*Contemptuous, yet unhansome...*

When he argues a case he sets his argument in a dramatic context which draws the reader's attention from the argument itself to the motives behind it. *The Extasie,* for example, sets out to prove that body and soul are mutually dependent and that soul cannot unite with soul except through the medium of physical love. The case is well argued, and yet it is doubtful whether Donne is really concerned to prove his point, or is just describing a successful seduction. The lovers lie side by side on an ominously "Pregnant banke", and when the lover has proved the philosophical necessity of physical love, there is more than a note of irony in the concluding lines:

*And if some lover, such as wee,*
*Have heard this dialogue of one,*
*Let him still marke us, he shall see*
*Small change, when we are to bodies gone.*

The girl has been befuddled by philosophy and the lover has got his way. The closest parallels to such poetry are to be found in Browning or the early poetry of T. S. Eliot. *Bishop Blougram's Apology* or *Gerontion* are doing the same sort of thing, for Donne's love poems always spring out of a particular dramatic situation. The lovers of the Songs and Sonets are lying in bed watching the morning sun, or being bitten by the same flea, or enjoying their first anniversary together. Donne's women are shadowy creatures, but they are real enough to provoke a genuine passion, and the poems are sufficiently vivid to suggest that they may be autobiographical.

The changed content of Donne's poetry demanded a new poetic diction, and Donne followed Sidney and the Drama in employing a more varied and colloquial diction than that of the Petrarchans. As his subjects are contemporary, so his language is racy and colloquial, full of imagery from the contemporary world in which his characters move. Divines are "Gods conduits"; a suspicious father who detects his daughter's lover by the perfume he wears is compared to "a tyran King, that in his bed Smelt gunpowder" (Elegy IV); a needy dramatist is

*One, (like a wretch, which at Barre judg'd as dead,*
*Yet prompts him which stands next, and cannot reade,*
*And saves his life) gives ideot actors meanes*
*(Starving himselfe) to live by his labour'd sceanes*
*(Satyre II. 11)*

The mathematical, astronomical and medical images which Donne consistently employs, the references to optics and globes, intelligences and spheres, meridians crossing parallels, are all a part of the intellectual life of his day and needed no gloss to make them comprehensible. There is, moreover, much accurate observation in Donne's poetry which appears not only in set pieces such as The Storme and The Calme, but is intrinsic in his imagery.

The comparison of a growing love to the circular ripples which spread out when water is stirred, or of thoughts compressed into verse, to the sea forced into "th'earths inward narrow crooked lanes", or of Lady Marckham's face refined by death, to the "embroder'd workes upon the sand" which the tide leaves behind it, are the work of someone who uses his eyes.

In his zeal for accuracy, Donne draws his comparisons from whatever source gives the most vivid visual impression, irrespective of Decorum and often in deliberate defiance of it. The comparisons in the Second Anniversary of Mistris

Elizabeth Drury's soul, as it flies upwards to heaven through the spheres, to a string which is threaded through beads, or to the pith

*... which, lest our bodies slacke,*
*Strings fast the little bones of necke and backe...*

are extremely vivid, but scarcely decorous by 15Ith-century standards. The spirit of scientific accuracy and the need for the truthful record of one's personal impressions unite to challenge the conventional canons of poetic diction. In doing so, they break down further the rigidity of the Kinds.

Donne, therefore, was an Elizabethan who was undermining Elizabethan poetic conventions, from within; and though he retained too many of the old conceits to set the predominant line of 15IIth-century verse, yet, in essentials, he looked forward rather than back. The dramatic quality of Donne's poetry is one example of this. The scientific curiosity of the Renaissance entailed, to an increasing degree, a study of the human mind, and "Know thyself" might have been the motto of the 15IIth century. Psychology formed the basis of philosophy in Descartes, in Hobbes and in Locke; and the preoccupation with human behaviour is already apparent in Middleton's ruthless analysis of human character in disintegration, or in Webster's curiously dispassionate villains who are not so much evil as interested in what happens when human beings are subjected to pain.

They are the practising psychologists of the 15IIth century, and Donne is essentially of their company. Like Thomas Browne who found "Africa and all her prodigies" in himself, and who loved to study the "Microcosm of my own frame", Donne delights in the play of his own emotions and the sudden vagaries of his own ideas. In the nineteenth of the Holy Sonnets, he analyses the vacillations of his faith: I durst not view heaven yesterday; and today

*In prayers, and flattering speaches I court God:*
*Tomorrow I quake with true feare of his rod....*

and he is at least as interested in his own mental processes as in the shortcomings which they imply. More than any other poet, Donne exploits the sudden change of mind as an occasion for drama or for humour. We can see this in the seventh Holy Sonnet, "At the round earth's imagin'd corners", when, after grandiloquently invoking the great pageant of Judgement Day and summoning all the souls and scattered bodies, he suddenly changes his mind, But let them sleepe, Lord, and mee mourne a space....

We can see it again in the frequent changes of direction which make the Songs and Sonets perpetually surprising, and so different from the shrewd but essentially moral analyses of character which appear in the Faerie Queene, or the miraculous blend of morality and psychology in Shakespeare's tragedies. Shakespeare always analyses the psychology of the Fall, and the moral judgement is inherent in the dissection of the sin. Donne, like the later dramatists, shows a weakening moral sense and an increasing scientific curiosity which anticipates the mood of the Restoration.

The extreme individualism of Donne's poetry is a further sign of his affinity with the main trends of the new century. The man of the 15IIth century was more isolated than his ancestors had ever been. Elizabethan society had been hierarchical, recognizing a rigid system of ranks and precedences, though allowing much freedom of movement to the individual within the hierarchy. Under the pressure of 15IIth-century economic expansion, the traditional conceptions of rank itself were weakening, as money played an increasingly important part in the establishment of social position, and the whole process was accentuated by the equalitarian tendencies of the Puritans who felt that all souls were equal in the sight of God. The individual was therefore less consciously part of a great social system, and less sure of his rights and obligations than he had been a century before.

At the same time, the reformed religion threw more responsibility for his salvation upon his own shoulders, and led to a growing egocentricity in religion, which is at its most extreme in Bunyan. Most important of all, though less immediately obvious in its results, was the new astronomy which, by gradually discrediting the Ptolemaic conception of the universe as a system of concrete spheres revolving round the earth, undermined also the belief in the great system of spiritual hierarchies from God and his angels down to man. Shakespearean morality rested on a belief that man is an essential link in the great chain of Nature. Donne, in contrast, lamented, in a well-known passage of the First Anniversary that thenew Philosophy calls all in doubt;...

*The Sun is lost, and th' earth, and no mans wit*
*Can well direct him where to look for it.... (1. 205.)*

Donne was ahead of his times in realizing what this implied, namely, the destruction of the whole conception of a hierarchical universe:

*'Tis all in peeces, all cohaerence gone;*
*All just supply, and all Relation:*
*Prince, Subject, Father, Sonne are things forgot.... (1. 213.)*

It is like the worst visions of King Lear, and, as Donne sees it, man will cease to be part of a great scheme and live in selfimportant isolation:

*For every man alone thinkes he hath got*
*To be a Phoenix, and that then can bee*
*None of that kinde, of which he is, but hee.... (1. 216.)*

For all these reasons, the early 15IIth century was a period of private philosophies and personal integrations. Donne's religion is an essentially personal one: he cannot take the preachings of any one Church on trust, but only those, which he has found by experience to be valid for himself. Another man may find the truth elsewhere. It is every man's duty, he argues in the third satire, to struggle up the hill, "Cragged and steep", towards the truth, and, having found it, to keep it because it is his own and not because "A Harry or a Martin taught thee this". There is no virtue for us in even a good creed if we follow it blindly, and no creed is the true one for everybody. Religion is becoming a relative and personal thing.

In the same way, Donne values love not on the philosophical grounds that it is the force, which sustains the universe, but on the personal grounds that it affords him a vision of more than earthly loveliness, and an escape from the tyranny of time and decay:

*Love, all alike, no season knowes, nor clyme,*

Nor houres, days, moneths, which are the rags of time.
*(The Sunne Rising.)*

The experience of love is its own justification, and there is a touch of mysticism in Donne's attitude, which is completely lacking in that of Spenser, for example. We can see the difference between the two poets, the old and the new, if we compare Spenser Epithalamion, with any typical love lyric of Donne. We might take Donne own Epithalamion made at Lincolnes Inne with its fine refrain, "Today put on perfection, and a womans name", if it were not spoiled by one appalling but not unexpected lapse of taste; Donne compares the bride awaiting the bridegroom to

*... an appointed lambe, when, tenderly*
*The priest comes on his knees t'embowell her.*

It is fairer to Donne to consider The Sunne Rising or The Good Morrow; and there we see the intensely personal record of an experience which obliterates everything else, transporting the lover, for the moment, to a world of perfection, "Without sharpe North, without declining West". Spenser's approach in contrast, is altogether more social and objective, though in no way less passionate. To Spenser, love is not an escape from the world but its most glorious expression; he is less conscious of the individual experience and more aware of the human elements, which it involves. He draws the bride in all her beauty and modesty; he handles the sexual relationship with supreme tact and delicacy, and he associates his love inevitably with the "fruitfull progeny" which is to be its justification. Spenser, to a far greater extent than Donne, gives an impression of the universal goodness and normality of physical love; it is at home in the world, and yet the whole weight of philosophy and religion is behind it, all nature rejoices with it. Love is right and natural, something fit to be celebrated as a holy occasion, with public ceremony and traditional rites.

Such a grasp of the essential human values and such a triumphant certainty about the fundamental necessities of life are to be found nowhere else in English literature, with the exception of Shakespeare's last plays. The Epithalamion has the force of nature behind it; and Donne's love poetry, with its element of conflict and escape, has no such universality. It is inevitable that we, who live in a period uncertain of its faith and afraid of its fertility, should read Donne more than we read Spenser. Spenser belongs to a simpler, more heroic age, the passing of which Donne himself lamented in his Anniversaries. Donne poem, The Broken Heart, might be a picture of the poet's own sensibility. His heart has been shivered like a lookingglass, and now, instead of giving a single whole reflection, it gives a variety of smaller ones:

*Therefore I thinke my breast hath all*
*Those peeces still, though they be not unite;*
*And now as broken glasses show*
*A hundred lesser faces, so*
*My ragges of heart can like, wish, and adore,*
*But after one such love, can love no more.*

The central truth is still there, but its reflection is disintegrated and no longer whole. Philosophy, for Donne, had ceased to be the great and unifying force which it was for Spenser. It had become something to be broken up and used, in its different facets, to reinforce a variety of unrelated attitudes. In this way, a doctrine concerning the nature of angels is removed from its context and made to define the relationship between man and woman, in Aire and Angels; or the belief in God's omniscience is perverted into an outrageous compliment to his mistress who knew his thoughts "beyond an Angels art" (The Dreame). In the same poem, Donne has already flattered the lady by comparing her to the Platonic Good:

*Thou art so truth, that thoughts of thee suffice,*

To make dreames truths; and fables histories. (The Dreame.)

On the one hand, Spenser's Mutabilitie is brought in to justify a philosophy of promiscuity, in such poems as The Indifferent or Communitie; on the other, the lover's timeless ecstasy is described in terms of the eternal love which emanates from the Godhead:

*If, as in water, stir'd more circles bee*

*Produc'd by one, love such additions take,*
*These like so many spheares, but one heaven make,*
*For, they are all concentrique unto thee. (Love's growth.)*

Donne's experience of love is no longer informed by any integrated set of values, and his poems mirror, instead, the uncoordinated impulses which his later religious poetry attempts to control. The analogy with modern life and literature is obvious. Virginia Woolf used the same image of a broken mirror to describe the XXth century in her novel, Between the Acts. The comparison is illuminating. It symbolizes our own deficiencies, and explains the affinity between Donne and the present day.

# Chapter 15

# Critical Essays

## Racism, Misogyny, and the "Othello" Myth

In this book, Celia Daileader has set herself a large task. Spanning four centuries, her study of what she calls "Othellophilia" or the "Othello Myth" also moves back and forth across the Atlantic. Rather than detail lovingly the historical variations on her theme, Daileader pursues with a clear singleness of purpose the process by which Othello's story not only retains its currency, but also edges out other ideological variations on interracial sexual relations. Racism, Misogyny, and the "Othello" Myth "proceeds from the simple observation that in Anglo-American culture from the Renaissance onward, the most widely read, canonical narratives of inter-racial sex have involved black men and white women". While a "desire to exorcise 'collective psychological demons'" might well be at work in the texts Daileader studies, she posits that Anglo-American culture's obsession with sex between black men and white women (a formula that inverts the sad realities of imperialism and slave culture) has less to do with race per se than with an imaginative appropriation of black men to control women, both black and white: "Othellophilia as a cultural construct is first and foremost about women—white women explicitly, as the 'subjects' of representation; black women implicitly, as the abjected and/or marginalized subjects of the suppressed counter-narrative". While she argues strongly against the absorption of "sex" as a critical category into "race" in a monolithic story of marginalization, Daileader is not just making a plea for taking women seriously in tales of interracial relations. From her perspective, the Othello figure who spies on and murders his unfaithful wife is a raced stand-in for the reader or spectator in masculinist-racist discourse. The Othello myth lets the (male) (racist) reader have it both ways. Thus, Desdemona gets what she deserves because pitch always defiles, so that Othello's blackness must rub off on her. At the same time, by virtue of his race, within the narrative of miscegenation Othello himself can be disposed of as a cultural afterthought or abjected as just another manifestation of dark femininity.

On the surface, Daileader's project might seem unwieldy, at once too grand and a bit tenuous. Some of the texts she studies make little or no direct reference to Othello or its principal characters, and building a broad cultural argument on paradigmatic works is always a tricky business. On the one hand lies the Scylla of synecdochic fallacy (these select texts prove a global thesis); on the other, the Charybdis of the critical hobbyhorse (Othello and Othellophilia are everywhere, especially where one expects them least). I am happy to say that Racism, Misogyny, and the "Othello" Myth steers a clear path between these critical dangers and that Daileader's argument is, in the end, both provocative and persuasive. One reason for the book's success is the author's careful selection of texts. The chapters pair familiar with lesser-known texts, a strategy in keeping with the book's concern with canonicity and the question of why the Othello myth is so entrenched in Anglo-American culture. Within each chapter, the chosen texts speak energetically to one another.

In some cases, the connection is historical; Harriet Jacobs, for instance, offered her story to Harriet Beecher Stowe before she gave it to Lydia Maria Child, establishing a factual connection among three of the authors discussed in chapter 4. Thomas Southerne's stage version of Oroonoko, discussed in chapter 2, is a clear revision of Aphra Behn's novel. More broadly, genre holds together the discussion of three Gothic tales in chapter 3. Daileader's talent for close reading solidifies the case for a persistent constellation of images and attitudes in the works covered by Racism, Misogyny, and the "Othello" Myth. Grounding her argument in earlier work about race in early modern literature that has been produced by Kim Hall, Arthur Little, Joyce Green McDonald, Patricia Parker and Margo Hendricks, and Ania Loomba, among others, Daileader begins her study of interracial relations with a close reading of Titus Andronicus, Othello itself, Thomas Dekker's Lust's Dominion, John Webster's The White Devil, and William Rowley's largely unknown All's Lost by Lust.Chapter 2 continues the story with Aphra Behn's Abdelazar and Oroonoko, followed by Thomas Southerne's stage adaptation of Oroonoko, Susanna Rowson's Slaves in Algiers, and Washington Irving's Salmagundi.

Chapter 3 attends to Othellophilia in the Gothic, treating Frankenstein and Dracula in tandem with Edgar Allan Poe's The Narrative of Arthur Gordon Pym. Chapter 4 moves to the United States, pairing Lydia Maria Child's Hobomok with Harriet Jacobs's Incidents in the Life of a Slave Girl and Harriet Beecher Stowe's Uncle Tom's Cabin with William Wells Brown's novel Clotel. Chapter 5 studies the "handsome devils" of Wuthering Heights, Gone with the Wind, and Alice Randall's parody of Margaret Mitchell's novel, The Wind Done Gone. Chapter 6 brings together William Faulkner's Light in August, Richard Wright's Native Son, and Ralph Ellison's Invisible Man. The book concludes with a glance at some film appropriations of Othello, including Spike Lee's Jungle Fever and Tim Blake's O.

Racism, Misogyny, and the "Othello" Myth makes an important contribution to the study of Shakespearean appropriation and of Othello's afterlives. It also engages vigorously with questions of canonicity by scrutinizing the ideological foundations of aesthetic endurance and attrition, the reasons why some texts seem eternal and others recede into oblivion. To some extent, Daileader's book is also an exercise in literary recovery. But her final, and most abiding, interest is in theory and models of critical practice.

The subterranean dialogue that Racism, Misogyny, and the "Othello" Myth carries on with critical discourses on race and sexuality is a crucial aspect of Daileader's project. In part, she wants to break free from the national and chronological boundaries that seem to have entrenched themselves in the wake of New Historicism. Not that Racism, Misogyny, and the "Othello" Myth disdains the theoretical frameworks that have brought us to the place in which literary study finds itself today. Post-structuralism, psychoanalysis, and most of all, feminist theory are always in play. At the same time, Daileader seeks a new kind of rapprochement between feminist and what she terms "black" theoretical stances. The shorthand "black/feminist" that she uses to describe her work indicates the theoretical position that she wants to achieve. Daileader builds the bridges she desires by careful and respectful reference to work on race being done in other time periods of English and American literature. She also courts a rapprochement between feminism and race studies with a frankly polemical appeal to a theoretical "sisterhood." In this search, Harriet Jacobs's Incidents in the Life of a Slave Girl poses in its clearest form the problem that Daileader wants to solve by revealing how white women (as mistresses in the slave household) are pitted against black women (as slaves) through the institution of marriage: "In its searchingly honest discussions of female interracial rivalry, the book lays bare marriage—at least in the slave-holding class—as a racist-masculinist institution that pits white women against black". The search for "Othello's sister" and the critic's own "sisters" is ongoing throughout the exploration of her chosen theme.

Racism, Misogyny, and the "Othello" Myth could have been a depressing book. After all, as Daileader concludes, "Racism will turn to misogyny on a dime; misogyny often obscures racism". But with a clear sense of how critical practice (and teaching) are by definition explorations of ethics when so much is at stake, Daileader not only faults characters and authors when they slip into the old attitudes of Othellophilia, but she also points out those promising moments when texts slip the yoke and begin to change the story. She is concerned not only to unmask the strategies of racism and misogyny, but also to celebrate small textual triumphs, such as a heroine's "refusal to commit suicide at the ideologically appropriate moment". With its strong voice, polemical stance, and rich content, Racism, Misogyny, and the "Othello" Myth: Interracial Couples from Shakespeare to Spike Lee would be an excellent text for classroom use as well as private pleasure.

### "Give me the glass, and therein will I read": Narcissism and Metadrama in Richard II

Over the last thirty years, Shakespeare criticism has demonstrated a growing awareness of the self-reflexive or metadramatic elements in his works. Lionel Abel's 1963 study, *Metatheatre: A New View of Dramatic Form,* provided perhaps the first significant analysis of the ways in which Shakespeare thematizes theatricality, in the broadest sense of the term, in his tragedies, comedies, and histories. In his discussion of *Hamlet,* he makes the observation—perhaps a bit commonplace and obvious to us thirty years later—that the famous "play within a play" is only the most blatant example of self-conscious technique found throughout the tragedy: once we begin to look closely, we notice that nearly "every important character acts at some moment like a playwright, employing a playwright's consciousness of drama to impose a certain posture or attitude on another". Elsewhere in his book, Abel argues implicitly that Shakespeare, though he often used metadramatic techniques more in the interest of developing character than creating "an event," the way later playwrights do, nevertheless composed plays which "are theatre pieces about life seen as already theatricalized". In making such statements, Abel laid the groundwork for a number of subsequent studies, from Thomas F. Van Laan's *Role-Playing in Shakespeare,* which appeared in 1978, to Judd D. Hubert's more recent *Metatheatre: The Example of Shakespeare.*

Critics following Abel's lead have been especially interested in Shakespeare's second tetralogy. James L. Calderwood, for instance, reads the Henriad as Shakespeare's reflection not only on a period of British history during which political authority, political "truth," gave way to corruption and falseness, but also on the potentially disturbing artificiality of his own work. Calderwood identifies the "fall of speech" as the main metadramatic theme in the Henriad, and outlines a progression in which words and their meanings are severed by political corruption and then gradually reunited. Bolingbroke, by usurping Richard's throne, in effect replaces a unified sacramental language, one in which "words have an inalienable right to their meanings," with "a utilitarian one in which the relation between words and things is arbitrary, unsure, ephemeral". Henry's son, Hal, eventually achieves "an earned kingship," thus restoring language for his people. Equally important, perhaps, is the process Shakespeare himself goes through, for in making "political affairs...metaphors for art," he ultimately establishes the legitimacy of his own dramatic medium.

Calderwood's reading of the *Henriad* as an allegory of Shakespeare's own development as a self-conscious artificer is intriguing, but of more interest to me here is his point that these plays dramatize a world in which signifiers and their signifieds are separated from one another. At the centre of this world stands Richard II, perhaps the most flamboyantly theatrical, the most self-consciously lyrical, of all of Shakespeare's characters prior to Hamlet. Richard personifies the disjunction between signs and meanings about which Calderwood writes; he is a man who, in losing his kingly name (signifier), subsequently loses the most basic vestiges of his identity (signified). Yet though he recognizes the disjunction, the "fall of language," he continually tries to use discourse—and not just any discourse, but discourse at its most creative, its most metaphorical—to maintain an identity, a sense of self.

Maintaining that sense is of paramount importance to Richard, whom more than one critic has called narcissistic because of self-absorption, his fanciful interiority. Marvin Glasser, for instance, has commented that "much of what Richard says sounds like a soliloquy because of his failure to relate to otherness," to the exterior world. His "vision, while consciously self-dramatic, conflates within and without, self and other"It is Richard's narcissism with which I am primarily concerned in this essay, for it, especially when considered in light of some of Jacques Lacan's theories, helps to illuminate the effect of Shakespeare's metadrama in this play. Like the narcissistic Lacanian subject, Richard paradoxically needs others, even as he shuns them in favour of his own interior reality; he depends upon others to provide him a "mirror" in which to see his own complete image perpetually. In theatrical terms, he must have an "audience" at all times for his "role" to mean anything. And like Lacan's subject, he is forever deluded; he is spoken by a discourse which he mistakenly believes he controls; he is just another signifier in a chain of signifiers for which there are no corresponding signifieds. Though Richard apparently recognizes his situation in the end, he nonetheless attempts to use language to deny his own lack of identity.

Starting in Act 1, Shakespeare sets Richard up as an actor who loves to put on a show. Yet the king's penchant for theatricality may be overlooked in the first scene, in which Richard hears the accusations of Bolingbroke and Mowbray against one another, because the ceremonial nature of that scene makes actors of *all* the characters. As Leonard F. Dean astutely observes, although Shakespeare deviates from his sources in much of *Richard II,* he evidently makes a "practical decision" to follow Edward Hall's account of the Bolingbroke-Mowbray incident, and to open this play and the entire Henriad with it. Beginning with this scene, in which "the real feelings of Richard, Bolingbroke, Mowbray, and even Gaunt are necessarily masked to a large extent by the calculated neutrality of the ceremony," allows Shakespeare to introduce immediately the "theatricalism of politics" and the extended analogy of "state" and "stage". Thus metadrama is used to meditate on the general nature of political affairs. But in 1.3, when Richard dramatically interrupts Bolingbroke and Mowbray's joust by "throw[ing] his warder down" and proclaiming, "Let them lay by their helmets and their spears", Shakepeare begins to focus on Richard's own individual theatricality.

As most critics have noticed, the soon-to-be-deposed ruler's narcissism, which results in his flair for drama, becomes more pronounced with his return from Ireland. Upon learning that he no longer has any forces with which to fight, Richard gives several extended speeches which, as Glasser remarks, sound more like soliloquies than dialogues with those around him. He seems to want to "wallow" in his misery:

*No matter where, of comfort no man speak;*
*Let's talk of graves, of worms and epitaphs,*
*Make dust our paper and with rainy eyes*
*Write sorrow on the bosom of the earth.*

The writing metaphor is significant here, because it suggests Richard's reluctance to give up his verbal powers as king even as he recognizes that they are diminishing. Even more important is the way in which Richard uses others to stage what is essentially a private performance directed at himself and by himself. "Let's talk," he says, and then ruminates until Carlisle protests, "My lord, wise men ne'er sit and wail their woes, / But presently prevent the ways to wail" (3.2.178-79). It is as if Richard uses his subjects as looking glasses in which he can see himself perform.

This, essentially, is the role Richard's subject play throughout. Although the king complains that "He does me double wrong / That wounds me with the flatteries of his tongue" (3.2.215-16), Shakespeare makes it clear that he has survived previously on such flattery. Even earlier in the crucial second scene of Act 3, Richard needs Carlisle to tell him "That power that made you King / Hath power to keep you King in spite of all", and the leader follows with a monologue whose self-assurance inspires in us both anger and pity toward him:

*Not all the water in the rough rude sea*
*Can wash the balm off from an anointed king.*
*The breath of worldly men cannot depose*
*The deputy elected by the Lord.*
*For every man shrewd steel against our golden crown,*
*God for His Richard hath in heavenly pay*
*A glorious angel. Then, if angels fight,*
*Weak men must fall, for Heaven still guards the right.*

Richard's performance here is only as good as his audience's reaction, however, and though there are no lines from Carlisle, Aumerle, or any of the soldiers present, in production, some directors have these characters express their agreement through physical gestures. What we come to realize about Richard is that his royal power, and even his imagination, ultimately stem from sources external to him.

The external nature of Richard's character, of his psychology, mark him as an excellent example of Lacan's conception of the narcissist. For in Lacanian thought, the notion that any person has a distinctive psychic substance, a complete, internally-determined meaning, is pure illusion. We are defined by other people and their discourses; our unconscious resides not within us, but outside of us. This is partly what Lacan means when he makes the famous statement, "the unconscious is the discourse of the Other"The narcissist is decidedly ambivalent toward others, but he nevertheless needs others for any conception of himself. This process of rejection and identification begins in the so-called "mirror stage," when a child first recognizes itself in the reflection of a mirror or, perhaps more often, in the image of another person. Throughout our lives, we feel bound to and alienated from ourselves and others. The relationship which the mirror stage sets up is one of signification, as Terry Eagleton lucidly explains:

We can think of a small child contemplating itself before the mirror as a kind of 'signifier'—something capable of bestowing meaning—and of the image it sees in the mirror as a kind of 'signified.' The image the child sees is somehow the 'meaning' of itself.

Though this process is modified as we grow older and are introduced into language, it basically defines how we deal with reality, according to Lacan; he notes in the opening chapter of *Ecrits* that this "mirror stage" introduces "the dialectic that will henceforth link the I to socially elabourated situations". And for the narcissist, the search for "meaning" is undertaken with an even greater sense of desperation than what the "average" person exhibits.

Richard II is, of course, precisely a narcissist in this mold. He puts on very theatrical performances, in which language is an integral prop, to give himself a definite position in reality, to perceive himself (through others) as a Gestalt. Why would a king, we might wonder, need to do so? If anyone is secure about his identity, it ought to be a ruler. Yet Richard's world is an increasingly ambiguous one, as Shakespeare (and astute critics such as Calderwood) goes to great pains to show: with the passing of medieval absolutism and the divine right of kings, appearances and realities, signifiers and their signifieds, do not harmonize. Despite Richard's several speeches confirming his faith in the old, unified order, he seems to know, at some level, the harsh reality of his world. This might explain why he "take[s] his correction" from Bolingbroke so "mildly," as the queen puts it.

Even if Richard has some understanding of his situation, his conscious recognition of it still comes only gradually. He begins to see that he is simply an empty signifier, dependent on other empty signifiers for any sense of identity at all, as early as the scene in Wales. Yet perhaps it is in 4.1, the deposition scene, that Richard becomes most fully aware of his plight. There, he performs with all of his earlier fervor but receives an entirely different response, and he acknowledges the changed situation when he says, "God save the King! Will no man say amen? / Am I both priest and clerk? Well then, amen". The struggle which Shakespeare presents in this scene is an intense one, as Richard summons all of his lyrical and dramatic powers to stave off loss of identity. He tries to turn his deposition, his very loss of self, into theatre, and thus, into a role. "Now mark me how I will undo myself," he says to Bolingbroke and his former subjects. But there is more than theatre in the question he asks after he has ceremonially "undone" his kingship: "What more remains?" The audience recognizes, with Shakespeare, and with Richard himself to some degree, that all along this king has been, to use Thomas F. Van Laan's words, a series of gestures; either those belonging to his social office or, as now, those arising from his own dramatization of losing that office. And he has also been a series of responses by others, who—*like mirrors*—have let him see reflected by them the success of his performance.

This realization is heightened when Richard asks Bolingbroke for a mirror. When it is brought to him, he says, "Give me the glass, and therein will I read", then proceeds to break it into "a hundred shivers". Paradoxically, the act of shattering the mirror makes clear the "truth" about Richard's subjectivity: that he has never been an autonomous individual, a self-determining *Gestalt*. His sense of self has been dependent on others; his little dramas have only been meaningful insofar as others have witnessed them. Within a Lacanian paradigm, Bolingbroke's typically terse response to Richard's histrionics here—he plays upon the former king's lament that "sorrow hath destroyed my face" by commenting that "The shadow of your sorrow hath destroyed / The shadow of your face" becomes intriguingly suggestive. The "shadow" of Richard's sorrow in this scene, or, in a more precise modern translation, the *reflection* of it, is Henry himself: he is the mirror, the other, who defines Richard from an external position, who dismantles from the outside Richard's identity as king (metaphorically represented in the broken "shadow" of his face, the image in the shattered looking glass), despite the narcissist's subsequent statement that "my grief lies all within". Again, it is Richard's audience, not himself, which bestows upon him an identity—an identity that can be taken away.

The newly deposed king's subsequent stay in solitude in Pomfret castle confirms this for him. Although his former groom arrives in 5.5 to offer a last bit of flattery, to call up in Richard's mind one more time his image as king by saying that he had relished the opportunity "to look upon my sometimes royal master's face", existence in solitude is disquieting for him. Prior to his conversation with the groom and his own death at the hands of Exton, Richard tries to perform once again, and though he knows that in his cell there "is not a creature by myself," he resolves to "hammer...out" a play. Yet in the end, he knows he needs another for his own narcissism to be satisfying. In this production, he plays "in one person many people," but is "contented" with none of them. One wonders if Shakespeare, who also, in a sense, played "in one person many people," was satisfied with his drama. He should have been. *Richard II* remains an important play in the Bard's canon because it illuminates the complex relationship between the individual and social institutions, between the private and the public, between self and other. Viewed from a Lacanian perspective, Richard's situation is our situation. As a king, he believes he is a stable signifier pregnant with meaning, when he is merely a variable sign with no ultimate substance of his own; he thinks he speaks the discourse of governmental, religious, and social authority when he is actually spoken by that discourse. Similarly, we conceive of ourselves "as free, unified, autonomous, self-generating individuals," though we are, according to Louis Althusser's reading of Lacan—once again summarized and clarified by Eagleton—merely "the 'decentered' function of several social determinants". If one follows such reasoning, one begins to see oneself as an actor, much like Richard (though he perhaps achieves, in the end, a modicum of awareness about his situation which Lacan would probably not afford to most). The goal is to establish a role, an identity, in the presence of others, in the presence of *the* Other, the entire set of institutions which make up our culture. This goal is probably not the effect Shakespeare intended when he wrote his metadramatic history. But if *Richard II* conveys ideas which can be considered relevant some four hundred years later, he probably would not have minded.

## Forget the Hee and Shee" Gender and Play in John Donne

Donne's ambivalence about self-other relations is well known to readers of Songs and Sonnets. Poised at the brink between leaving and lingering, Donne's speakers navigate the competing urgencies of intimacy and autonomy, what Roy Roussell has described as "the twin inevitabilities of distance and desire." In fact, we can think of the dilemma as a quadrupled one, over determined by the paradox that staying behind with the beloved entails both the pleasure of contact and the risk of being consumed by that contact, while parting rewards the adventurer with independence but no guarantee of his lover's faithfulness. To strengthen a self made vulnerable by the conflictual demands of this crowded psychical threshold, Donne deploys his linguistic skill—the "masculine perswasive force" so often invoked by critics—in terms that can seem to denigrate the very women for whom the poet professes love and to undermine even the most apparently genuine expressions of devotion.

Yet the threshold is not simply or consistently a space of anxiety in Donne's love poetry, and against the need to safeguard his male identity from threatening contact with women runs a countercurrent of playful transgressiveness where Donne exhibits not only an ability to recognize women's separate identity, but also, at his most explicitly revisionary, a desire to exceed the restrictions of binary gender roles. My goal here is to suggest that Donne frequently depicts self-other dynamics in ways that extend beyond the familiar accounts of his encounters with women (e.g., pleading or arguing with them, curiosity and fear about their difference from—or similarity to—him, worry that he will never fully know them) toward a more radical gesture of testing the boundaries of gendered identity. Overlapping realms of self and other, male and female, appear throughout the Songs and Sonnets, in ways that suggest less a rhetorical (and ultimately aggressive) exchange of positions than an eager dissolution of outline the speaker of "The Relique" claims "we lov'd well and faithfully, / Yet knew not what wee lov'd, nor why, / Difference of sex no more wee knew" (lines 23-25); the speaker of "The Dampe" ambiguously exhorts his audience to "Kill mee as Woman, let mee die / As a meere man" (lines 21-22); the lover of "The Undertaking" suggests we "forget the Hee and Shee" (line 20). Even the "expansion" endured by the parting couple of "A Valediction Forbidding Mourning"—who like gold are pounded into an "ayery thinnesse" (lines 23-24)—transforms the distance between them as polarized, gendered selves into a continuum of connectedness, uncovering the paradox of a separation that is also a form of union. Often, too, when Donne preserves a sense of self in relation to women without feeling annihilated by proximity to another's psyche, the connection is articulated through metaphors of sovereignty that describe both speaker and mistress the lovers in "The Anniversarie," who "Prince enough in one another bee" (line 14), or in "The Sunne Rising," whom "Princes doe but play" (line 23).

Donne's manner of blurring boundaries between male and female has typically been regarded as a way of reentrenching conventional gender roles and of suppressing the assertiveness of female sexuality. In her discussion of the elegies, for example, Achsah Guibbory argues that the "effect" of "transferring conventionally `masculine' terms... to the woman is not to question traditional distinctions," but rather acts as a "strategy" designed to expose the essential monstrousness of the female body and "reassert masculine dominance" with a vengeance. Far from transgressing gender difference in any potentially liberatory way, Guibbory contends, Donne's acts of positioning himself as feminine or rendering the female in traditionally masculine terms are ultimately antifemale, motivated both by intense anxiety about the literal fact of a woman's monarchical rule and by a more general worry about women's potential influence over him in psychological or sexual ways. Diana Benet has similarly maintained that the poet is "generally conservative," his elegies depicting sexual transgression in derisive terms that reinforce gender distinctions, making violation a crime to be "guilty" of. It has become something of a commonplace to speak of Donne's coercive "ventriloquizing," as Elizabeth Harvey does in her discussion of "Sapho to Philaenis." Harvey asserts that Donne's identification with Sappho "turns out to be an act of colonization" in which the male poet-speaker overpowers the woman by taking on her voice. Stanley Fish reiterates this notion of Donne as a desperate egotist because "Donne occupies every role on his poem's stage," he is "protected" from "the intrusion of any voice he has not ventriloquized." Fish also suggests that Donne's attempts at gender reversal are doomed to collapse "in the face of a fierce and familiar desire to be master of his self" —a fate that Janel Mueller once described, somewhat differently, as Donne's inevitably "gendered consciousness, his identity as a man."

Such discussions of Donne's efforts to consolidate his

masculine identity through rhetorical force recall Thomas Laqueur's well-known claim that seventeenth-century conceptions of gender were bound up with a one-sex model of human physiology, in which the anatomical similarity between male and female bodies required elabourate discursive and educational codes to stabilize difference. Following this idea that gender preceded rather than derived from a sexed body, Mark Breitenberg writes that early modern male subjectivity is "inherently anxious," because the body offered no certain ground of identity "humoural psychology comprehends the male body as constantly in need of regulating its dangerous but nonetheless essential fluidity." "If masculine identity is fundamentally unstable," argues Breitenberg, "then the assertion of gender difference... functions as a way to compensate for the lack of anatomical guarantee of difference." At the core of this struggle between body and discourse is the fact that "male and female seed were not seen as sexually specific," as Anthony Fletcher explains, so that "there was seen to be in everyone some trace at birth of gender doubleness." Breitenberg's claim that early modern male writers "stage masculine loss and vulnerability for the purpose of maintaining control of the performance of one's gendered identity" suggests that the very conceptual ambiguity that allows for Donne's poetic "inversions" of gender might also be what produces, as Harvey and others maintain, a rhetoric of cementing difference.

Yet Donne's recurring articulation of gender as a fluid realm of experience indicates that he was able to construe subjectivity and intimacy alike outside of a patriarchal ideology in which "woman" is first constructed and then regulated as a threatening Other. In an article on the sapphic epistle, Janel Mueller describes Donne's "`what if' imaginings" as the poet's efforts to "[bond] with Sappho across gender difference as a subject of otherwise unimagined or unimaginable possibility," and to "[write] his way beyond the confines of a Renaissance social context." Contrary to the notion of gender play as a carnival of transgressions that always, ultimately, reaffirms power hierarchies, I would agree with Mueller that a "what if" dynamic is at work in a number of Donne's poems. As I hope to show, Donne's courting of liminal experience often registers a disruption in discursively enforced gender identity and thus offers the possibility of both identification with women and recognition of their separateness. By blueprinting Donne's play within the space-between, such familiar tropes as teardrops, maps and globes, windowpanes, and the compass bring into view this ability to resist the static constraints of the pairs (self-other, attachment-loss, male-female) that they themselves contain, as well as the poet's fascination with destabilizing gendered identity in a pleasurable, rather than a strictly policing, manner.

The notion of playing with and in threshold spaces, a central concern of object relations psychoanalysis, allows us to think anew about what might be at stake in a seventeenth-century male writer's figuration of gendered selfhood. D. W. Winnicott's concept of the "potential space" between subjects in which psychical play occurs provides an especially useful model for considering the ways in which Donne manipulates the paradox of an identity always both "male" and not fully male. (Winnicott himself notes that the "intermediate area... appears in full force in the work characteristic of the so-called metaphysical poets.") By definition a borderland activity, to play in Winnicott's sense is to invite the paradox of simultaneity; the field of play is at once illusory and real, solitary and connected. In the dialectic of this "intermediate area" between self and other, the individual's "potential" for creativity and wholeness can be fostered, even as—or perhaps precisely because—the play space imbricates internal psychical reality with the external world. Winnicott defines play as a coalescence of reliability and intimacy, a psychic activity dependent on the self's trust that the other will neither abandon it nor intrude upon the privacy of its imagination. Anticipated by the "holding" space of nursing, play is intimate and intersubjective, a paradoxical realm in which self and other, interior and exterior, reality and fantasy, autonomy and attachment all coincide. It is the notion of loosening the borders of self in contact with the other—a way of being both "me" and "not-me" at once—that can help us to recognize how a writer like Donne might pose alternatives to his culture's construction of gender.

Winnicott's focus on the care giving "environment" leads to a theory of selfhood in which no individual exists outside of its object relationships "self" emerges from the "relational matrix," a subject's ongoing engagement with real people in the external world as well as with internalized imagos. Because object relations theory does not, then, in Jane Flax's words, "require a fixed or essentialist view of `human nature,' it becomes a useful method of exploring the representation of self-other relations in Donne's poetry, particularly in view of what Breitenberg calls "the specifically social basis of subjectivity in the early modern period." A notion of intersubjective "play" founded on mother- infant interaction also accords with recent historical studies of childhood that have contested earlier conclusions about the formality and emotional indifference of parent-child relations in the early modern period. In an article addressing seventeenth-century attitudes toward infancy and nursing, Patricia Crawford argues that "contemporaries were aware of the close bonding which occurred between mother or nurse and child," and that "maternal love was recognized as a strong bond," a very symbol of "the closest human love." Crawford offers evidence that breast-feeding was believed to provide "comfort" as much as nutrition to babies and to be a source of "pleasure" to infant and woman alike Linda Pollock cites similar evidence that children were "wanted and valued," regarded with "concern and interest" by their parents in the seventeenth century, and she contends that "the closeness of the parent-child bond" was "very much a dyadic one."

A further connection between object relations theory and early modern subjectivity derives from the peculiarly indeterminate nature of the body. I would argue that the early modern male infant resided, in effect, in a space of Winnicottian play, always "in-between"—subject to the instability of anatomy as well as to the absence of culturally enforced gender differentiation in the first years of life. To dissolve gender difference in poetic potential spaces—as Donne does—or to rest from the perpetual task of maintaining it is to evince the ambiguity of the body and to call up the psychical doubleness of a male infant's experience of the wholly female domain into which he was born. As Anthony Fletcher shows, early modern "manhood" was equated with "separation from the mother," signaling an end to the "sexual twinship which began with conception and the concoction of male and female seeds." But rather than insisting that Donne is forever at work to enforce that separation, denying a changeable self or the possibility of full engagement with women who might remind him of the discomfiting possibility of his own inconstancy, we can instead explore the way in which he plays with that very paradox. In this way, Winnicott's central paradigms—holding, play, and potential space—help advance a reading of those poems where Donne's speakers evoke the autochthonous pleasures of relaxing the borders of subjectivity.

Other readers of Donne who make use of psychoanalytic theories of play, most notably Anna K. Nardo in her formidable book, The Ludic Self, have tended to discuss threshold experience as the poet's way of assuaging conflicting fears about separation and engulfment. In Nardo's study, play becomes a mediatory outlook as much as an actual activity, taken up by the adult poet in order to cope with the resurgence of childhood conflicts newly triggered by the turbulent landscape of widespread social change. Describing the witty contradictions of so many of Donne's images and poems, Nardo presents Donne as a self-conscious "player," fully aware of the fragility of the play world his language creates. In a richly contextualized essay, William Shullenberger draws on both Nardo's and Lagan's discussions of mirroring in the mother-infant dyad, but focuses instead on triangulations in which a third party is invoked to witness acts of lovemaking (and acts of poetry making) so as to guarantee the self's stable identity. But while proposing that the most trusting moments of connectedness between adult lovers "have their experiential basis in the totalizing and exclusive intimacy of mother and child," Shullenberger does not address the possibility that Donne's male speakers get beyond an emphatically male identity. Indeed, they remain stably, steadily male. And while Nardo does assert that "the conflict [Donne] felt so keenly between separation and union" necessarily entails the female other, her descriptions of Donne's play vis-a-vis that other do not connect the intermediate space with a specific interest in transgressing gender or with reconfiguring male-female relations.

Yet it is in such moments of trespass that Donne articulates what may be his most nuanced sense of identity and of gender. Donne's overt linguistic wittiness suggests "play" in a literal sense, but he seems most actively to solicit the dialectic of play when his speakers move beyond the rules of logic and boundary and into intermediate psychical areas where they can enjoy what Winnicott called "rest"—a secure, pleasurable overlap of inner and outer, of self and other. Modern Donne scholarship seems to have moved away from an interest in the poet's "metaphysical" ingenuity and toward accounts of strain and incompletion, particularly in terms of his relation to women. Psycho-analytic readings tend to combine the two perspectives, suggesting that verbal inventiveness masks, exposes, and assuages anxiety all at once. But there is perhaps another way of thinking about gender and emotion in Donne. In what follows, I understand Donne's playfulness to serve less as a public display of his clever intellect, or as a defence against social upheaval, than as a way of rethinking the possibilities of gender and erotic connection. Through the liminality of teardrops, windows, even the transitional act of breathing, Donne creates poetic potential spaces in which speakers enjoy intimacy without threat and—even as they enter into imaginative revision of the contours of their own identity—respect the subjectivity of the women they address.

The opening stanza of "The Flea" provides a compelling example of Donne's play with gender. Here, the male seducer becomes identified with the female seduced through the mutual sucking of the insect

*Marke but this flea, and marke in this,*

*How little that which thou denys't me is;*
*It suck'd me first, and now sucks thee,*
*And in this flea, our two bloods mingled bee;*
*Thou know'st that this cannot be said*
*A sinne, nor shame, nor loss of maidenhead,*
*Yet this enjoys before it wooe,*
*And pampered swells with one blood made of two*
*And this, alas, is more than wee would do.*

The stanza radically revalues the domineering, "male" sexuality that the poem seems to be urging the woman toward. The speaker takes on the position not of the invasive flea whose behaviour serves as vehicle of his argument, but rather that of the woman herself. He announces that he was "suck'd... first" (line 3), and the ambiguity of "this" in line 5 suggests that what "cannot be said / A sinne, nor shame" is at least on some level the speaker's experience of having been pleasured by that sucking—in addition to, or even superseding, the "mingled" blood that represents a more overtly heterosexualized genital coupling (and thus loss of virginity). Coursing beneath the overt terms of the seduction is a longing to do the passive thing, not just to penetrate but to be "pampered," not simply to suck but to be sucked (with implications both of being nursed and of being "fucked"). And this sucking occurs before seduction and erection, which emphasizes that pleasure can be obtained prior to the more explicitly and conventionally masculine forms of sexual arousal signaled by "wooes" and "pampered swells." Thus the stanza shifts its forward motion of desire and seems instead to linger in a moment of jouissance—where sucking and "being fucked" take precedence over the more obvious sequence from solicitation to tumescence to coitus to completion. Moreover, what the flea "enjoyes" seems identified as the specific pleasure of being able to suck both male and female bodies—and at least in part it is this, "alas," that is more than the male speaker will do. Thus through the knotting of one elabourate conceit, Donne manages to identify himself both with the female body and with a kind of "bisexualized" erotic pleasure.

The speaker of "The Good-Morrow" stakes a similar claim

for a kind of sexuality that transcends the binarism of heterosexuality. The mood of wonder that opens the poem feels rich and tactile, and the stanza luxuriates in a polymorphous, sensual pleasure that is childlike and erotic at once

*I wonder by my troth, what thou, and I*
*Did, till we lov'd? were we not wean'd till then?*
*But suck'd on countrey pleasures, childishly?*
*Or snorted we in the seaven sleepers den?*
*'Twas so; But this, all pleasures fancies bee*
*If ever any beauty I did see,*
*Which I desir'd, and got, t'was but a dreame of thee.*

The speaker meets the morning with innocent fantasy and curiosity, as if paying a kind of marveling, rapt attention to the surprise of good feeling. What the speaker wonders about, of course, is what they "did," prior to a moment of loving that represents being "wean'd" from childish escapades. But the pleasure the stanza records is not the moment of adult sexuality that ostensibly inaugurates this "good morrow"; in fact, it is the pleasure of not being weaned. To be weaned is to be removed from and deprived of nursing at the breast; the speaker remembers—quite delightedly—having "suck'd on countrey pleasures, childishly" (line 3). "Countrey pleasures" may be, as C. A. Patrides glosses in his edition, "rustic; hence unrefined," but the phrase also connotes something instinctual and unruled. The allusion to the seven sleepers' mythic two-hundred-year sleep heightens the atmosphere of snug satisfaction, because it implies not just a space in which danger may be escaped but also dragnet replenishment. The speaker increases the sense of restful content with "den" and "snorted," which suggest a self so deeply comfortable that it can be unconscious of its surroundings. In these first few lines, pleasure is associated with deliberately and intensely "childish" behaviours—the greedy orality of suckling, the swaddled protectedness of sleep. Moreover, it is pleasure itself that the speaker sucks (rather than a breast or a body), as if it could be absorbed directly into the self—pure and undistilled.

The first is a stanza of affirmations, culminating in the

speaker's unequivocal "'Twas so." The abundance of pleasure emerges through repetition ("countrey pleasures" and "all pleasures"), as well as by the fact that in both instances the word is plural pleasures proliferate. Indeed, in the speaker's compacted phrasing, "all pleasures fancies bee" (line 5) suggests not so much that all those prior pleasures are mere fancies, but rather—and more emphatically—that all pleasures and fancies exist. But for this adult, complicated, divided love, he seems to hint, pleasure could actually be. The ontological importance of the stanza lies in this metaphorical childhood, as a time of immediate gratification. In "The Good-Morrow," desiring means getting, with no intervening wait to survive "If ever any beauty I did see, / Which I desir'd, and got" (lines 6-7). It is also a time in which being emerges out of a bond between self and other defined by sucking and experienced not as a connection between two ultimately separable things but as undifferentiated pleasure itself. The "dreame"-like quality of this prior existence reinforces its evocation of early attachment between infant and caregiver and the infant's capacity to "create," through the illusion of omnipotence, what it needs. But the dreaminess also suggests a desire to do away with the barriers that make adult love so fraught with dangers. Here, difference itself is annulled "all pleasures fancies bee."

The fact that those prior pleasures are made meaningful in "The Good-Morrow" by their relation to the speaker's current love affair reminds us that the explicit comparison also works to affirm the rapture of the "adult" present love over "childish" past dalliances. The poem has traditionally been read in just this way, as a statement of mature, "mutually successful love-making," to borrow David Daiches's phrase, in which younger flirtations are dismissed as insignificant. Yet the way in which the first stanza overlays a nostalgic fantasy of infant joy with those previous "fancies" complicates the idea that the poem charts a clear progression toward reciprocal, adult love. The first stanza of "The Good-Morrow" does not so much depict the activities of a literal childhood as it "wonders," through the relational vocabulary of play and potential spaces (not being "wean'd," "suck[ing]," sleeping, and seeing), about the possibility of an intersubjective eroticism free from anxiety and vigilance, physical "slakening" (line 21), or even actual death.

This is made apparent in the first lines of the second stanza—"And now good morrow to our waking soules, / Which watch not one another out of feare" (lines 8-9)—which usher in the spectre of doubt and surveillance. Where many critics take the speaker at his word, supporting his bid for the strength of the relationship ("we are not afraid of anything"), I would argue that these lines are haunted by distrust, by a surprising unease that deepens through the remainder of the poem. Why the insistence that their looking at each other is not done "out of feare"? Is it possible that fear prevents them from looking at each other? The hopeful myth, that love "controules" one's "sight" (and so might stop a woman from looking at other men), leads only to the poem's poignant, final conditional—"If our two loves be one" (line 20)—a sudden contingency which seems to undermine its own confident assertion of mutuality. Wondering signals openness, but also wariness; the speaker begins the poem by working hard not to ask outright about his lover's prior loves. That the stanza then moves so quickly to a fantasy about childhood may point less to a kind of self-protective "regression" than, more provocatively, to a way of rearticulating the dynamics of intimacy. It is twoness that troubles the end of "The Good-Morrow," as if the very difference seemingly required to maintain what Stephen Orgel has called "the integrity of the perilously achieved male identity" ends up unraveling the pleasurable sameness captured by the repetition of "we" at the start of the poem.

If "The Good-Morrow" exalts the love of "thou and I" by rendering all else mere childish trifling, I would argue that it also inverts that trajectory, contrasting the intersubjective "we-ness" of potential space with doubt about the viability of intimacy in an era when conventional narratives about women make "sexuality itself... misogynistic." The valediction poems tell similar stories of friction. As speakers prepare to depart across complicated thresholds, their ability to trust their lovers' faithfulness seems acutely stressed, and often some expression of the imminence of betrayal seeps into the frame of the poem. Nonetheless, Donne registers alongside the fretful worry an important recognition of women's separateness from the men who leave—an autonomy often indicated by speakers' suspicions that women have already "departed" long before the literal voyage that may occasion a valediction poem. While Donne may experience separation as a kind of trauma, his fear does not prevent him from acknowledging a woman's independence from his efforts—literal or poetic—to hold onto her. Again and again, the poems locate in women the very sensation of centered wholeness male speakers wish they themselves could experience. And, recurringly, these poems contain nodal points of pleasurable exchange between male and female subjectivity.

In "A Valediction of My Name, In The Window," for instance, the speaker's concerns about what will take place in his absence—about who might take his place—both result from and give rise to a sense of his mistress's power over his emotional and bodily integrity. As the name in the window expands to represent the body of the absent lover, and as the boundaries between this name-body and the face-self of the mistress begin to merge, he comes to depend upon her eyes' ability to hold his body and self intact. Far from becoming dismembered by the gaze of a woman that reminds him of his inadequacy, and farther still from being able to strong-arm her vision, this speaker dismembers himself when he senses he is outside of a look that can restore and reconfigure him to wholeness. The power and importance of her look throughout the poem strongly counters such claims as Barbara Estrin's that "his vision controls." And it strongly evokes the power of the mother's look, in the mirroring exchange of gazes in which the infant arrives at its own subjectivity even as it learns to negotiate the separateness of the mother who "holds."

The "name engrav'd" (line 1) into the window, and by extension the self it represents, is rendered harder than glass, as hard even as the diamond that engraves it. In the first stanza, both the pane of glass and the self embodied there gain value by the lover's "eye," which gives "price enough" to the name-engraved window (line 6). She—the female "other"—does the looking. In Barbara Estrin's reading, this happens only because the speaker "limit[s]—by contraction—the woman's vision." Yet the imagined overlap of name and face within the window requires a specifically dialectical exchange of looks; she sees both herself and him when she looks into the window, as does he, looking back. The complex visual dynamics of Donne's windowpane anticipate Winnicott's notion of a cohering maternal gaze which establishes a fundamental sense of self-integration even as it introduces the presence, and therefore the separateness, of the other. Winnicott describes mirroring as intersubjective and mutual, because what mother and infant see as they gaze into each other's faces is the simultaneity of their own and the other's desires. In Thomas Ogden's words, "this constitutes an interpersonal dialectic wherein 'I-ness' and otherness create one another and are preserved by the other." To look in this sense is thus once again to blur distinctions of subject and object. "Loves magique... undoes" those "rules" (line 11) that demand separate bodies, separate consciousnesses, separate positions from which to "look"; to undo such rules is to transport oneself psychically, to confound the static linearity of gazer and gazed upon, so that the speaker becomes not "more himself" but rather her "Here you see mee, and I am you" (line 12). Transparent, the window "confesses" (line 8) all that occurs on either side of it—glass will not conceal her actions once he has gone, but neither will it hide his watching. At the same time that glass is looked through, however, it can also superimpose their two "bodies" her face looking, his name being seen. The speaker's manipulation of the frame of the window to capture her gaze and superimpose them leads Estrin to claim that "the 'I' binds the woman to him by imposing himself on her." "When the 'I' says 'I am you,'" Estrin writes, "he means 'I want you to think I am you—and I want to make myself think you are I—so that I can be confident that your fidelity and love are what I propose them to be unfoundering.' But his 'I am you' really is a way of saying 'you are I.' The lady is urged to give up her identity for his."

But the fact of being seen by her ("you see mee") leads less to a consolidation of his autonomous existence through appropriation of her (not "I am me") than to a collapse of their positions as separate selves ("I am you").

Rather than imprisoning the woman within its boundaries, the windowpane functions as a play space whose threshold both speaker and lover cross over, moving beyond their real, physical selves and thus also their divided, gendered identities. It is this blending together, I think, far more than any scopic pleasure produced by, or masculine power producing, the exchange of looks, that brings forth a sense of "intirenesse." The name engraved in the glass retains its shape because it manages to achieve the physical permanence that is otherwise elusive, denied by the kind of "departure" this valediction marks (the "plot" of parting provides a context for more psychological forms of separation). Its integrity cannot be "outwash[ed]" by the inundating fluidity of "showers and tempests" (line 15). But a certain kind of "intirenesse" (line 17)—to be so whole as to include each "point" and "dash," all the smallest "accessaries" of one's "name" (lines 13-14)—the speaker finds only within his lover. She contains the "patterne" (line 18) of him within; he becomes her as she looks upon the overlay of their two "bodies" in the window. Thus while the engraved name may independently claim "firmnesse" and constancy—"all times," he tells her, "[shall] finde mee the same" (line 16)—nevertheless he needs her to "better... fulfill" the "intirenesse" (line 17) that will bridge the space between, salve the hurt of parting.

The speaker's experience of being attached to his mistress is not univocal in "A Valediction of My Name." If in one stanza he appears to celebrate their closeness so fully as to dissolve the distinction between them, in the next he reacts to the demands of that intimacy by losing hold of identity altogether, by breaking down into a variety of bones and body parts barely held together any longer by the name carved into the window. In stanza 3, the woman is filled with him in the way her face is "filled" with his name as she looks into the window, and somehow she brings the potential of his entirety into reality by containing the "patterne" of him within her. But no sooner is this sense of being housed within her uttered than it defracts into the "ragged bony name" (line 23) of the following stanza. It is as if the speaker's own expression of being so deeply embedded in the body of his lover (now figured explicitly as mother), so thickly entwined with her identity, overpowers the viability of the name that once withstood "showers and tempests." If, without her, there is nothing to hold him together, if he must depend on her for the blueprint of himself that will "repaire / And recompact" him (lines 31-32), and if there is no fundamental "patterne" of him without her, then the leave-taking this poem commemorates must bring forth fears of chaotic unraveling, a dismembering that leaves his body-self "scattered" (line 32). Simultaneously, though, intimacy is itself a danger precisely because his lover becomes too large—or too constricting. What independent existence can his "self" attain if its very architecture relies, in order to be built, on a pattern she controls?

Thus the "scratch'd name" burgeons into a "deaths head," ominously warning her of "lovers mortalitie" (lines 20-22). The name that could not be "outwash[ed]" (line 15) just the stanza before now signifies the awful temporality of a love unguaranteed and unguarantee-able, no longer impervious to the effects of tempests both external/poetic and internal/ psychic. The glass that was both charmed and "grav'd" (i.e., made serious? legitimized?) by the name it held now shows not a gracefully "accessorized" name that sloughs off rain but a "ragged bony name," a "ruinous Anatomie" (line 24) that itself seems to "ruin" the glass and the love it is meant to solidify. His fantasy of a window that places them one upon the other seems both to manifest an awareness of and to display back to him the extent to which his identity (signed by his name) is contained within her face, the sign of her personhood. To be her ("I am you") is specifically to experience himself as within her, to want to be and to feel himself as contained. But this connectedness then evokes fears of being frighteningly loosened and dissolved. No small feat, then, that in the fifth stanza the speaker rebuilds himself. Declaring to his lover that "all my soules bee / Emparadis'd in you" (lines 25-26), he is newly confident that this core of connection between them will refashion again the "house" (line 30) of "Muscle, Sinew, and Veine" (line 29), literally fleshing out the skeletal "rafters" (line 28) that remain following the self-annihilation of the previous lines.

In his absence, she will "repaire / And recompact" his "body" within her (lines 31-32). The casement that contains the name works as a barrier and a passageway between the room within and the world beyond. When he imagined her face reflected in the window surrounding his name, the window became a limit; both her image and the name would look back at her (he would look back at her), inverting and turning inward her act of looking outward. Now, as he imagines her receiving and greeting a new lover, the window once again opens outward—literally, symbolically—to the world the speaker has himself entered, but from which he cannot help looking back, over his shoulder.

These shifting attempts to manipulate and respond to space suggest forms of attachment that are liberating and threatening at once. Framing himself in the casement—to be "encased"—provides some firm sense of embodiment. To be embodied within the "face" of his lover is also to feel whole and (re)integrated. But the window that performs the superimposition also measures the limits of security, for there is a world beyond, one that seems excitingly full of possibilities and disturbingly populated by potential rivals for his lover's attentions. What happens to his name, his body and identity, if her face no longer looks through it in the window—if, indeed, the window is thrown aside to allow her clear view to another man's "name"? More central an image, perhaps, than even the name itself, the window is defined by a transparency evocative of a desire to "see-through," to know but also to be known. Glass can be looked through as well as "look back," like the eyes of a lover.

The fantasy of experiencing himself contained seems to allow the speaker to stop a motion that is both inevitable (the poem "bids farewell") and feared. He is like a child looking in at a doorway to remind himself that the mother is there, reacquainting himself with her by her reassuring glance. Since he cannot look through the window in fact (and there is perhaps a voyeuristic wish here as well), he leaves something behind in fantasy and in the poem a body scattered; a ruined anatomy; his bones, sinews, veins, and muscles—in short, himself, barely held together. In this context the phrase "being still with you" (line 29) takes on multiple meanings. The parts of him are still with her, with her as yet and always, waiting to be "bodied" again at his return. But there is also, I think, a wish to be in a kind of motionless overlap with her. This is what makes engraving so important; it grants a motionlessness to the speaker's body (and emotions, devotions?) that is itself an expression of her movement away from him and toward other lovers.

Estrin suggests that the speaker, by pinioning the face of his mistress against his name in the window, denies the possibility of an "other" capable of moving out of the frame he has created. But the very engraving of the name in the window suggests how far the poem goes to acknowledge her separateness from him. The engraved name will never move as his real body and her real face so emphatically do. The repetition of "Till my returne," "till I returne" (lines 31, 41) signals visions of the blank space of his absence, which is also her absence from him, conveying both his anxiety about these absences and his determination to return. If there is a subtle warning here, he is also assuring her, and himself as well.

Like the windowpane, the teardrop is one of Donne's most evocative representations of the delicate boundaries that separate as well as connect the self and the external world. Fragile, rarely solitary, of a shape so distinctively recognizable and yet so easily ruptured, the teardrop's thin membrane perfectly imitates the edges between people that Donne is always testing. The teardrop itself, though knowable, meaningful, and extant only on the outside surface of the skin, is also somehow always "looking" inward, because it is so much of the body's interior, always representing some internal state. Winnicott writes that "there comes into existence what might be called a limiting membrane, which to some extent (in health) is equated with the surface of the skin, and has a position between the infant's `me' and his `not-me.' Accordingly, it is through images of teardrops that Donne articulates his sense that boundaries can be so easily defocused in ways both pleasurable and threatening.

The tear—like an eye or window—behaves like a tiny mirror, reflecting the face of the lover looking toward it; at the same time, the exquisitely delicate surface of a teardrop gives it its paradoxical quality, vulnerable to dissolution, but also, thrillingly open to exchange.

The dynamics of looking become ever more taut on the threshold of parting in "A Valediction Of Weeping." The implied face-to-face positioning of "Let me powre forth / My tears before thy face" (lines 1-2; he specifies her face, rather than her eyes) suggests that looks are being exchanged, that he looks into her face in search of her whole expression, which he then encapsulates in his tears. His tears, not her eyes, accomplish the reflecting he is the reflecting surface; he looks at her to capture what she looks like and then integrates that look into himself, reproducing her in his tears while she faces him with her own face and being. It seems vitally important to this Donnean speaker that there is another body there, a face that looks back in a mutually-created experience.Produced from within himself but reflective of her, his tears are now of self and other simultaneously; he seems to experience her as something that both originates from within himself and is superimposed onto his tears and then looked at through the commingling medium of his fluidity.

With her image contained in the tears that course across his face, the speaker can "stay" (line 2) and be still; it is as if her face "stays" him from the imminent leave-taking. "Here" (line 2) suggests, therefore, "with you" (and thus not "out there"), but also "over here, where I am, on my side of the boundary between us." With her image imprinted upon them, but shed only in the "absence" of her as one lover faces another, tears measure an irreducible distance between them. At the same time, however, they contain an impression as vital as the seed of her, as if they could give birth to her. Such fullness is intensely pleasurable—he can contain her within himself, if only on the outskirts of his body, within the fragile membrane of the tear. (The metaphor of pregnancy is prefigured in line 3 by "beare"; they are "something worth" [line 4] for containing her in this way.)

But the fantasy of being pregnant with her—of needing, as it were, to give birth to her—implies that he does not already have a connection to her that fulfills him the way her image "fulfills" the tear. Those tears are, as he quickly remembers, produced by "much griefe" (line 7), and while the ostensible meaning is clear (he is leaving), the phrase connotes as well something far more interior, as if "griefe" has been accumulating within him over countless unspoken betrayals. Indeed, the rest of the line—"emblemes of more..." (line 7)—trails off vaguely, as if he cannot find adequate words with which to articulate the many reasons for these tears. His own descriptive metaphors work to belie what might seem important here to disguise the progression from tears coined by her image to tears "pregnant" (line 6) with the "seed" of her leads him to the paradox of "fruits" (line 7), a word which carries suggestions of transgression and delight at once, as if the very objects by which he tries to hold her to him (in place?) become symbols of the kind of act that could breach that connection. The tears perform the transgressiveness, in fact, by "fall[ing]" (line 8) as he cries them.

The parts of him that successfully "contain" her—those tears—are always already on the move away from him as soon as they achieve shape and meaning outside of his eyes (he, his body and "self," can never really hold her as his tears do). Tears always fall; they can never go back in, never return to connect with the body that forms them. It is this incessant "falling" that triggers the shift in tone and emotion in the second part of the first stanza.

It is as if his own image of pregnant tears, seeming to grant a wonderful wholeness, requires that he track back to the dangerous sexuality of which pregnancy is a literal fruit and which causes even further pregnant tears. The tears that "bore" (line 8) her detach from his eyes and give birth to a "fallen" her. His desire, and attempt, to retain a sense of her in his tears ends up "falling," measuring as it does so how little he can ensure that she will not "fall" after he departs (or, perhaps more acutely, even prior to this moment). Nor can he guarantee in her the stasis that is so important to him; as if to counter his own assurance that "I stay here" (line 2), he seems to accuse her, "thou falst" (line 8).

Nevertheless, the tear maintains its transformative powers, as the speaker redoubles his efforts to locate spaces in which their two subjectivities can experience a pleasurable melding. As the empty "round ball" (line 11) devoid of meaning becomes an identifiable, navigable "All" with maps of the world pasted upon it (line 14), so the value of a tear increases with her reflection "worn" within it; the "impression" (line 16) of her face makes the tear an all, the way she—if she could also be contained within him—might grant him the completeness of a world. It is as if she covers him like the overlain "copies" (line 11) of the continents and fills him from within like tears "pregnant of" (line 6) her, until the space they share "overflow[s]" (line 17) with tiny crystalline worlds of which both have been the creators—she with her face and looks and presence, he as the "workeman" (line 11) who cries the englobing tears. And while it seems that she too has begun to cry—"Till thy teares mixt with mine doe overflow / This world, by water sent from thee, my heaven dissolved so" (lines 17-18)—"thy teares" may also refer, in a way that underscores the spatial and psychic entanglements the poem depicts, to his own tears, which "belong" to her because her face gives them meaning and worth, because it is her relation to the speaker that elicits them, and, too, because they wet her face as he weeps. In the dissolution of tears, then, what is "hers" becomes indistinguishable from what is "his."

The penetrability of the teardrop further demonstrates the exciting experience of exceeding the limits of one's boundaries. When lovers cry together, their tears intermingle, blurring distinctions by combining the positions of mourned-mourner, performer-spectator, self-other. The act of crying itself here repeats the reorientation of the gaze enacted by "A Valediction of My Name" initially, it is the man's tears that are "pregnant" and pour forth uncontrollably, the man who is uncontained, flowing, fluid, while the woman watches.

The many distortions of space (the proportions of the cosmos are stretched from micro- to macrocosmic, with teardrops reflecting faces and encapsulating worlds and a woman expanding to become the moon) exaggerates the poem's willingness to ignore outline and limitation, its eagerness to experience a comfortable at-one-ness. While it seems clear that, as Mark Breitenberg points out, water imagery symbolizes a constellation of anxieties in early modern texts—from maternal engulfment to the frightening fluidity of a humoural body to the real danger of shipwreck—Donne's use of the tear also unthinks anxiety, measuring a sensitivity to edges and to various ways of crossing or even dispensing entirely with boundaries—of the body, while crying; of tears, which dissolve; of the self, in love with another. Of course, these suggestions are not intended to supersede entirely the poem's culminating tone of despair. "More than Moone" (line 19), the woman here is an omnipotent woman who can house or fragment the body of her lover, look back in a mutual gaze, or look away with murderous unconcern. The woman who is more commands his very life; to be close to her is to experience his self as dangerously loosened, so unpredictable is her "spheare" (line 20). She can, and might, "draw up seas" (line 20) to drown him. And the imagined mourning seems to record what is coursing beneath this poem that once he is gone ("dead" [line 21]), she is free ("dissolved"? [line 18]) to pursue other lovers. Indeed, his pleas to her to "forbeare / To teach the sea, what it may doe too soone" (lines 21-22), to "Let not the winde / Example finde" (lines 23-24), disclose the worry that sadness and separation may happen "too soone" (which sounds like "soon enough" and suggests an inevitability); that whatever actual danger exists in the literal plot of the poem is outweighed by the increase in harm she could cause (she sets an "example" that is more than the moon, the sea, and the wind together). Even the personified "winde"—already perceived as a malevolent force that "purposeth" (line 25) to do him some degree of "harme" (line 25)—might be impelled toward "more harme" by her example. So much danger may be offset by the possibility of them "holding" each other and of being held in a space that staves off unstoppable floods. The intermingling of breaths—her body contains his, his body her breath—works to control their lives and deaths. He wants them to "hold" each others' breaths by not sighing, and so maintain a feeling of keeping-in, of repletion and completion. But of course they cannot hold their breaths forever, and the inevitable breathing out (which he seems to watch and wait for in an agony of anticipation) is thus an unfathomable cruelty that "hastes the others death" (line 27). Yet the very imagery that conveys grief and doubt in "A Valediction of Weeping" serves also to modify, on a perhaps more subterranean level, the poem's tendency toward such expressions. Tears, coins, fruit, globes, maps, tides, sighs—each of these suggests overlap and exchange within liminal spaces that allow the speaker to play with the indeterminacy of selfhood and the undulating limits of relationality.

"A Valediction Forbidding Mourning," in a similar way, complicates our sense of which subject position (self-other, male-female, traveler-left-behind) the speaker identifies with most emphatically. The opening analogy between parting lovers and dying men who "passe mildly away" and "whisper to their soules, to goe" (lines 1-2) makes the separation as natural—and the reunion as inevitable—as that of "virtuous" (line 1) bodies and souls. It may be the certitude of rejoining that renders death a mild passing (so subtle is this parting, in fact, that it is nearly imperceptible to others; as Geoffrey Hartman points out, "the evidence of life [hangs] on a word, on less than a word, on a vocal inflection or quantity, the difference between `now' and `no'"); on the other hand, the stanza confuses one's sense of which—body or soul—is figured as leaving. It is as if they both "leave" the one "passes," the other is whispered at "to goe," they move away from each other as if simultaneously, and neither "stays." Saying goodbye, the speaker suggests, might be just as internal an event as this parting of body and breath—so private, others can't perceive it; so "mild," it feels less like a wrenching breakage than like melting. Let us part, he seems to say, as if only gradually dissolving, separating out of oneness and into twoness in a way that is simultaneously a melding; and let us do this so quietly that no one else will notice. If the parting of body and soul will look like just one more exhalation of breath, so their parting should feel like just another normal parting.

Despite the speaker's confirmation that it is he who physically leaves ("I must goe" [line 22]), the poem expresses a familiar ambiguity notice that it is the breath that leaves, not the men who hold the breath; and the soul that goes, not the male body that houses the soul. And if the instruction to "make no noise" (line 5) stems from a wish to protect "our joyes" from the misunderstanding of others, it also serves to soften the distress of separation, to allow each individual to "melt" (line 5). Such blending together seems delicious, rather than inundating. Mere earthly lovers, dependent on the body with its simple sensuality and reliance on the senses, cannot tolerate physical absence. But a love that can withstand "motion" is one independent of physical connection. Not having to rely on sight, touch, even the sound of each other's voices, their love is of the spheres, "innocent" (line 12) of the requirement of constant contact. So "refin'd" (line 17) is that love, they are made pure by it—made so subtle and precise, that they cannot even define what it is that they experience together, though they nonetheless escape the dull interpretation already belittled in the third stanza. The speaker makes explicit the terms of so fine a fit to withstand physical separation, lovers must have internalized each other as sustaining imagos, carried within and related to as vividly as their physical selves. To be "inter-assured of the mind" (line 19) is to experience reciprocity and understanding as guaranteed—and "inter-assured" seems just the right phrase, since it conveys the mutuality and exchange that are so vital, along with the sense of being reassured of a continued affection. Separation means destruction to an infant; it feels annihilating, as if both object and self might never return. But when (or more specifically here, because) there is such psychical connection, the lovers' physical disconnection feels neither obliterating nor even disruptive of love itself they can "care less" (line 20) about the absence of lips, eyes, and hands. In turn, the speaker can be "careless" about togetherness he seems jaunty, playful, and confident.

Not to know "what [love] is" (line 18)—to be beyond (even prior to) explanations and definitions that would require observation of oneself and consideration of the self's interaction with another—suggests a doubled state of simultaneous union and exchange in which conceptions of "twoness" have no meaning. The "inter-assurance" of their minds creates an experience of oneness that, far from presupposing knowledge and experience of dualities, smudges all delimiting outline between their separate selves. So their "two souls therefore,... are one" (line 21) and, equally paradoxically, the space that keeps them apart is but a continuation of themselves and thus of their bond, just as the ends of a sheet of gold hammered to thinness stand apart, yet uninterruptedly attached

*Our two soules therefore, which are one,*
*Though I must goe, endure not yet*
*A breach, but an expansion,*
*Like gold to ayery thinnesse beate.*

This last image of "gold to ayery thinnesse beate" is an index of the speaker's willingness to tolerate distance, and it sounds less like a buttressing of a vulnerable self (increasing its sense of identity, in effect, by adding her identity) than like a liberating continuum of connectedness in which confident selves expand toward the other and lose rigid definition in that intimacy. Whatever disappointment might be felt by the loss, even abandonment, that parting entails is assuaged by the ability to remember good feelings and to remain "in contact," as it were, intrapsychically.

The compass metaphor complicates this fantasy, if only because the physical reality of the device necessitates that the two souls previously figured as one are suddenly returned to a condition of divided twoness. Like one leg of a compass joined to the other, each lover's motion is now contingent upon the others. She is "the fixt foot," which "makes no show / To move, but doth, if the other doe" (lines 27-28); he, "the other," which "far doth rome" (line 30). She is "the centre" (line 29), still and sure, that marks the home base of the circle circumscribed around her by the speaker's roaming. This would seem to substantiate some critics' belief that the compass is used here as an emblem of constancy and that the speaker means to express his belief in (or anxious wish for) his lover's fidelity. But the image also, once more, works to destabilize what the solidity of the compass would seem concerned to assure. That the "fixt foot" "makes no show" to move implies that it might at any moment, unpredictably, or perhaps that she moves internally, imperceptibly, emotionally—in short, in some way that cannot be measured by outward show. Her immobility is hardly guaranteed. The apparent readiness to follow after the "the other" foot, then, along with the joint that holds the two legs of the compass together, are both undone by doubts only the grammar works to evidence.

The speaker allows that "though [the fixt foot] in the centre sit / Yet when the other far doth rome, / It leanes, and hearkens after it, / And growes erect" (lines 29-32). In a poem that has already subverted its own fiction through implications that it is the female other that "goe[s]" (line 22), and in which issues of selfhood and subjectivity are very much at play, the phrase "the other" seems suddenly to reverse the positions man and woman occupy in the terms of the compass analogy. Imagistically, "the other" defines the roaming man, but rhetorically it hints, once again, that the "self" of this poem—its male speaker—is aware of the potential roaming of his mistress. At the same time, he fashions himself as a wandering, transgress other in terms of a stable "centre" meant to establish origin and to contain his motion around her. Donne maximizes such "misidentifications" by relying on ambiguous pronouns in four lines, three instances of "it" and one of "that," detached from their referents, inhibit firm assignment of self and object (indeed, at line 31, "it" applies both to the man and to the woman). Furthermore, the fixed foot moves (already a paradox) not simply in a barely measurable circle controlled by the movement of "the other"; it actually "hearkens after" the other and "growes erect, as that comes home." In the "hardly gendered bodies" of the seventeenth century, sexual arousal was not imagined in clearly differentiated terms; a woman's genitals were thought to "swell" and her "seed" to be ejaculated much like a man's. Thus the "firmness" of the centre foot of the compass, its excitement at the return of the wandering leg, may emphasize the speaker's need to ensure his lover's continued desire for him. At the same time, however (and granting that the fixed leg of a widened compass would, literally, straighten as the other moved inward), the overtly masculine image reverses conventional expectations about constancy, furthering the hint that it is the man who perceives himself as stationary. As she roams in a circle around him—a circle that will be narrowed only by her moving toward him—he wonders after her and grows erect at her return.

"Such," then, "wilt thou be to mee, who must / Like th'other foot, obliquely runne" (lines 34-35). "Such" here sets up a comparison whose elements are already deeply conflicted and unclear. On the surface, the word recovers the terms of the analogy from whatever may have problematized them in the previous stanza, and seems to confirm that she will be the one to lean and hearken after him. The syntactical progression of these lines, however, pulls out of shape what the simile at first tries to render. "Such" seems to work backward to the immediately preceding phrase—as if to say, "you will be to me 'as [the one] that comes home'"; to the degree that the penultimate stanza has already confused one's sense of who stays, who leaves to roam, such a succession reinforces the subtext he experiences himself as left behind by her. Thus "who" (in "Such wilt thou be to mee, who must... obliquely runne") also seems detached, applicable to either of them grammatically as well as thematically. And which of them is "like th'other foot"? Must she, too, run? Do they both move, both grow erect at the prospect of reunion? Tellingly, the trope that is meant to show the two lovers in relation to each other in fact doubles them at first they are "twin compasses" (line 26), identical.

The effect of so much layering of language and subjectivity (which may also be its point) is to call radically into question both the nature of the mourning the poem seems to prohibit as well as the identity of the individuals involved. The poem piles up images of attachment and motion, only to deny the fixity of meaning those very images seem to strive so much to assure. In the highly determined, seemingly stabilized space inside of which the poem comes to a close—the circle drawn by the compass in which, the speaker says, "Thy firmness... makes me end, where I begunne" (line 36)—a kaleidoscopic interplay of position and movement threatens to bulge the outline of that perfect circularity (the course of "th'other foot" is "oblique"; the poem ends by being "begunne"). Thus the other must be invested with "firmnes" to make things "just," to make him stop "running." She must stand firm, straighten up, perhaps, even get excited for him, in order for him to return. He depends on that reliable durability to counter his own ambivalent roaming, to reassure him that his own wanderings are "just," right, and safe, and to bring him around again to himself. And yet, simultaneously, she is the one moving, circling, and wandering. The poem's figurative language allows two stories to be told at once.

I will conclude with a brief reading of "The Sunne Rising" as one of Donne's most singular poetic acts of playing with space. Thomas Docherty writes of the poem that the "fundamental point at issue is that the space is relativized and made mutable." The world beyond the bed that contains the intertwined lovers is controlled by the speaker, first by a gesture of audacious dismissal, then by an act of encompassing inclusion. The window through which the voyeuristic sun intrudes is both barrier and passageway between two realms (as in "A Valediction of My Name"); the pair luxuriates in a loving "wee"-ness (line 25)—reinforced by the repetitions of "us" (lines 3, 23, 28), of "bed" (lines 20, 30), of "warme" (line 28), of "all" (lines 20, 21, 24)—that is distinguished from the particulated world of "boyes," "ants," and "the rags of time" (lines 6, 8, 10). It is just this sense of a union so solid as to be condensed into the solemnity of "Nothing else is" (line 22), that infuses the speaker with an illusion of magical control over the objects of the world. Secure in his bond with his lover/other, the speaker can make the "out-there" accord with his own expectations and desires—he can define not only the movement and proportion of the world (e.g., "the King will ride" [line 7], and "both the' India's of spice and Myne... lie here with mee" [lines 17-18]), but also the very configuration of the cosmos as well ("This bed thy centre is, these walls, thy spheare" [line 30]). The bed and then the room the lovers inhabit in "The Sunne Rising" are first isolated from the bother of kings and suns and "ants," then expand to encompass all of that, to become the whole world. In Robert Wiltenburg's words, "The Sunne Rising" strikes us with its "imperative mood, gigantic, engorged with the physical and emotional immediacy and sufficiency of its experience of love," an experience through which the self discovers "the power not only to shape itself... but to shape the world to itself."

But there is something else at work in the poem, too, other than a childlike belief in magical omnipotence. Rather than representing separation, with disturbing implications of unknowability and loneliness, the window in "The Sunne Rising" takes on the intermediate nature of potential space, allowing the speaker imaginatively, and pleasurably, to push away ("goe chide," "goe," "tell" [lines 5-8], "call," "looke" [line 16]) or pull in ("shine here to us" [line 29]) what lies beyond. The speaker mediates his perception of what lies beyond the threshold of the window through his trust in the depth and durability of his relatedness to his lover. The intensity of the poem's articulation of potential space (neither "all-me" nor objects beyond the self's control) renders the "contract[ion]" (line 26) of the final stanza more an experience of "holding"—in which "wee" are "happy" (line 25) and "warme" (line 28) and the "centre" of "every where" (line 29)—than the oppressive space of "The Good-Morrow's "one little roome." In that in between area, the speaker articulates not so much a fantasy of self-centered omnipotence as an absenting of self in deference to his mistress. Thus the line that critics so frequently seize upon as proof of Donne's colonizing stance toward women might be more provocatively read as a profound acknowledgment of one woman's utter completeness less a strident "she is all the states, and I am all the princes" than a loving She is all states and all princes. Aye.

The cumulative evidence of the readings I have presented here suggests that the genderedness of Donne's poetic imagination is not as emphatically, certainly not as consistently, "masculine," or masculinity, as has so often been claimed. In a recent study of Donne's "articulations of the feminine," H. L. Meakin juxtaposes "Donne's attempts to `emprison' the various figures of the feminine" with "the `excess' which is woman beyond the margins of patriarchal discourse." In the threshold spaces mapped out by images of liminality, however, it is just this sort of hierarchical schema that Donne reconfigures, repositioning male self and female other in ways that elude stock oppositions of "centre" and "margin." If certain poems in Songs and Sonnets point up the limitations of identifying Donne as consistently evacuating or appropriative of women, so, too, do they suggest that Donne's recognition of women extends beyond simple tributes paid from uncomplicatedly conventional, gendered positions. While there can be no intermediate space without eventual separation, no recognition of separate subjectivity without acknowledging the difference-between, the question of what Donne does with difference remains an intricate one.

The very breadth and richness of recent Donne scholarship points to the impossibility of confining Donne to a unified style of relating to female others (there may be no poet so capable of rhetorical escape as Donne), yet I would argue that it is equally untenable to maintain that Donne's identifications with women serve unequivocally, or univocally, to suppress them and to reassert the primacy of his own masculine identity. Through the conceptual metaphors of play and liminal space, Donne liberates his speakers from anxieties about gender by exploiting the very notions that tend to produce anxiety in the first place, maximizing rather than reductively denying the ambiguity of gendered identity. In the kinds of moments explored in this article, acts of identification become ways of questioning—transgressing—the very terms of being male, being a self, and loving each other.

## Critical Opinion

Critical opinion has rarely been united as to the appropriate response to Doctor Faustus. In the same year (1817) that Henry Maitland, arguing that Faustus harmed no one but himself, could pronounce his fate undeserved, Francis Jeffrey endorsed the fall of "a vulgar sorcerer, tempted to sell his soul to the Devil for the ordinary price of sensual pleasure, and earthly power and glory."As the nineteenth century wore on, however, general opinion strengthened that the quality of the scholar's passionate desires and of the language in which they found expression easily counteracted his impious audacity in sealing a bond with the Devil.For Francis Cunningham in 1870, the last hour of the doctor's life filled the soul "with love and admiration for a departed hero"; for J.A. Symonds, Faustus, "the medieval rebel," was animated by Marlowe's "own audacious spirit," and in 1887 Havelock Ellis exalted Faustus as "a living man thirsting for the infinite." Such eulogies continued into the present century, Una Ellis-Fermor discovering in him "dignity, patience, tenacity and a certain profundity of thought." The most extreme statement of this view emanated in 1910 from the American philosopher George Santayana, for whom "this excellent Faustus" was a good Protestant, "damned by accident or predestination."He goes on,

See an essentially good man, because in a moment of infatuation he had signed away his soul, driven against his will to despair and damnation.... The evil angel represents the natural ideal of Faustus, or of any child of the Renaissance; he appeals to the vague but healthy ambitions of a young soul, that would make trial of the world.In other words, the devil represents the true good, and it is no wonder if the honest Faustus cannot resist his suggestions. We like him for his love of life, for his trust in nature, for his enthusiasm for beauty.... Marlowe's Faustus is a martyr to everything that the Renaissance prized, - power, curious knowledge, enterprise, wealth, and beauty.

Some may consider such an approach partisan and partial, but the spirit behind these claims bears witness to a general belief in Faustus's fundamental significance as a human being. He is not a character to whose aspirations or plight we can remain indifferent. While not necessarily endorsing Santayana's fervent testimony, most of us find more to Faustus than simply an arrogant, foolish, immature or blasphemous man whose appetites betray him into overreaching himself, as both Prologue and Epilogue would have us believe.

However, if we are unable to simplify his fate as the inevitable progression of a self-centered hedonist who flouts God's just laws, it is another thing to portray Faustus as more sinned against than sinning, as one whose intellectual passion and aesthetic awareness justify his "disobedience." Such a view has persisted, however, and Nicholas Brooke's essay "The Moral Tragedy of Doctor Faustus" remains its most sophisticated and discerning exposition. Brooke regards Faustus as one who sets out to achieve "the supreme desires of Man," describing these as "the only positive ideas advanced" in the play and seeing the magnificence with which they are endowed as obliterating all the trite moral exhortations.

Admitting that Faustus's ambitions are formulated as a jumble of disparate pursuits, Brooke still insists that "all the positive statements of the play, supported by the finest verse, are against the declared Christian moral," while statements which advance the "heavenly" case remain "vague, flat, meaningless." For this critic, the piece becomes an inverted morality play in which Faustus appears justified in refusing to assume a position of humble servitude to God. Even the traditional technique of introducing Good and Bad Angels becomes a device for satirizing the divine regime through anachronism. The hero's rejection of Heaven for Helen of Troy is construed as an act of glorious defiance, placing appetite above intellect, and exposing the full irony of a creation which can only fulfill its highest potential by bypassing God's laws and paying the price. Brooke insists that Faustus's bargain does bring worthwhile satisfactions with it, and that his actions in the central scenes appear trivial only because it was impossible to demonstrate him exercising a command of the secrets of astronomy and cosmography in adequately theatrical ways.

Brooke's reading of the play deserves careful thought, but we may still feel that it ignores the less admirable traits in Faustus's behaviour, and the less noble aspects of his ambition. Over against Brooke we have to set the ardent belief of other critics that the play remains predominantly an updated medieval morality play which may accord its protagonist an individual name and personality, but which still presents his story as that of an archetypal sinful man recompensed for his wicked acts in the traditional manner.

Those who hold this opinion point to the overtly Christian imagery and machinery of the play, for example the terminology of Faustus's final hour soliloquy, the stern language of the Prologue and Epilogue: "swollen with cunning of a self-conceit" (Prologue, 2); "falling to a devilish exercise" (Prologue,); "Cut is the branch that might have grown full straight" (Epilogue,).

Thus amid Victorian adulation in 1877 Wilhelm Wagner wrote, "Marlowe's Faustus is anything but a hero... though we can sympathize with his fear and lamentations, yet we cannot but feel that his end is the appropriate conclusion of his career."In more recent years others have adopted the view that it is only by dint of an excess of critical sophistication that Faustus can be interpreted as anything other than an admonitory drama, however skilfully varied from its medieval predecessors.James Smith in "Marlowe's Doctor Faustus" and Greg in "The Damnation of Faustus" argue in favour of such an interpretation, which Leo Kirschbaum in "Marlowe's Faustus: A Reconsideration" expresses trenchantly if a little too forcefully the doctor as a "blatant egotist... self-deluded, foolishly boastful," and "a wretched creature who for lower values gives up higher values," Kirschbaum concludes, "the

Christian view of the world informs Dr. Faustus throughout - not the pagan view.... Whatever Marlowe was himself, there is no more obvious Christian document in all Elizabethan drama than Dr. Faustus."

Typical is the attention which such critics pay to Faustus's encounter with Helen of Troy in Act V, Scene i.Arguing that his off-stage copulation with a disguised demon (which they take Helen to be) is the ultimate act that puts salvation irrevocably beyond his reach, they attach great importance at line 102 to his cry of "Her lips suck forth my soul," and to the blasphemy of the preceding request that she should make him immortal with a kiss.Sexual intercourse with a demon has been taken to be a damnable offence, and Kirschbaum, Greg and others highlight the Old Man's comment in lines 119-21 as Faustus leads Helen off: Accursed Faustus, miserable man, That from thy soul exclud'st the grace of heaven, And fliest the throne of his tribunal seat.

Several commentators have challenged this reading, arguing, like J. C. Maxwell in "The Sin of Faustus," that it overemphasises Faustus's sin of sensuality rather than pride, or, like T. W. Craik in "Faustus Damnation Reconsidered," that the Old Man's valediction does not necessarily refer to copulation with a demon, which does not necessarily follow Faustus's exit with Helen. Moreover, Nicholas Kiessling in "Doctor Faustus and the Sin of Demoniality" points out that the Second Scholar still holds out the hope of salvation after Helen has become Faustus's mistress, and that sex with a demonic spirit was never considered as being "beyond redemption."

So, while there is much to support a reading of Faustus on strict morality lines, there is evidence to refute it too.For one thing Faustus is a complicated man whose motives for behaving as he does, while not explicit, are none the less discernible and plausible.Unlike the earlier morality hero, he is no one-dimensional creation without a psychology: we recognize our common humanity in him, and, even though we may disapprove of what he does, most of us acknowledge that his fate cannot be explained entirely satisfactorily as that of a wicked sinner whose end induces in us a smug feeling that we have seen justice done.

Faustus is sympathetic and credible enough for us to believe that his downfall results from a human failure, like that of Macbeth or Oedipus, to understand the enormity of what he is proposing to himself, he is an unhappy figure who acts against his own better nature, and whose agonized death is a matter for regret rather than applause. This is what gives him tragic stature for all his personal weaknesses and defects.

## What is the Theme of the Play Which Bears Faustus's Name?

Some might reply that it is to be found in humanity's blindness to the reality of its own immortal essence, that in thinking Hell a fable and his own soul a trifle Faustus is denying the spiritual truth about himself.Others, unable to adopt a position essentially Christian and yet unwilling to surrender entirely to the allure of Brooke's portrait of the martyred humanist, find the core of the tragedy in the Epilogue's first line.

For them "Cut is the branch that might have grown full straight" epitomizes that sense of human wastage and avoidable pain lying at the root of all tragic art.The man who might have lived contentedly and profitably lies dead, having dared the impossible and lost.

To such people the fact that Faustus enlisted diabolic aid is probably less important today than his pathetic need to transcend his own limitations.Perhaps at the base of Faustus's tragedy lies a fundamental inability to accept himself as a man, a self-disgust at discovering himself to be human after all. If he ends "cut off from all contact with humanity," as Brooke suggests, it could be his own fault for seeking to become more than human in the first instance.

## Failed Superman or Foolish Sinner?

Each of us can privately resolve the debate, but the choice is ours, for Marlowe does not attempt to influence us one way or the other.Preserving a neutral stance, he leaves us free to make up our own minds.In this he shows himself a pioneer by comparison with his immediate predecessors in the field of English drama, and appreciation of this remarkable fact can also assist us to accept Marlowe's ambivalent presentation of his hero's dilemma.

Most early sixteenth-century drama was didactic: it sought less to examine problems of human behaviour and personal conduct than to illustrate the consequences of right- and wrongdoing.

Only slowly did dramatists show interest in ethical complications or moral predicaments, in what led people to behave antisocially or in ways which the Church deemed worthy of punishment here or in the afterlife.Plays generally upheld the belief that men and women were free agents confronted by a choice between two modes of living, one acceptable and encouraged, the other unacceptable and condemned.

No extenuating circumstances could be permitted to mitigate wrongdoing, no explanatory pleas could disguise the commission of sins.Last-minute repentance might secure last-minute salvation, but it was not the business of drama to question the hallowed system of rewards and punishments, to challenge the traditional pieties, or to explore the moral, spiritual, or psychological reasons which had led an individual to select the wrong path.

Marlowe lived in an age and moved in circles which had started to query the old orthodoxies, and he, like many thinking people of his day, could not fail to be aware of the new agencies at work in the Western world, guaranteeing mankind more say in its own future, boosting its confidence in its own abilities and in its right to shape its own environment.

The rigidly limited and defined "world-picture" beloved of medieval thinkers was beingdismembered, and Renaissance men and women were left contemplating in bewilderment the clash between the outdated but still reassuring cosmic framework familiarized by tradition, and a more scientifically demonstrable pattern which was still alarmingly novel and untried.Little wonder that John Donne could comment in An Anatomie of the World (1611) that "wise nature" observ'd that every sort of men

**Did in their Voyage in this Worlds Sea Stray and Needed a New Compasse for their Way?**

Marlowe was acutely aware of the predictably mixed reactions of his contemporaries to the fresh set of dilemmas which "the pressures of modern life" posed for them.For many, the changes in politics, religion and morality, the almost daily discoveries in the natural world and in the realm of ideas, the unleashing of acquisitive and aspiring instincts in social and economic affairs, would have seemed unsettling and unacceptable, forcing them to cling resolutely to old beliefs and opinions.Others, eager to embrace the "new Philosophy," were convinced that, the sooner the old mental lumber was got rid of and man's energies were released from guilt-ridden restraints, the sooner a brave new world would come into being in which humanity could enjoy a more fulfilled existence.

Without some understanding of the divided mind of the English Renaissance, one cannot fully appreciate Doctor Faustus, which typifies the transition from the old black-and-white ethical scheme which underlies the morality play and conditions its audience's judgment, and the more colourful, empirical, exploratory investigation of moral issues and psychological conditions which we associate with the best Elizabethan and Jacobean dramas.Marlowe invites us to see the splendor of man, but to contemplate the species at its most abject too.

On one hand we have the boldly defiant, self-reliant figure of the opening, a man of boundless confidence whose egotism is at once awe-inspiring and terrible; on the other hand we find a pitiful, grovelling creature seeking to hide from the consequences of his ambition in the bowels of the earth, vulnerable, and stripped of all dignity and self-assurance.

On one level Doctor Faustus may be treated as a study of the split personality of the Renaissance; on another as an exploration of just what controls human beings should expect to find laced on their own development given such limiting factors as character and environment. Marlowe has left us ample room for speculation on the issues involved.The Prologue to Tamburlaine invites spectators to applaud its hero's fortunes as they please; that to Doctor Faustus suggests that we assess the scholar's fortunes as "good or bad". Preserving authorial neutrality on these matters, Marlowe created a revolution in English drama by refusing to pass overt judgment on his leading figure's conduct. Prologue and Epilogue may speak harshly of Faustus, but the play itself compels us to ponder and debate and decide for ourselves where the key to the truth lies.Its author will not arbitrate for us.All he does is present the paradox of the clash between human aspiration and restrictions placed on it not only by an inexorable theological scheme but by human fallibility too.

Marlowe makes most effective and yet subtle dramatic use of Biblical allusion in Doctor Faustus as shown by R.M. Cornelius in Christopher Marlowe's Use of the Bible.The reader's persistent consciousness, throughout the play, that things are out of joint and even upside down is due to Marlowe's reverse use of the Bible.

Three types of reversal appear: the reversal of role, the reversal of values, and the reversal of meaning.Analysis of various passages will clarify these terms.Marlowe makes straightforward use of Biblical allusion, as in most of the speeches of the Old Man, but more characteristic and more effective are his reversals.

Reversal of roles happens when words spoken by or of a righteous person (usually Christ) in the Bible are associated in the play with a wicked person like Mephistopheles or Faustus.The effect is shocking - much more shocking, for example, than the device of dressing Mephistopheles in the garb of a Franciscan friar.Given, the full significance would come only to those capable of recognizing the context of the allusion.Yet even those unread in the Bible heard Scripture every Sunday.At any rate the references suggest passages that would have been known to most Elizabethan playgoers.The reversal of roles, therefore, though the audience in many instances may not have consciously analyzed what was wrong, could hardly have failed to produce a sharp sense of something bent out of shape.

When Mephistopheles promises Faustus, "And I will be thy slave and wait on thee, / And give thee more than thou hast wit to ask" (II. i. 47-8), the audience is reminded of the passage, "Now unto him therefore that is able to do exceeding abundantly above all that we ask or think... Be praise" and is brought up short.A devil ascribes to himself a power that the Bible ascribes to God; Marlowe presents a world of theological and moral ideas seen in reverse.This is in accord with the quest of Faustus, who, believing that he cannot get what he wants from God through the study of divinity, aims to satisfy his lusts through recourse to Lucifer.

Dr. Faustus even becomes a kind of perverted Christ who sheds his blood not to save the souls of others, but to damn his own soul and then appropriates the death cry of the Biblical Christ to emphasize the blasphemy.As Faustus prepares to sign away his soul with his own blood, he says, "View here this blood that trickles from mine arm, / And let it be propitious for my wish" (II. i. 58-9). Paul said of Christ: "Whom God hath set forth to be a propitiation through faith in his blood" (Romans 3:25); but Faustus thinks of his blood as being propitious in his suit to Lucifer. Then he exclaims, "Consummatum est, this bill is ended" (II. i. 75), an echo of Christ's "It is finished". According to traditional Christian theology, these were a cry not of defeat but of triumph that the work of redemption by the blood of Christ was completed and that now the souls of men could be freed from Hell.On Faustus's lips, however, the words became a grim statement of a diametrically opposed transaction: by his own blood Faustus seals his own soul's condemnation.The Scriptural language used makes a horrifying situation more horrible by adding a blasphemous parody of holy utterances.

A second type of Biblical allusion in Marlowe reverses values.Marlowe often used such reversals without Biblical allusion, as when Faustus speaks of divinity, traditionally the most exalted of studies, as "basest of the three, / Unpleasant, harsh, contemptible, and vilde" (I. i.). But, as in the case of the reversal of roles, a wicked act or a blasphemous sentence appears even blacker if it involves abuse of Scripture.Before Faustus has signed away his soul, he sits alone in his study awaiting Mephistopheles, vacillating between a desire for salvation and a lust for all that magic can bring him, and deliberately he attempts to reverse his standard of values. For hope and faith in God, he would substitute "Despair in God, and trust in Beelzebub" (II. i. 5) and he seeks to make firm wavering purpose by making blasphemous claims of what he will do for the devil. "The God thou serv'st is thine own appetite, / Wherein is fix'd the love of Beelzebub" (II. i. 11-2). Faustus, Doctor of Divinity now turned necromancer, has found support for his new creed in the New Testament: "For they that are such [heretics] serve not the Lord Jesus Christ, but there own belly... whose end is damnation, whose God is their belly, and whose glory is in their shame, which mind earthly things" (Romans 16:18; Philippians 3:19). Here Paul describes those who have exactly reversed Christian values: for the spirit, the belly; for heaven, damnation; for God and his Son, their own appetites; for glory, shame.This credo Faustus struggles to adopt as his own, but he never entirely succeeds in substituting his appetite for his belief in that God made the world.

The opening scene in Faustus's study, containing the final rejection of divinity in favour of magic, turns on a reversal of meaning in the passages Faustus reads from Jerome's Latin Vulgate.The reversal is brought about, not by a perversion of the portion alluded to, but by a deletion of part of the context which considerably modifies the meaning of the portion read.

*Jerome's Bible, Faustus, view it well.*
*Stipendium peccati mors est.Ha!, Stipendium, etc.,*
*The reward of sin is death.That's hard.*
Si pecasse negamus, fallimur, et nulla est in nobis veritas. If we say that we have no sin we deceive ourselves, and there is no truth in us.
*Why then, belike,*
We must sin, and so consequently die. Ay, we must die

an everlasting death. What doctrine call you this?Che sera, sera. What will be, shall be.Divinity, adieu! (I. i. 38-48) first passage Faustus reads is the first half of Romans 6:23; the full verse is: "For the wages of sin is death; but the gift of God is eternal life through Jesus Christ our Lord."In the second passage, Faustus reads the first full sentence, but not the one which follows: "If we say that we have no sin, we deceive ourselves, and there is no truth in us.If we acknowledge our sins, he is faithful and just to forgive us our sins, and to cleanse us from all unrighteousnes".

The original meaning - that although men are sinners doomed to death, a way of escape from that doom has been provided in Jesus Christ - is reversed and a fatalistic doctrine is falsely drawn from the Bible.Even Faustus's reaction - "That's hard" - and his adieu to divinity are based on the New Testament story of those who turned back from discipleship when they decided that the doctrine of Jesus was too hard.Directed by Mephistopheles Faustus deliberately reverses the meaning of the passages he reads because he is ravished with a desire for the intellectual and physical power that can be his through making the spirits his subjects; determined to close his eyes against the light, at the same time he wishes to blame his determination on fate.His set purpose to view himself as irrevocably damned in spite of his references to passages containing the promises of God's grace and forgiveness is made even more evident when he writes a deed to bequeath his Soul to Lucifer.

Consummatum est: this bill is ended and Faustus hath bequeath'd his soul to Lucifer. But what is this inscription on mine arm? Home fuge: Whither should I flie?

If unto God, he'll throw me down to hell (II. i. 75-9).

The question "Whither should I flie?" echoes the cry of the psalmist: "Whether shall go from thy Spirit? Or whether shall flee from thy presence?If I ascend up into heaven thou art there; if I lie down in Hell, thou art there.Let me take the wings of the morning, and dwell in the uttermost parts of the sea; yet thether shall thine hand lead me, and thy right hand hold me". The reversal of meaning involved in the words of

Faustus attacks the willingness of God to receive those who come to him.The question of the psalmist implies the answer that there is no place where the love and direction of God will be denied him; the question of Faustus implies his belief that wherever he might flee, condemnation is sure.The psalmist believes God will be with him even in Hell; Faustus believes God will reject him even from Heaven.Such use of Biblical allusions by Faustus increases the tragedy of his end, for in one as accomplished in the study of divinity as he, reversals of meaning can only be deliberate, springing from his desire to gain power and wealth through a pact with the devil and from his consequent need to consider himself already damned anyway.The tragedy of Faustus is the tragedy of a man who perversely rejects every advanced means of redemption through a desperate conviction, self-imposed, that he cannot repent and that even if he could God would not save him.

Yet there is an inner struggle as Faustus seeks to find some glimmer of hope for salvation in spite of his soul's having been signed over to Lucifer.At one point Faustus consoles himself with the thought: "Tush, Christ did call the thief upon the cross, / Then rest thee, Faustus, quiet in conceit" (IV. iv. 26-7).But still the meaning of the Bible is reversed.His allusion is to the story of the repentant thief in the Gospel of Luke who said to Jesus, "Lord, remember me when thou comest into thy kingdom" (Luke 23:42).It is not Christ who calls the thief,but it is the thief who calls upon Christ, believing that Christ will receive him.Faustus wavers in fear and thinks of Christ and his saving blood, but instead of calling to Christ as the thief did, he calls upon Lucifer to spare him and upon the mountains and hills to fall upon him and hide him.After seeing the blood of Christ momentarily, he says:

Where is it now? Tis gone: And see where God Stretcheth out his arm and bends his ireful brows: Mountains and hills, come, come, and fall on me, And hide me from the heavy wrath of God. Here, in the moment of his end, Faustus's allusion to the Bible emphasizes his despair: according to Scripture, when God's judgment upon earth was envisioned in the Apocalypse, the great men of the nations hid themselves "and said to the mountains and rocks, fall on us, and hide us from the presence of him that sitteth on the throne, and from the wrath of the Lamb"

The function of the Old Man in Act V, Scene i seems to be in the early English tradition of having a reliable commentator on the events in the play - one who, like the Doctor in the mystery cycles, can be counted on to give the audience the "right" view.Almost everything the Old Man says to Faustus is traceable to Bible texts, and, with one possible exception, all of his statements are Biblically phrased presentations of the orthodox Christian view of Faustus and the jeopardy in which he has placed his soul.One image used in the Old Man's exhortation to Faustus to repent and be saved indicates, perhaps, Marlowe's intention to raise a question not about the validity of the advice given, but about the possibility of its being accepted.The Old Man says,

*I see an angel hovers o'er thy head,*
*And with a vial full of precious grace*
*Offers to pour the same into thy soul.*
*Then call for mercy and avoid despair.*

The image is Biblical, but the significance in the source is the reverse of that in the Old Man's speech."And I heard a great voice out of the temple saying to the seven angels, go your ways, and pour out the vials of the wrath of God upon the earth".The pouring out of these vials of God's wrath is followed by noisome sores, the seas and springs turning into blood, the scorching of men with the heat of the sun, and other such plagues.Although the surface meaning is just the opposite, the image used by the Old Man suggests that judgment, not grace, hovers over Faustus's head.Only a few lines later he refers to Faustus's "hapless soul" (V. i. 69), and when Faustus goes off with Helen, the Old man calls him "Accursed Faustus".

The chorus closes Doctor Faustus with an allusion to Psalm.Cut is the branch that might have grown full straight, And burned is Apollo's laurel bough,That sometime grew within this learned man.

"And the vineyard which thy right hand hath planted,

and the branch that thou madest strong for thyself; it is burned with fire, it is cut down: they perish at the rebuke of thy countenance...Turn us again, O Lord of hosts, cause thy face to shine; and we shall be saved".The devils take Faustus away, but it is the rebuke of the countenance of God ("My God! My God! look not so fierce on me!" cries Faustus) that seals his doom.The branch that was strengthened for the service of God and might have grown full straight is cut and burned; Faustus is gone; his "waxen wings" have mounted "above his reach" as "melting, heavens conspir'd his overthrow" (Prologue, -). That God could have turned Faustus to himself whereas Faustus was powerless to repent was the view to which Faustus kept returning, and it was this fatalism, this casting of the full responsibility for salvation upon God instead of exercising faith, which makes the play a tragedy.If Faustus really had no choice of his own, there is no tragedy. Although the chorus closes the play with an allusion to a Scriptural passage which seems to support the view that Faustus held, Marlowe uses it as a basis for exhorting the wise to "Regard his hellish fall" - perhaps to emphasize that as Cole says "the human will is always the observable agent of destruction and pain."Faustus owes much of his complexity and power as a dramatic character, as well as the success of the play, to the Marlovian use of Scripture, through which a reversal of conventional conceptions is accomplished and an additional force given to the dramatic statements.

# Bibliography

- Introductions and preliminary course programme discussion
- *Main Spenser texts:* The Shepheardes Calender (1579), Januarye, Februarie, Aprill
- *Contextual primary source:* Thomas Sackville, 'Sacvyles olde age' (1566-7?) [cf. Shakespeare, Songs of Heims and Ver (see end of Love's Labours Lost) (1598)]
- *Spenser:* Shepheardes Calender, October, December; with EK's epistle to Gabriel Harvey (1579).
- Contexts Philip Sidney, The Defence of Poesie (1580-2) (also known as The Apology for Poetry) also extracts from *Thomas Nashe, Pierce Penniless his supplication to the Devil (1592).
- *Spenser:* Muiopotmos: or the Fate of the Butterflie (pr. 1590).
- *Context:* Arthur Golding, tr. Ovid, Metamorphoses, ed. M. Forey (Penguin), Bk 6, lines 1-181 (Pallas/ Minerva & Arachne) (1567).
- *Spenser:* Amoretti and Epithalamion (1595).
- *Contexts:* choose a selection of love lyrics from: either Sidney, Astrophil and Stella, ca 1582-3 (pr.1591); or Shakespeare, Sonnets and A Lover's Complaint, ca 1590s (pr.1609); or John Donne, Songs and Sonnets, ca 1590s (pr.1633).
- Reading
- *Spenser:* The Faerie Queene, Bk 1 (pr. 1590), see also Theatre for Worldlings (1569), sonnets 12-15

- *Contexts:* The Revelation of St John the Divine (omitted from some translations of the Christian Greek Bible)
- *Spenser:* The Faerie Queene, Bk 3 (pr. 1590) [Britomart and Chastity]; cf. end of Bk 2.
- *Contexts:* Cf. Arthur Golding's Ovid, Metamor-phoses, Bk 15, lines 171-300 (Pythagoras & recycled life forms, cf. FQ 3,vi); cf. also Shakespeare, Venus and Adonis (pr. 1593).
- *Spenser:* The Faerie Queene, Bk 5 (pr.1596) [Britomart, Artegall and Justice].
- *Contexts:* Sidney, Old Arcadia, ed. K. Duncan Jones (Oxford World's Classics), Bk/Act 5 (1580?); cf. extracts from [Spenser?], A View of the Present State of Ireland (1596).
- *Spenser:* Faerie Queene, Bk 6 (pr.1596) [Courtesy] Cantos 9-12 especially.
- *Context:* B. Castiglione, tr., Thomas Hoby, The Book of the Courtier, Bk 4 (pr. 1561).
- *Spenser:* The Fowre Hymns (1596).
- *Contexts:* Selected metrical psalms by Sidney (d.1586) and his sister Mary Herbert, countess of Pembroke (by 1599); religious lyrics by Donne.